OPEN WHEN

WISDOM FOR THE LEADERSHIP MOMENTS THAT MATTER

Camille Nicita Higley

CNH Holdings

Beverly Hills, Michigan

Open When: Wisdom for the Leadership Moments That Matter/Camille Nicita Higley

First edition 2026

ISBN: 979-8-9954478-0-1 (paperback) ISBN: 979-8-9954478-1-8 (eBook)

For Anthony Nicita, my first example of what leadership could look like.

And for John Gongos, who trusted in my potential to become one.

TABLE OF CONTENTS

FOREWORD

In June 2012, I was in Chicago with a client and friend, John Gongos, co-presenting at one of his company's industry conferences. Two weeks later, I joined John and his executive team for a quarterly strategy session, a discipline he had instilled a decade earlier. Just weeks after that, in a tragic turn of events, I found myself attending his funeral. John had died unexpectedly of cancer in the prime of his life.

He was a well-respected leader. The company he founded, Gongos Research (later simply known as Gongos), helped shape its industry for over 20 years. The chances of a business surviving a loss like this are...well, rather small. The company was in shock. The industry was in shock. As a business advisor, I have seen events like this conspire to put companies out of business. Many likely assumed that would be the case here.

But Gongos didn't cease to exist. One of John's executive leaders stepped into the role of owner and CEO. As unlikely as it seemed in July 2012, the company not only survived, it thrived. Over the next decade, it grew in both size and influence. How does that happen? How does a new CEO/owner guide a company through the devastating loss of its founder, while navigating growth, technological change, market shifts, and even a pandemic, and emerge stronger?

That leader was Camille Nicita Higley, the author of this book. In these pages, you will learn directly from a leader whose courage, fortitude, and learning mindset enabled her to accomplish what few would have thought possible. Few have been thrust into the CEO/owner role so suddenly. Fewer still have navigated such odds with the level of grace and effectiveness Camille demonstrated.

While Camille may have been an unlikely owner, she was not an unlikely leader. Camille embraced leadership early in her career. Over 30+ years, she has been an avid learner and practitioner, continuously honing her leadership and business acumen. I had the privilege of knowing Camille as a member of the Gongos leadership team while John was still CEO, and later as a business advisor working alongside her through a decade of growth. During that time, Gongos became a thought leader and pacesetter in customer- centricity.

What I saw consistently was Camille's purpose in action: creating a positive impact on the world through employees and clients. She is a humble, thoughtful learner, but one of Camille's super skills is diligently putting what she learns into practice. The insights in this book are grounded in real-world experience. If she shares it, she has lived it. Learning isn't academic for Camille, and I can assure you, what she has put into this book isn't the theoretical material you find in business school programs. Her insights come from real-world experience.

Her Flywheel for a healthy and sustainable organization is exactly that, a "lived model. "I witnessed Camille and the company she led, live out the elements of the Flywheel she presents in this book – Great People focused on doing Great Work with Great Clients achieve Great Impact. I also saw her wrestle with the very challenges she writes about here. Camille is sharing her wisdom from a position of authority, having lived it as a CEO.

I'm especially grateful she includes wisdom "Beyond the Flywheel," particularly for those in the CEO/owner role. Not all executives are owners, and ownership carries unique responsibilities, pressures, and perspectives. While Camille didn't initially aspire to ownership, she embraced it fully; learning, growing, and ultimately using that position to create meaningful impact for her team, clients, and the industry.

The *Open When* structure is well-suited to today's business leaders. Our lives are busy. We rarely have the time to read a book cover to cover or in one sitting. What we need is relevant insight, accessible when we need it, and in the right amount. This book delivers exactly that.

Camille's approach allows you to turn directly to the moment you're facing – accessible topics based on key situations all senior leaders are likely to encounter. Its format is designed not just for reading but also as a resource and a repeated reference for leaders.

When Camille and I began conversations about her eventual leadership succession and business exit, she wanted to maintain a purposeful, ongoing impact on other business leaders. One way she accomplishes this is through her individual coaching. I believe this book will now be a far larger part of fulfilling her envisioned outcome. *Open When* allows Camille to share her insights with many leaders she cannot work with directly. I'm grateful Camille has invested her time in writing this book. It is an extension of who Camille is as a leader – an authentic voice on business leadership – and it will be a well-used resource for business leaders in the years to come.

So, to the curious leaders: keep this book close at hand. I trust you'll find what you need as you open it in the moments that matter most in your own leadership journey.

Troy Schrock, *Owner/Advisor, The CEO Advantage*

March 2026

PREFACE

I never aspired to be the sole owner of a business. *A founding member of a start-up? Absolutely. A leader of teams and people?* Without question. But owning a company outright was never on the bucket list.

Until the day everything changed.

Our CEO, my business partner, mentor, and friend, John Gongos, called to tell me that after a series of inconclusive tests, he had been diagnosed with stage 4 cancer. We had a succession plan, and yes, I knew I was the one to step in if duty called. But John was only 51, vibrant and active. In our minds, succession was years away, with him riding off into the sunset, but only a phone call away.

That phone call never happened. Within eight days of his diagnosis, John was gone. And I, then COO, found myself standing in front of our 75-person team, announcing that our beloved founder had passed away.

I was stunned. Numb. Heartbroken. But alongside the grief came something else: resolve. This company that I had helped build from day one was now 20 years in the making. It was special, and I would do everything in my power to ensure it endured.

In the years that followed, our task was not simply to preserve what had been started with John, but to prepare it for a changing world. We evolved from a traditional marketing research firm into a broader, customer-centric consulting organization, expanding our capabilities, bringing in diverse talent and new skill sets, and deepening the value we deliver to clients. That evolution strengthened long-standing client partnerships while attracting a wider range of organizations seeking more human-centered approaches for growth.

Through economic cycles, industry shifts, and internal reinvention, the company grew steadily while working hard to nurture the culture that made it unique. Employee retention remained strong, client relationships endured for decades, and the organization ultimately transitioned into a global firm. What began as stewardship became transformation: proof that purpose-driven leadership can also be adaptive and durable.

The day that John passed not only marked the moment I became a business owner; it marked the day I discovered my "why" more clearly than ever. Owning a business wasn't about exerting control. For me, it was about impact. Impact on people, clients, partners, our industry, and the communities we touch.

But let's be honest: leading and growing a people-centered business is hard work. There were countless times I wished for a companion, someone I could turn to in moments of uncertainty or possibility that would offer perspective, encouragement, or reassurance that I wasn't alone. "It's lonely at the top" isn't just a saying; it's a reality.

Over the years, I pieced together and applied guidance through mentors, boards, executive peer groups, books, articles, podcasts, and plenty of trial and error. This book is my attempt to gather those lessons into one place for you. Think of it as a mentor at your fingertips; a voice of experience to turn to when you need clarity, courage, ideas to jump-start your thinking, or simply a fresh lens on your work and your "why."

A note up front: this book is not for the faint of heart. It's written for courageous, purpose-driven leaders: founders, business owners, and executives who believe business can and should be more than a financial mechanism. For those who see their company and influence as a force for good, creating meaningful work, belonging, and outcomes bigger than any one individual. Yes, financial results matter. But here, they're treated as outcomes of meaningful goals, not the goals themselves.

There are plenty of books on the mechanics of business: strategy, finance, legal, and operations. This isn't one of them. This book is about the human side, the part that often gets less attention but ultimately determines whether everything else holds together. *After all, when we spend so much of our lives working, shouldn't we focus on the humans who lead, work in, and buy from our businesses?*

My passion for purpose-driven leadership started early in my career. From the moment I first managed people, I felt accountable for their growth. I studied what I could: courses, books, mentors, and hard-earned experience, while relying heavily on emotional intelligence, perspective-taking, and staying close to what people truly needed to thrive.

After settling into my role as a CEO and business owner, I was intent on cultivating an environment where people not only felt cared for and respected but also challenged and supported to do their best work and become the next best version of themselves over time. We aimed to create a place where people could grow professionally without losing themselves personally, where high expectations and humanity coexisted.

This people-first ethos truly shaped everything: how we hired, how we developed talent, how we made decisions, how we developed new capabilities, and how we showed up for clients. I believed deeply that our employees were the most powerful representation of our brand. Every interaction with colleagues, candidates, clients, partners, or our community had the potential to leave a lasting impression.

I often said that whether someone came in for an interview and didn't get the job, an employee chose to pursue an opportunity elsewhere, or a Fortune 500 executive walked through our doors, each person should leave feeling better for having experienced our company, encouraged by the knowledge that a culture like ours existed, and hopeful about what workplaces could be.

I came to understand that when people have clarity, feel valued, and are challenged, they produce exceptional work. Exceptional work strengthens client relationships. Strong relationships create an impact that extends far beyond any single project or transaction. These elements are not separate priorities competing for attention, but parts of a single system. When one strengthens, the others follow.

Now, after more than three decades of leadership experience, including building, transforming, and ultimately selling a business, leading another through significant change, advising Fortune 500 executives, and coaching founders of emerging companies, I've seen just about everything leadership can throw at you. From hypergrowth to crisis, from succession to reinvention, from uncertainty to opportunity, the contexts differ, but the themes are remarkably consistent.

I don't claim to have all the answers. I will remain a lifelong student of business and leadership. But I have lived enough of the questions in everyday leadership moments, boardrooms, and crises to know what tends to help and what tends to harm. Whether you're a team leader in a multinational firm or a founder of a small start-up, many of the challenges and inflection points are strikingly similar. The lens changes, but the underlying principles hold steady.

This book is for you, wherever you are on your leadership journey, especially in the moments that matter, when things feel heavy, uncertain, or unexpectedly full of possibility.

A Note on the Organizations Referenced in This Book

Throughout this book, I reference two organizations central to my leadership experience.

Gongos, Inc. was a U.S.-based firm founded in 1991 that evolved from custom marketing research into broader, customer- and employee-centric consulting for Fortune 500 companies and industry leaders. In 2022, it became part of InSites Consulting.

Human8 is a global customer insights consultancy formed by integrating InSites Consulting and several complementary firms, including Gongos, Inc., with a shared mission to help organizations stay deeply connected to the people they serve.

INTRODUCTION - HOW THIS BOOK WORKS

Whether or not you're familiar with *Open When* letters, here's a quick refresher. The concept of writing letters to be opened during specific moments dates back centuries, to a time when handwritten correspondence was the only bridge across distance. In more modern times, *Open When* letters found new meaning in long-distance relationships, most notably among military families and loved ones separated by service. Each letter carried an act of presence: words written in advance to offer comfort, confidence, celebration, or perspective in a future moment of need.

There's something profoundly intimate about being known and supported by someone who isn't physically there, but who somehow anticipated what you might need most.

I received my first set of *Open When* letters from my daughter more than a decade ago, just as I was stepping into the unexpected role of business owner after my mentor and partner passed away. It was a stressful time filled with travel, client reassurance, and the weight of newfound responsibility. Her letters offered perspective and encouragement at a pivotal moment. One of them simply read, *"Just trust yourself. That is some of the best advice you've ever given me, so I am passing it back to you."* The reminder that someone believed in me, especially when I needed it most, was part of their power.

Years later, when I began advising entrepreneurs and executives, I saw the same need: **leaders searching for perspective at moments of decision, doubt, possibility, and often helping to facilitate an experienced lens on what may lie ahead**. I wanted to find a way to scale the one-on-one mentoring I was doing, so this book was born. I hope that each letter feels like a trusted voice in the room with you: a mix of reflection, real-life experience, encouragement, forethought, and practical tools you can use right away.

Here's what you'll find inside:

- **The Flywheel Framework:** most of the book is organized around a simple, human system focused on four elements essential to operating a healthy, sustainable organization: Great People, Great Work, Great Clients, Great Impact. An in-depth explanation of this framework and how to use it are provided in the next section: The Flywheel Explained.

- **Signature Letters:** These letters open each major section of the book. They set the tone by providing context, perspective, and a sense of what's to come.

- **Open When Letters:** Each letter offers perspective for a specific leadership moment or milestone in your journey. Think of these letters like coaching sessions on paper designed to meet you right where you are.

- **Reflection, Activate the Flywheel, Lead the Moment, Your Turn:** these are headings used throughout the book to indicate reflection prompts, short playbooks, frameworks, and other similar tools designed to help you translate insight into practice and action as it relates to the topic of a specific *Open When* letter.

- **From My Journey:** Brief, real-life stories from my own experience to demonstrate how the *Open When* moments played out and what stayed with me long after.

I know your time and attention are stretched, so each entry is designed to be brief, human, and actionable; something you can apply immediately.

THE FLYWHEEL EXPLAINED

Early in my tenure as a CEO and business owner, I knew I needed a straightforward, human framework to connect the dots of value creation for my team; not something theoretical, but something clear and relatable enough that everyone, from a new hire to a seasoned leader, could see themselves in it and understand how their everyday choices contributed to the larger picture.

The result was our **Flywheel**

At its core, the Flywheel captures how healthy organizations actually grow and endure through the intentional alignment and connection of people, work, client relationships, and impact. Central to the model is the belief that high expectations and humanity can coexist. When people feel valued, supported, and challenged to grow, they are inspired to do their best, not only for themselves but also for one another and for the stakeholders they serve: clients, partners, communities, and owners alike.

When a business invests in strengthening each element, momentum builds. When one element stalls, or is neglected for too long, friction creeps in, and that friction can throw the entire Flywheel off balance. This isn't a sequence; it's a system where each element matters and reinforces the whole.

Flywheel:

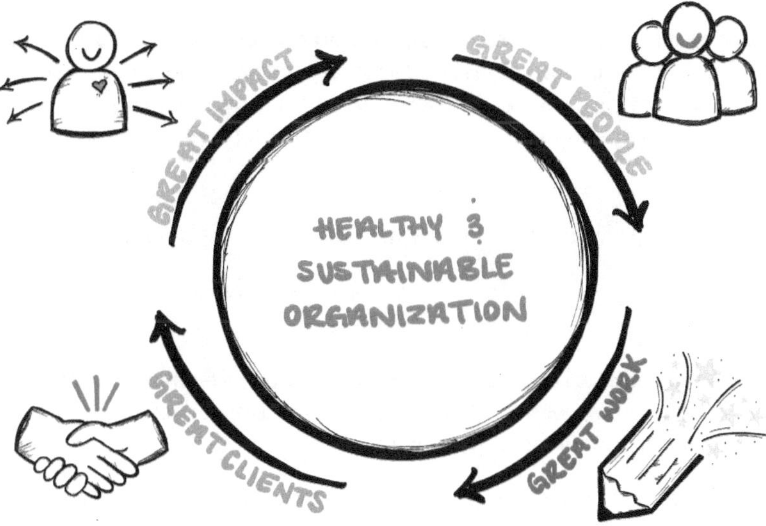

The Flywheel consists of four interconnected elements:

- **Great People:** Attracting, developing, and retaining individuals that embody your values and are aligned with your purpose and mission. This includes creating an environment where people can do meaningful work, grow, and stay engaged over time.

- **Great Work:** Delivering excellence with consistency, thoughtfulness, and pride. When people are clear on what "great" work looks like and feel ownership over the work, quality increases, and the work itself becomes something they are proud to build and sustain.

- **Great Clients:** Building trust, growing partnerships, and creating shared value. Strong client relationships aren't transactional. They are built when great work is delivered by people who care, resulting in loyalty, advocacy, and resilience through the inevitable challenges that arise.

- **Great Impact:** Extending influence beyond financials to your people, clients, industry, and broader community. This is where everyday decisions reverberate over time and where meaning claims equal, if not greater ground, than margins. Great impact strengthens your brand reputation, which, in turn, enhances your ability to attract and retain great people and clients - feeding momentum back into the Flywheel.

Flywheels aren't new. Jim Collins popularized the concept in *Good to Great,* illustrating how reinforcing cycles build momentum over time. Simon Sinek's *Start with Why* similarly emphasizes the power of purpose in sustaining organizations. Both are excellent reads, and if you haven't explored them, I highly recommend doing so.

What makes *this* Flywheel distinctive is not novelty, but usability:

- **Simplicity:** Four pillars that are real-world, concise, memorable, and actionable.

- **Accessibility:** Designed for leaders, founders, executives, and team leaders alike, yet relatable to everyone, making it useful for everyday communication and decision-making.

- **Balance:** Intentionally connecting the internal (People, Work) with the external (Clients, Impact) in a distinctly human-centric way.

This Flywheel isn't theoretical or aspirational; it's operational.

It became the guiding framework for our company, Gongos. It later translated easily when I introduced it to the global leadership team at Human8. It gave us a shared language, clarity of focus, and a compass for decision-making. Over time, it became part of our culture as a shorthand for how we grew together.

Importantly, the Flywheel is not growth for growth's sake. The aim is organizational health and sustainability. Financial performance matters, of course, but when the elements of the Flywheel are intentionally connected and reinforced through momentum, performance tends to follow as a natural outcome rather than the sole objective.

In practice, this meant making deliberate choices, sometimes slower, sometimes harder, in favor of purpose, people, clients, and culture. As you will see in many of the "From My Journey" stories throughout this book, we could likely have grown faster or bigger by prioritizing short-term gains. Instead, we chose longevity and meaning.

Even so, the organization achieved steady top-line growth of roughly 10% annually over 30 years, alongside high employee satisfaction and engagement, lower-than-industry employee turnover, and strong client satisfaction and retention. Those outcomes were a byproduct of focusing on what makes organizations worth building and belonging to.

When the Flywheel is working well:

- People feel valued and invested in outcomes
- Work carries both meaning and standards
- Clients experience trust, relevance, and genuine partnership
- Impact compounds across stakeholders

With each turn, positive momentum builds. And that is where the real payoff lives: an organization that endures because it is healthy enough to adapt, grow, and create value for all its stakeholders. Leaning into the Flywheel creates an organization that is connected through a shared rhythm of what matters most and a clear understanding of why.

How the Open When Letters and Flywheel Fit Together

"The future is not a linear progression of the past." Leadership Team, Gongos, Inc.

This was a phrase my leadership team and I used often, a reminder that change is inevitable and that we must be ready to adapt. The same idea applies to your leadership journey: it rarely unfolds in a straight line. It's a collection of moments:

decisions, trade-offs, doubts, turning points, heartbreaks, and breakthroughs that, together, begin to shape who you are and define how your organization grows.

That's why each *Open When* letter is designed to meet you *in the moment*. Whether you're facing a challenge for the first time, leading through change, ready for reinvention, seeking foresight into what may lie ahead, or taking a brave leap into the unknown. These letters are meant to be opened as guides: human, empathetic, practical, and real.

But leadership moments don't happen in isolation. They accumulate, not just as measurements of time, but as the lived inputs that shape how you lead and how your business or team operates. Each moment influences the next, creating patterns, habits, and over time, momentum.

As those moments stack, they begin to form a rhythm.

As explained in the previous section, that rhythm is what I refer to throughout this book as the Flywheel—a simple, human system built around four essential forces: Great People, Great Work, Great Clients, and Great Impact.

This is where the *Open When* letters and the Flywheel come together.

Think of the *Open When* letters as **entry points into the Flywheel:** guidance for the leadership moments that matter most. Each letter aligns primarily with one element of the Flywheel, helping you make sense of a specific moment through a broader system of value creation. A decision you're facing today may present as a people moment, a work moment, a client moment, or an impact moment, but because of their interconnectivity, it rarely stays contained at its origin.

Each conversation and decision either reinforces or strains part of the Flywheel. Over time, those experiences compound and determine the kind of organization you build and the impact you create.

While not every leadership moment you face fits neatly inside the Flywheel (and we'll explore those, too), most of the *Open When* letters are aligned to its elements. My goal is to meet you in the lived reality of leadership, using the Flywheel as a connective tissue that links individual moments to long-term organizational health and sustainability.

BEFORE YOU OPEN THE FIRST LETTER

Additional Overarching Themes

Two additional philosophies run throughout this book. They reflect not only my own leadership style but also the principles that underpin human-centric, purpose-led leadership.

One Foot in the Present, One Foot in the Future

One of the hardest and most important balancing acts for founders and senior leaders is staying grounded in today's realities while remaining clear-eyed and committed to the future you're building.

For some, this balance comes naturally. For others, it requires constant discipline. The goal isn't to operate in both modes at all times, but to ensure that both perspectives are intentionally represented within your organization. Some roles focus on optimizing today's performance; others are designed to imagine and develop what comes next.

The most effective leaders engage with both: guiding the present, shaping the future, and holding themselves and their teams accountable to each other. You'll see this theme woven throughout many of the *Open When* letters and reinforced by the Activate the Flywheel tools, which invite both a present-day and future-focused lens when making decisions.

Blending Employee Experience and Client Experience

Two of your most important stakeholders and critical contributors to the Flywheel are your employees and your clients. Blending **employee experience** and **client experience** is fundamental to creating a truly human-centric organization.

When both are aligned with your purpose and values, a powerful reinforcement loop begins. A strong employee experience, inclusive of understanding customer needs, clarity around the desired customer experience, and the empowerment to deliver it, enables employees to be the most authentic expression of your brand promise.

The relationship is mutually reinforcing:

Happy, empowered employees create better customer experiences › which create happier, more engaged employees.

This reciprocal dynamic underpins many of the leadership moments explored in this book and sits at the heart of a healthy, sustainable business.

> Finally, remember that most challenges leaders face won't fit neatly into one part of the Flywheel. Business is messy, and leadership rarely follows linear logic. For clarity, I've grouped each *Open When* letter where it most logically fits, and where overlap exists, I'll reference related sections along the way.

Shared Language, Shared Meaning

Throughout this book, you'll start to notice certain words and ideas recurring, such as courage, clarity, intentionality, rhythm, organizational health, and sustainability. This isn't an exhaustive list, but you'll get the gist.

These aren't buzzwords to me. They're the language I relied on while leading teams and businesses, and I continue to lean on them today in my work with founders and executives. Each one carries a specific meaning associated with a mental picture, a discipline, or a way of showing up. Over time, they are something of a personal shorthand: reminders of what it takes to build something resilient, human, and healthy.

Here's what I mean when I use them:

- **Adaptability:** The willingness to flex without losing your footing and staying rooted in purpose while adjusting your approach to meet new realities. Often grounded in a growth mindset.
- **Clarity:** Knowing what matters most and communicating it simply enough that others can align, act, and rally around it.

- **Courage:** Moving forward even when the path ahead isn't certain. It's the confidence to make choices aligned with your values, even when fear is present.

- **Growth Mindset:** The belief that learning and action, not perfection, drive progress. That people and organizations can evolve through challenges, feedback, and curiosity.

- **Intentionality:** Choosing with purpose, not by default. The discipline of aligning time, energy, and resources with what truly drives impact and helping others do the same.

- **Organizational Health:** The ability of an organization to stay aligned around a clear vision and strategy *and* operate effectively day to day. Reliant on strong communication, trust, and accountability, healthy organizations create flow in the work, make decisions stick, and renew themselves over time so that they remain relevant to their stakeholders and build genuine affinity with the people they serve and employ.

- **Rhythm:** The intentional cadence that creates flow across the organization. It's the repeatable drumbeat of meetings, decisions, communication, and follow through that helps people and systems move in sync and reinforces clarity instead of chaos.

- **Sustainability (Endurance):** Building with a long- term lens for your people, your customers, and the business itself. It's not about doing more or being the biggest; it's about lasting longer and being stronger.

- **Stewardship:** The responsibility to care for what has been entrusted to you—people, culture, resources, direction, with the intent of leaving it stronger, healthier, and more capable than you found it.

- **Value Creation:** The ongoing practice of delivering meaningful outcomes for customers, employees, and shareholders alike. It's the "why" behind every decision that endures.

As you read, you'll see these words surface repeatedly, not as theory, but as habits of thought and practice that I welcome you to try on for yourself.

AUTHOR'S NOTE ON SOURCES & INSPIRATION

Like most leaders, I've been guided by the ideas and experiences of many others: authors, mentors, colleagues, clients, and teams I've had the honor to work with. You'll see familiar concepts throughout this book: purpose, mission, vision, culture, customer centricity, and more. These ideas aren't mine alone, but the way I've lived, practiced, and taught them is.

Where I reference well-known thinkers or companies, I've noted them directly. Otherwise, the insights shared here come from years of learning in real time, often the hard way, and from translating those lessons into language that you can use.

ESTABLISHING (OR RE-SETTING) YOUR FOUNDATION

In this section, you will find letters and guidance to ***Open When*** you're starting something new or re-grounding what already exists: a team, department, or entire company.

Because establishing your foundation is so essential to long-term success, **this section is intentionally different**. It includes just two letters, with deeper guidance woven between them to help you slow down and build with care.

As your leadership journey unfolds, I encourage you to return to this chapter whenever you need it.

Open When:

- You're Defining Your Fundamentals
  - Purpose
  - Mission
  - Vision
  - Core Values
  - Brand Promise
- You're Ready to Define Your Culture

BEFORE YOU BEGIN

Whether you're building a company from the ground up or re-setting the direction of an existing team, **clarity at the foundation matters**. The concepts you find in this section aren't just for the C-suite; they're equally valuable for any group seeking alignment, accountability, and shared meaning in how they work together and the outcomes they create.

In this section, we will explore **five fundamentals** that form your foundation: *Purpose, Mission, Vision, Core Values, and Brand Promise.* Together, they provide the grounding forces that hold everything else in place. Think of them as the platform your Flywheel will ultimately rest upon. Alongside each fundamental, you'll find practical tips to help you define your own.

When uncertainty strikes, these fundamentals offer direction. When momentum builds, they remind you why. They remain the backbone as you grow and scale, providing cohesion across people, work, clients, and impact.

Finally, you will begin to see how these foundational elements come alive through people, forming the culture that is the heartbeat of your organization.

OPEN WHEN: YOU'RE DEFINING YOUR FUNDAMENTALS

Dear Leader,

Starting something new is exhilarating and overwhelming. Whether you're building a company, a department, or a team, the early days are full of architecting: ideas, ambition, and more decisions than there ever seems to be time for.

The temptation is to sprint ahead, chasing growth, launching your ideas to market, and celebrating those early wins. But here's what experience has taught me: if you can balance that sense of urgency with the discipline to invest in a strong foundation, **your future self and your people will thank you**.

When I say *strong foundation*, I mean one sturdy enough to carry the weight of future challenges, yet flexible enough to evolve as the world around you inevitably changes.

That foundation is more than your business plan, org chart, or administrative setup. It's clarity about your **purpose beyond making money**. It's alignment around **what you stand for and the commitments and behaviors you'll hold yourselves to**. A shared understanding of **where you're headed**, even if the path isn't fully mapped yet. It's also the space to dream by **envisioning the ideal future** state you're aiming for.

Over time, these fundamentals: your purpose, mission, vision, core values, and brand promise serve as reference points. They inform how decisions get made, how trade-offs are determined, and how progress is measured. When they're clear, people don't have to guess how to behave or what to do. When they're not, even the best intentions can cause confusion and drift from what you intended.

Clarity at this foundational level brings people, work, clients, and impact into closer alignment. It's what allows momentum to build; eventually, the Flywheel begins to turn.

As you set or re-set your foundation, resist the pressure to get it perfect. Focus instead on what must be **clear now** so it doesn't get lost later. The words you choose and the decisions you make in this moment may feel small, but they will echo for years in your culture, your relationships, and your results.

This moment is precious. You won't get it back. So slow down just enough to honor it for what it is...the start of something meaningful. Build it with care.

With you at the starting line,

Think of this section as your starting block. Come back to it often...when you need stabilizing in the midst of uncertainty, or when you need reminding of how far you've come. The foundation you build today will be the red thread that weaves throughout your story, and you'll one day look back on it with pride.

DEFINING YOUR FUNDAMENTALS

At the core sit **five** essentials: **Purpose**, **Mission**, **Vision**, **Core Values**, and **Brand Promise**. Developed with intention, these aren't just statements. They're thoughtfully crafted, lived guides for how you and your people show up for one another, for clients, and for the world you serve. Without them, growth can be unanchored, culture can drift, and decisions can feel reactive rather than intentional. Defining your fundamentals can take days, weeks, or months. As with many things in this book, the key is progress over perfection. Carve out some time to thoughtfully put a stake in the ground, then reflect on it, and iterate until you've crafted something that feels uniquely and authentically you.

As you explore this section, these elements may feel abstract to you at first. But if you invest the time to define them, and the discipline to live them, they will guide thousands of everyday decisions, who you hire, what you prioritize, how you lead under pressure, and what you say yes or no to when trade-offs arise. Organizations with clear fundamentals move with greater coherence and less friction, attracting people and clients who resonate while naturally filtering out those who don't. Over time, that alignment translates into culture, performance, and impact that become a true competitive advantage.

You can search and find plenty of books, articles, podcasts, and online videos on each of these five essential business fundamentals. I'm not trying to replicate that here. The point of this section is to give you a high-level overview of each, along with practical tips for creating your own and a few examples for inspiration. After explaining each individually, I've provided a side-by-side comparison. Hence, it's easy to distinguish among them, as I found in working with clients, this was sometimes the most difficult part. Also, remember, this is not a science; it's an art. Make it yours!

The examples I've given throughout this section include well-known brands so that they are recognizable to you. They also reflect publicly stated purposes, values, and other key principles. They are included to illustrate clarity and intent, not to suggest a single right answer or to imply perfection in execution.

PURPOSE

Your reason for being beyond making money. Purpose is timeless and unchanging; it answers *why you exist* and **points inward** to inspire your people.

Why it matters:

- Serves as the ultimate "North Star" daily and in times of uncertainty or change.
- Creates emotional connection with employees and clients alike.
- Helps attract talent who want to work for more than a paycheck.

Tips for development:

- Ask: *What would the world be missing if our company didn't exist? Is this meaningful and valuable to others?*
- If you are beyond start-up, involve a cross-section of employees in early brainstorming. Purpose should be discovered, not invented.
- Keep it short, memorable, and timeless.

Examples (Publicly Stated Purpose Statements):

Nike: To move the world forward through the power of sport and unite the world through sport for healthy, active communities.

Ikea: Create a better everyday life for the many people.

MISSION

The roadmap for living out your purpose. Mission is what you do, how you do it, and for whom. **Unlike purpose, it can evolve as your capabilities and market evolve**.

Why it matters:

- Brings clarity to day-to-day operations.
- Turns abstract purpose into something measurable and actionable.
- Provides direction as teams prioritize initiatives.

Tips for development:

- Articulate *who you serve, what you provide, and how you deliver it.*
- Anchor it in today, but allow for evolution over time.
- Test it with employees, clients, or advisors. *Does it sound like what you actually do?*

Examples (Publicly Stated Mission Statements):

Apple: To bring the best user experience to customers through innovative hardware, software, and services.

Starbucks: To inspire and nurture the human spirit -- one person, one cup, and one neighborhood at a time.

VISION

A vivid picture of the future you wish to create. You may not know exactly how you will get there because the Vision timeframe is longer term: 5-10 years out. The Vision describes the destination your purpose is leading you toward. It should be bold yet believable and an energizing source for people, giving a shared sense of possibility.

Why it matters:

- Provides direction and inspiration; a long-term view that fuels persistence and progress and can sometimes provide a sense of measurement.
- Creates alignment by helping people see how their work contributes to something larger.
- Sparks innovation by focusing energy on a common horizon, not just the tasks and urgency of today.

Tips for development:

- Start with your purpose, ask: *Aligned with our purpose and in the context of our mission, what would the future look like?*
- Paint the picture vividly: *In our envisioned future, what do we feel, see, hear, and know? What have we accomplished? What are we known for?*
- Keep it emotionally resonant and forward-looking (with a 5–10-year horizon). Complete a gut check: A*re people excited about this future? Can they see themselves in it?*
- Revisit it regularly; unlike the timelessness of Purpose, Vision should evolve as your business grows and as you learn.

Examples (Publicly Stated Vision Statements):

Habitat for Humanity: A world where everyone has a decent place to live

LinkedIn: Create economic opportunity for every member of the global workforce

 ***Key insight:***

In my experience, distinguishing among Purpose, Mission, and Vision causes the most confusion for people. Let's pause here to instill some shared clarity. Think of the difference this way:

- **Purpose** is your *why*; it fuels belief, meaning, and motivation.
- **Mission** is your *how*; it translates purpose into focused, everyday action.
- **Vision** is your *where*; it paints the picture of the future your purpose and mission are driving toward.

Together, they create a powerful throughline for your organization; connecting what inspires you, what you do about it, and where you're headed.

CORE VALUES

The behavioral tenets of your organization. Core values define how people treat one another, your clients, and anyone you encounter.

Why they matter:

- Translate culture into daily behaviors.
- Help leaders make tough decisions and trade-offs.
- Signal to employees and clients what you stand for (and what you don't).

Tips for development:

- Start with what's already lived, not what sounds good. Observe: *What behaviors do we admire here? What behaviors make us, us?*
- Keep them actionable and accompany one-word descriptors ("Excellence," "Integrity") with specific behaviors to create clarity. The

articulation and behaviors of "excellence" by your organization could be very different from how this shows up in another organization. Clarity leaves no room for misinterpretation or assumptions.

- Stress test: *could you hire, coach, and exit people to these values?* If not, they're not real.
- Point to them in daily interactions and celebrate them often!

Examples (Publicly Stated Values or Guiding Principles):

- **The Walt Disney Company:** Curiosity, collaboration, optimism, and innovation—brought to life through inclusive and supportive environments
- **Google:** Focus on the user, innovation, openness, and trust

BRAND PROMISE

The experience and outcomes you consistently deliver to clients or customers. It's as much about how people feel when they work with you as it is about what you deliver.

Why it matters:

- Serves as your external differentiator.
- Builds trust and repeat business when delivered consistently.
- Provides clarity to employees: "This is the experience we owe every client."
- **Remember:** employees, especially those who interact with clients, are the most influential representation of your brand.

Tips for development:

- Ask clients: *Why do you choose us?* And *What disappoints you most in our industry?*

- Test your promise against reality. *Do employees recognize it in their work? Can you reliably and consistently deliver it?* If not, you will erode trust.
- Empower frontline employees with examples and freedom to deliver the brand promise authentically.

Examples (Publicly Stated Brand Promises):

- **FedEx:** "When it absolutely, positively has to get there overnight."
- **Geico:** "15 minutes or less can save you 15% or more on car insurance."

THE FIVE FUNDAMENTALS AT A GLANCE:

Fundamental	Core Question	Time Horizon	Primary Focus	Summary
Purpose	Why do we exist beyond making money?	Timeless and unchanging	Inspiration & meaning	Your reason for being, the "North Star" that guides your people and connects your work to greater impact.
Mission	What do we do, for whom, and how?	Present to near-term	Action & direction	The roadmap for living out your purpose, what you do every day and how you deliver value to those you serve.
Vision	Where are we going? What future are we creating?	5-10 years	Aspiration & ambition	A vivid picture of your desired future; bold yet believable; energizing people around a shared sense of possibility.

Fundamental	Core Question	Time Horizon	Primary Focus	Summary
Core Values	What beliefs and behaviors guide how we work and make decisions?	Timeless	Culture & conduct	The behavioral tenets that guide how people treat one another, make choices, and live the brand every day.
Brand Promise	What experience and outcomes do we consistently deliver to our clients or customers?	Present and enduring	Experience & trust	The external expression of your culture; how your organization shows up and delivers value in a way that builds trust and differentiates you.

Reflection: Foundation Check

Before you move forward, pause and ask yourself:

- *Is the foundation beneath my business (department, team) clear, strong, and flexible enough to carry me where I want to go?*
- *If I'm setting up or re-setting a team or department within a larger business, what should I consider in the broader context?*
- *What beliefs, values, or intentions must be clear now, so they don't get lost in the speed of growth later?*

Making and Keeping Fundamentals Alive

Defining your fundamentals is only the beginning. The power comes in how they live beyond presentation decks, your website, or the wall.

- Communicate them frequently using a variety of channels.
- Point to them in decisions.

- Coach against them.
- Hold people accountable to them, even if that means letting go of those whose behavior does not regularly demonstrate these important tenets of the business.
- Celebrate them!

When alive in the culture, your fundamentals are a true competitive advantage, advancing not just *what* you do, but *how* you do it.

Which leads us to an important next letter...

OPEN WHEN: YOU'RE READY TO DEFINE YOUR CULTURE

Dear Leader,

I hesitate to even put the phrase "define your culture" on paper because culture isn't something you write down once and file away. It's intangible, dynamic, and ever evolving. It lives in your hallways and video calls, in how people feel when they show up to work, in how your clients feel when they work with you, and in the stories people tell about what it's like to interact with your organization.

Every company has a culture: good or bad, intentional or accidental.

As a founder or leader, **you are your company's loudest signal**. What you model through your words, decisions, and everyday actions reverberates across the organization. Over time, those signals take root as norms, and those norms form culture. Which means defining your culture starts with something deceptively simple: **being deeply self-aware of your own influence.**

Placing this letter within *Defining Your Fundamentals* is intentional. The fundamentals: your purpose, mission, vision, values, and brand promise, are what you stand for. **Culture is how it feels to live them.** It's the human expression of everything you've defined on paper.

Culture connects abstract ideals to real, lived experience. It's the activation layer of your fundamentals; the part that turns aspiration into daily behavior. When it's healthy, there's no gap between what you say and what you do. When it's misaligned, even the most inspiring words can ring hollow.

So, as you define your culture, don't start with slogans or delegate them to a single person or department. Culture is shared by all. Not owned by one individual or team. Instead, start with reflection:

- *How do people experience your purpose and values through your behavior and your organization's actions and decisions?*
- *What does it feel like to work here—and does that feeling match what you intend?*
- *Where might your culture be unintentionally excluding, discouraging, or disconnecting people from your mission?*

The goal isn't perfection or control. Its alignment people can truly feel. The more aligned your people feel between what's said and what's lived, the stronger and more sustainable your organization is.

Culture, ultimately, is your company's heartbeat. It's the way your fundamentals and norms come alive through people. Nurture it. Keep it alive and healthy. And most importantly, remember: **you are the strongest role model for the culture you desire.**

Warmly,

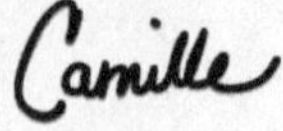

Reflection: A Culture Alignment Check

Culture isn't built in statements, and it isn't something you invent. Culture is built in moments through behaviors and actions. To reach its potential, culture must be understood, modeled, and nurtured.

Take a few minutes to pause and look at your organization through the lens of your fundamentals and your everyday lived experience.

Ask yourself and your team:

- **Alignment:** *Where do our daily actions and conversations clearly reflect our purpose, values, and brand promise, and where do gaps appear between what we say and what we do?*
- **Experience:** *What three words would employees use to describe what it feels like to work with us? Are those the words we'd want them to use?* Repeat the same exercise with clients and any other important external stakeholders.
- **Influence:** *How am I, as a leader, reinforcing or eroding the culture that I want through my everyday choices and behaviors?* Ask others you trust for feedback.
- **Intention:** *What rituals, practices, or conversations could we intentionally create to strengthen the culture we aspire to live?*

THE FLYWHEEL IN MOTION

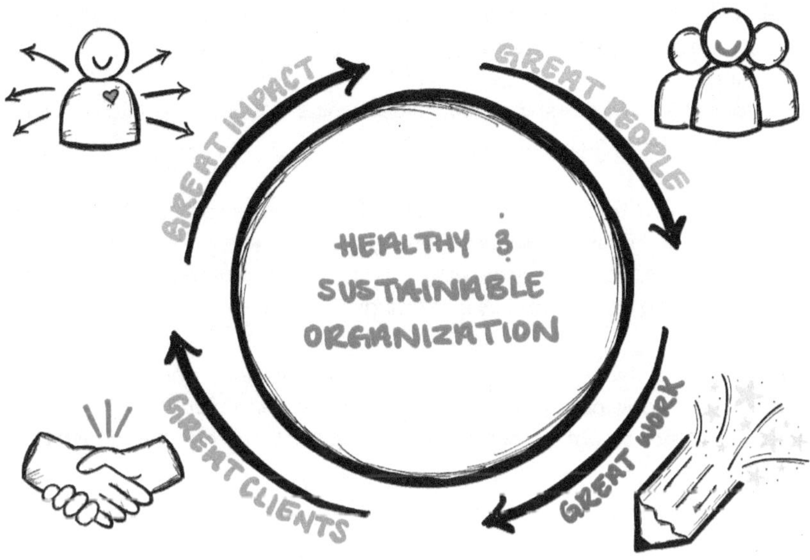

Here you will find **four sections of letters** designed to help you build healthy momentum and sustainability through your people, your work, your clients, and the impact that you create together.

Reminder: The Flywheel is not sequential; it's a system where each element matters and reinforces the whole. Strengthening one element has ripple effects across the others. At the same time, prolonged neglect in any area introduces friction that can weaken the system.

At its core, the Flywheel is not about growth for growth's sake. It is about organizational health and endurance. When people feel valued and challenged, they are more likely to produce meaningful, high-quality work. Great work deepens client relationships. Strong relationships create a sustaining impact. Growth, performance, and resilience follow naturally from a healthy system.

This framework rests on the belief that high expectations and humanity can coexist. Excellence does not come at the expense of care; it's strengthened by it. When people feel respected, supported, and stretched, they are more likely to bring their best to one another and to the stakeholders they serve.

Each letter in the sections that follow is designed to help you strengthen one part of the Flywheel in a specific moment. But no action exists in isolation. A decision about your people may influence the quality of your work. The quality of your work shapes your client relationships. Your relationships with your people and clients ultimately determine the impact you create.

As your team, department, or organization grows, leaders at every level influence the system through everyday choices: what you prioritize, reward, tolerate, nurture, or guard. When there are clarity and alignment around what matters most, friction diminishes and momentum builds into energy that begins to sustain itself.

These letters are designed to meet you in the moment and to be used for reflection, action, and conversation. The goal is not perfection in any single area but intentional movement toward balance, alignment, and healthy growth across the whole.

GREAT PEOPLE

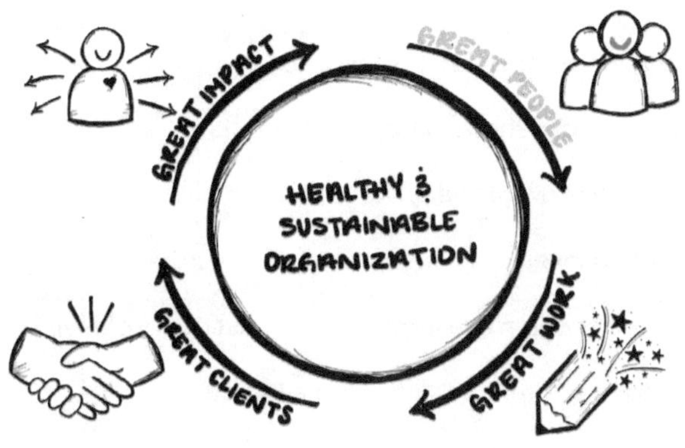

In this section, you will find letters to **Open When** you're attracting, developing, and retaining the people who make everything else possible.

Open When: (Attract)

- You're Hiring Your First (or Next) Team Member
- You're Tempted to Settle for a Hire
- You're Hiring (or Promoting) Your Highest Level Roles
- The Talent Market Feels Competitive
- You Need to Clearly Articulate Why Someone Would Want to Work Here (Employee Value Proposition)

Open When: (Develop)

- You're Onboarding New Employees
- You Realize Feedback Isn't Leading to Change
- A Team Member Shows Untapped Potential
- You Need to Grow Leaders, Not Just Doers
- You Need to Invest in Learning to Fuel the Future
- It Feels Easier and more Important to "Just Do It Yourself"
- You Need to Address a Difficult Issue Directly
- You Want to Future Proof Your Team
- You're Navigating Change

Open When: (Retain and Grow)

- Your Best People Are Burning Out
- Turnover Creeps Up
- You're Questioning if Pay Matches Value
- You Need to Re-Inspire Your Team
- Fixing Weaknesses Isn't Working (Managing to Strengths)
- You Need to Let Someone Go

BEFORE YOU BEGIN:

This section meets you in the real, human moments of leadership. The ones that may not make it into your strategic plan but touch everything around it. It's the decision to hold out for the right person when you're short-staffed. The tug between doing it yourself or slowing down to develop someone else. The conversation you wish you didn't have to have but know you must.

Attracting, developing, and retaining the right people is the lifeblood of a thriving organization because everything begins with and flows through them. People aren't just a resource to manage; they're the source of your energy, ideas, and resilience. When the right people are in the right roles leveraging their strengths, they fuel the Flywheel inspiring great work, delighted clients, and lasting impact.

Through the letters in this section, we'll navigate the often underplayed but defining moments of attracting talent in a competitive market, developing emerging leaders amid change, and retaining engagement and grace through cycles of fatigue or transition. Together these practices form your toolkit for building a people-first culture; one that inspires, stretches, and sustains by investing in the humans behind it.

Dear Leader,

"You're only as good as the people you surround yourself with." Unknown

It's a truth I've carried through every seat I've held. Yet it's easy to treat talent like a line item: something to acquire, manage, and measure. But people aren't a commodity. They're the greatest multiplier of value for your business and for your own fulfillment as a leader. The moment you see talent as transactional; you begin to erode the engine that fuels lasting success.

Maximizing value through people means treating talent as a strategic discipline on par with finance, operations, and marketing. Every decision about your team deserves the same rigor and intention as those you make about clients or capital. When talent strategy aligns with business strategy, you unlock exponential potential: the right people, in the right roles, doing the right work.

Your employees, especially those on the front line, carry your brand promise into the world. They translate strategy into action and turn experiences into loyalty. Viewed through the lens of **reciprocity**, great leadership creates a **win-win** dynamic between people and the organization. When your employees grow, your company grows. When they feel seen, supported, and stretched, they bring their best. You're offering an opportunity for meaning, not just a paycheck.

Building a great business requires more than managing people. Greatness comes from ensuring that the humans behind your strategy have what they need to thrive today and tomorrow.

With you in growing greatness,

P.S. In today's world of automation and generative AI, this alignment between people and strategy has never mattered more. As technology evolves, so must our definition of human value. The opportunity isn't to compete with AI, but to complement it by equipping people with the skills technology can't replicate: empathy, creativity, critical thinking, and the ability to read between the lines for meaning. It's also about fostering an environment where continuous learning, innovation, and even a little serendipity helps people do their best work. These are the capabilities that will continue to set your business apart, not just keep it running.

GREAT PEOPLE: ATTRACT

OPEN WHEN: YOU'RE HIRING YOUR FIRST (OR NEXT) TEAM MEMBER

Dear Leader,

Bringing someone new into your business is exciting but can also be daunting. This person's livelihood and career are now influenced by you. Whether it's your very first hire or your hundredth, the decision always carries weight. For me, this was never just about filling a role, it was about inviting someone to join our mission, our culture, and our story. No matter how short or long the person would stay, they leave an imprint on the business.

Attracting and hiring can be an expensive and time-consuming endeavor, but here's a truth that can increase your effectiveness: **skills matter, but values matter more.** Skills can be taught, sharpened, and expanded. Values and character, on the other hand, are innate and are difficult to "unlearn." When you hire someone who shares your core values and fits your culture, everything else simplifies. When you don't, no amount of talent can make up for the misalignment.

Keep these guideposts close as you step into hiring:

- **Start with who, not what.** Before writing any job description, define the type of person you want by clarifying the values and behaviors that make your business thrive. All people are culture carriers, but alongside you, your first few hires act as culture definers, whether you like it or not.
- **Hire for alignment, not clones** A strong culture isn't about cloning yourself or those you've already hired. It's about shared values and clarity of purpose alongside diverse perspectives and strengths. Diversity in thought, background and lived experiences matters when it comes to weaving a vibrant and resilient fabric for your organization.
- **Test for values and behaviors in action.** Go beyond résumés and interview questions. Ask candidates to share real stories that reveal how they've handled challenges, collaboration, or integrity. When appropriate, introduce exercises to provide an opportunity to demonstrate behavior in action.

- **Don't let urgency lead to settling.** The wrong hire will cost you more in time, energy, and culture than waiting for the right one.

Each hire changes the company in ways you won't fully see until later. Choose people who don't just want a job but want to belong to what you're building. If you get the *who* right, the rest has a way of catching up.

With you in the search,

ACTIVATE THE FLYWHEEL: QUESTIONS TO TEST FOR VALUES FIT

When interviewing, weave in questions that go beyond technical skills and reveal character and culture alignment:

- Tell me about a time you worked on something that really mattered to you. *What made it meaningful?*
  - » Reveals what motivates them at a deeper level.
- Describe a time you faced a conflict with a colleague at work. *How did you handle it?*
  - » Shows integrity, collaboration style, and problem-solving under pressure.
- *What kind of environment helps you do your best work?*
  - » Surfaces alignment (or misalignment) with your culture.
- Tell me about a time you had to make a difficult decision when the *right* thing wasn't the easiest or most popular decision.
  - » Reveals courage, ethical compass, and how they prioritize values over what's easy.

- Tell me about a piece of feedback that was hard to hear. *What did you do with it?*
    - » Surfaces humility, self-awareness, openness to growth.
- *What behaviors from teammates or leaders energize you? Which ones drain you or shut you down?*
    - » Gives you early insight into culture friction points.

FROM MY JOURNEY

In our early days, we didn't have a talent strategy or even a clear sense of our core values. We were moving at light speed, jumping through hoops for clients, and building the plane as we were flying it. One of the best ways we discovered to hire for fit was through our intern program. It gave us a chance to see people in action: how they worked, learned, collaborated, and handled challenges, all before either side made a longer-term commitment.

The intern program helped us recognize something important: the people who thrived with us weren't just those with the strongest credentials, but those who naturally aligned with our (then unspoken) values. But as we began hiring at higher levels, it became much harder to assess that fit. We couldn't see people "in action" ahead of time, as we could with interns. And while many candidates had impressive resumes, something often felt off once they joined. It wasn't about capability. It was about fit.

Things began to shift only when we paused to articulate our core values (the behavioral tenets that defined how we expected to interact with each other, with clients, and with anyone our business touched) and built them intentionally into our hiring process. We translated our values into observable behaviors and structured interview questions to assess not just expertise and experience but alignment with how we wanted to work and build together.

We still had misses because that's part of being human. But our hiring success rate improved dramatically, and new team members felt a faster sense of connection and fulfillment not just from doing the work, but from doing the work with us.

It was the moment we stopped hiring only for what people could do and started hiring for who they were that everything changed.

For additional guidance, see: *Establishing (or Re-Setting) Your Foundation, Open When: You're Defining Your Fundamentals.*

OPEN WHEN: YOU'RE TEMPTED TO SETTLE FOR A HIRE

Dear Leader,

I know the feeling much too well. You are in growth mode, or perhaps a key role has been open for too long. Your team is stretched thin, burning out, and may even threaten to go elsewhere if the workload doesn't improve. The pressure to "just get someone in the seat" is palpable. A candidate appears who isn't quite right but seems *good enough*, and they are available now. You tell yourself they'll grow into it, or that you'll work around the weaknesses.

It's sooo tempting, but the risk is high.

Here's the kicker: the wrong fit is almost always costlier than an empty seat, because a mismatch can eat away at your culture and damage client trust. The time and energy you spend trying to fix, coach, or cover for the wrong hire will far exceed the time it would have taken to hold out for the right one.

When you feel that temptation, remember this:

- **Short-term relief, long-term pain.** Settling may ease today's pressure, but it often creates fires in the not-too-distant future.
- **Your team is watching.** The team antenna is sharp, and they notice quickly when the fit is wrong because they are experiencing front-line action with this person. Especially if you've compromised on values or capabilities. It sends a message, one you may not intend, about what "good enough" looks like here and that the leader doesn't walk the talk of the core company fundamentals.
- **The right fit multiplies.** The right person not only delivers the work but also lifts the energy, creativity, and confidence of those around them. The wrong one drains it.
- **Patience is an investment.** Every extra day of searching is an investment in the future health of your team and business.

It's not easy to wait. But waiting preserves the integrity of your culture and the credibility of your leadership. Know that the right person is out there and remind yourself: an empty seat costs less than a misfit one.

With you as the right one comes along,

ACTIVATE THE FLYWHEEL: GUARDRAILS AGAINST "SETTLING"

1. **Define your non-negotiables.** Be crystal clear before you start interviewing on the values, experience, skills, and character traits you will not compromise on. Write them down to be used as a consistent filter.

2. **Name the pressure you are under.** Ask yourself: *What's driving the urge to settle: speed, workload, fatigue, fear of missing out?* Naming the pressure can help bring clarity and reduce the power over the decision.

3. **Set a "settling signal."** If you hear yourself saying, *"They're not perfect, but..."* pause. That phrase is often a red flag signaling you may be solving today's problem at tomorrow's expense.

4. **Engage your team.** Bring experienced team members into the hiring process. They'll often spot misalignments you might overlook under pressure.

5. **Create a stop-gap plan.** Instead of rushing, consider contractors, fractional leaders, or temporarily redistributing work. It buys you time to find the right fit.

6. **Play the decision forward.** Ask: *If this person is still here in 12-18 months, how does that feel?* If the answer gives you pause, listen to it. The effects of a culture misfit can add up faster than workload.

FROM MY JOURNEY

Because great people were so central to our value equation, and because we'd been burned by settling before, we eventually adopted a simple mantra:

We will only grow as quickly as we can find, develop, and keep great people.

It was a strong statement, especially at the time we made it. Client demand for our work was high, and our Detroit-based talent market offered limited access to the skills we needed, and client growth opportunities were right in front of us. But this mantra became our boundary – **a promise to ourselves to grow with intention, not impulse.**

We were never trying to be the biggest; we were trying to be the best. That clarity permitted us to be selective in hiring and forced us to get creative about attracting, developing, and retaining talent.

We expanded our search beyond geography, long before remote work was common. We accelerated mentorship, shadowing, and training programs to grow talent from within. We invested in progressive benefits and recognition structures that made great people want to stay.

It wasn't always easy, but it worked for us. **By refusing to settle, we protected the culture we were building and created a foundation for growth we could actually sustain with pride.**

OPEN WHEN: YOU'RE HIRING (OR PROMOTING) YOUR HIGHEST-LEVEL ROLES

Dear Leader,

Those who sit in your highest-level seats are more than executives; they're your closest partners in steering the organization forward. They're both symbols of culture and shapers of strategy. Inviting someone into these roles isn't just a hire or a promotion; it's a signal to the business about what truly matters. Choose well, and they'll multiply your impact. Choose poorly, and you may spend more time repairing than advancing progress.

At this level, skills and experience are table stakes. Of course, you need competence, and your process should dig deeply into capability and results. But what matters even more is **your ability to lead through these people**. That requires alignment in values, vision, and leadership philosophy. Senior leaders live under a microscope: your people will watch them for cues about what's acceptable, aspirational, or off-limits. Those who embody your purpose will amplify it; those who don't will erode it faster than you think.

A few reminders as you prepare for this pivotal choice:

- **Hire for values and behavioral alignment first, expertise second.** Skills can be strengthened; character is far harder to rewire.
- **Look for multipliers, not solo stars.** The best leaders make everyone around them better.
- **Weigh "inside vs. outside" thoughtfully.** Internal promotions honor loyalty and sustain culture; external hires inject fresh perspective and new capabilities. Ask what your business needs most right now.
- **Prioritize chemistry.** Mutual respect and partnership matter as much as competence. If you can't imagine sharing both hard truths and hard days with them, keep looking.
- **Beware the résumé trap.** Big titles or big-name companies don't guarantee success in your context. Ask whether they can thrive in your culture, at your pace. And never assume the "book of business" they claim to have ready will translate to new revenue for your business.

This decision is about so much more than filling a seat; it's about weaving the next layer of your leadership fabric. Treat it with the patience and discernment it deserves.

With you in this crucial choice,

ACTIVATE THE FLYWHEEL: HIRING FOR FIT + ABILITY

Whether you are promoting from within or hiring from the outside, filling a high-level role means you are placing someone in a position of influence. Careful consideration is a must.

- **Start with values.** Before diving into technical expertise, explore how they lead, make decisions, handle conflict, and define success. Skills can be learned. Values misalignment is costly. High-level positions set the tone for the organization.
- **Team chemistry check.** Include future peers or direct reports in the process, as they'll feel the effects of this hire the most. Pay attention not just to their feedback but also to their energy as they provide it. *Are they excited? Is there a sense of confidence and ease in how they respond to this person?*
- **Scenario testing.** Pose both strategic challenges and day-to-day situations your business is currently facing, and explore how they'd approach them and why. Case-style conversations reveal thinking and character.
- **Assess readiness differently for internal candidates.** When considering someone internal, don't assume culture fit equals role readiness. Explore what will change in expectations, influence, and relationships, and whether they are prepared for that shift. Clarify where they'll need support to succeed at the next level.

- **Check your gut.** Intuition matters, especially at senior levels. If something feels off, don't ignore it. Ask yourself *why. Is it a real signal or your own discomfort with change?*

- **Get them out of the office.** Break bread, take a walk, or create some informal time together. When the formality of the interview process recedes and scripts drop, you can see the whole person more clearly.

- **Fast forward.** Ask yourself: *How will this person influence culture, decision-making, and leadership norms two years from now?*

FROM MY JOURNEY

Getting higher-level hires right was tough for us. In truth, we got it right only about half the time. We had a solid, well-tested hiring process – one designed to assess not just skill but alignment with our culture and values. And still, we didn't always get it right. Sometimes, even when we followed the process, things didn't work out. But the hires where we skipped steps? Those were the ones that hurt the most.

One instance still stands out. We were hiring a leader to build a new capability, a critical step in our transition from data collection to consultancy. A trusted friend referred someone who seemed like the perfect fit: technically brilliant, deeply experienced, and highly respected. Confident in the referral, we relaxed our own rigor. Only a few of us did a brief interview, and his expertise wowed us. It was the end of the year, and I wanted to kick off January with momentum. New capability, new leader, big announcement.

At first, it looked like we'd nailed it. He helped us accelerate learning and added instant credibility in a space that was new to us. But soon, the cracks started to show. The say/do gap was real. Not just in how he delivered to clients, but in how he worked internally. Our people noticed it first, and, regrettably, our clients soon did too; trust was eroding both inside and outside the business. We addressed behaviors head-on and coached as best we could, but eventually we agreed to part ways. What started as an exciting leap forward became a reminder that capability alone isn't enough when values and cultural alignment aren't there.

Looking back, I can see how badly I wanted that new capability to succeed and how that desire became a blind spot. Every senior hire deserves the full rigor of the process, no matter how well-respected the source, how strong the résumé, or how urgent the need.

When you shortcut the process, you don't just risk a bad hire; you risk culture, credibility, and trust both inside and outside your organization.

OPEN WHEN: THE TALENT MARKET FEELS COMPETITIVE

Dear Leader,

If your experience is anything like mine, the talent market is almost always competitive. This is because you know the right people are a strategic asset, and you aren't willing to settle for just anyone. After decades of hiring, I've learned that the talent landscape moves in waves, sometimes shaped by generational expectations, other times by broader societal forces. Whatever the cause, there are periods when people reconsider their relationship with work itself, not only where they work, but what they want their work to mean in their lives and how they want work to fit into their lives. During these periods, organizations that treat people as fully human, not merely productive resources, are the ones talented people increasingly gravitate toward and build their careers within.

That's why you can't win on compensation and perks alone. Those may attract interest, but they aren't a competitive advantage in attracting and retaining top talent. What truly differentiates you is **purpose and culture**: the clarity of why your business exists, the culture you build and nurture, and the way people feel when they belong to it and produce meaningful work.

Here's what to hold onto when you are vying for the best and brightest:

- **Lead with meaning, not just money.** Pay fairly, of course, but don't assume that higher salaries alone will win hearts. People want their work to matter.
- **Show your culture, don't just describe it.** Candidates can tell when words on a careers page don't match reality. Invite them to meet your team, hear stories, and feel the energy. If it's a pivotal position, spend time with the candidate yourself.
- **Elevate HR to strategy.** Long ago were the days when HR was considered an administrative and compliance function. You need HR to contribute as a business partner, understand the business, anticipate talent needs, and help instill the employee experience as a growth driver.

- **Hire for fit, not volume.** The right person will amplify your culture and attract more like them. In fact, you can encourage employees to do so by offering referral bonuses. The wrong person, even if they're technically brilliant, can drain energy and momentum. As the Container Store famously puts it one great employee can deliver the impact of three merely good ones - the "1=3" effect."
- **Think of talent attraction as an always-on engine.** In my experience, two engines should always be running: talent attraction and business development (we'll touch on business development in the "Great Clients" section). That is not to say that these engines are always on at the same rate of acceleration, but losing your focus on either can put you on the back foot. Even when you have no open positions to fill, keeping a pulse on the talent market, networking with potential candidates, and investing in your employer branding are essential activities.

Hiring people, especially in a competitive market, isn't just about recruiting people; it's about building trust. The organizations that win are the ones that create belonging, clarity, and purpose that people can believe in.

With you in the search,

ACTIVATE THE FLYWHEEL: WAYS TO DIFFERENTIATE IN A COMPETITIVE MARKET

- **In a crowded talent market, be intentional about why your organization is worth choosing.** Tell your "why" in every job posting. Instead of starting with duties, lead with purpose: why your company exists, who you serve, and the impact you're making.
- **Bring candidates into your story.** Share real examples of life inside your organization – team testimonials, client impact stories, or cultural rituals. Help candidates feel what it's like to work with you, not just imagine it.

- **Elevate the HR function to a strategic role.** Whether internal or external, ensure someone owns talent at a business level – linking attraction, development, and retention to your vision and strategy. This shifts HR from policy and process to a true growth accelerator.

- **Be honest about who you are – and who you are not.** Clarity attracts the right people and deters the wrong ones. Talk openly about your pace, expectations, values, and trade-offs.

- **Position your people as ambassadors.** Encourage current employees (and even alumni) to share their experience. Authentic voices carry more weight than marketing messaging – and this serves to reinforce pride and belonging internally, too.

FROM MY JOURNEY

For the first several years we were in business, we didn't have an HR department. We were operating on a tight budget while trying to control overhead costs. Our CFO handled payroll and benefits, and hiring was something a handful of senior leaders squeezed in between client work, strategy, and everything else on our plates. In those early years, that scrappy approach worked well enough...until it didn't.

By the time we reached around 45–50 employees, it was clear something needed to change. We were growing, but recruiting was slow and reactive. Strong candidates slipped away. Internally, people were starting to feel the strain. Development conversations were inconsistent, career paths felt unclear, and managers were stretched too thin to give hiring the attention it deserved.

That's when we realized: in a competitive talent market, treating people as an "extra" responsibility was costing us momentum. **If people were truly our growth engine, then we needed to invest in that belief.**

Hiring our first dedicated HR leader was a game-changer. Recruiting became intentional instead of scrambling to fill seats. We told our people and culture story more clearly. And just as importantly, we finally had someone focused on the full employee journey from attraction through development and retention.

The lesson was simple but powerful: when the talent market feels competitive, it's often a signal to elevate how seriously you treat recruiting, developing, and retaining your talent. Investing in talent leadership flipped our view from business overhead to a true growth accelerator for the future.

For additional guidance, see: *Great People, Open When: You Need to Clearly Articulate Why Someone Would Want to Work Here (Employee Value Proposition).*

OPEN WHEN: YOU NEED TO CLEARLY ARTICULATE WHY SOMEONE WOULD WANT TO WORK HERE (EMPLOYEE VALUE PROPOSITION)

Dear Leader,

Most organizations invest significant time and energy defining their **value proposition to the market:** how they create value for clients and customers. But in a purpose-led organization, an equally important question is this:

How do we create value for our employees in exchange for their time, energy, and talent?

Talented people have choices. They can take their skills anywhere. The best organizations make it abundantly clear why *here* is where someone can grow, belong, and make a meaningful impact.

That's where your **Employee Value Proposition (EVP)** comes in.

An EVP is so much more than sharing information on your compensation and benefits. It is the full story of what it *feels like* to work in your organization: the culture, development opportunities, sense of belonging, and connection to a mission that matters. It's the emotional and practical exchange between your people and what they experience being a part of your organization.

Your Employee Value Proposition is the promise your organization makes (and keeps) to its people.

When crafted thoughtfully, it serves as the throughline between who you are, how you work, and why it matters, and who you will attract because of it.

The best EVPs aren't written by the leadership team or in a vacuum; they're *co-created* with the people who work there. The most authentic language, the most noteworthy differentiators, come from listening to employees describe their lived experience: *Why did you join? Why do you stay? When have you felt most proud to work here? What do you tell your family and friends about working here?*

The magic happens when you take those insights and express them clearly in words, actions, and daily behaviors that affect how people feel every day.

An EVP is the **brand strategy of your workplace**, and, like all great brands, it must be lived to be believed, so it must transcend marketing jargon or verbiage on your website.

When done right, your EVP is a promise that attracts the right people, inspires belonging, and reminds everyone, from candidates to long-tenured employees, *not just why this place matters but how it creates value for them.*

With clarity and care,

ACTIVATE THE FLYWHEEL: BUILDING BLOCKS OF AN EMPLOYEE VALUE PROPOSITION

A strong Employee Value Proposition answers these questions:

Why should talented people choose to grow with us? What makes us different than other employers they may be considering?

Use these building blocks to help you define, create, and deliver that answer. Remember, co-creating with your people, those who are living your brand now, will increase authenticity.

- **Purpose:** Why we exist and how our work contributes to something meaningful beyond the financials.
- **Growth**: How we help people learn, stretch, and advance their skills and careers.
- **Connection:** How individuals feel seen, valued, and part of something bigger; a community, not just a business.

- **Rewards:** How we recognize contribution through fair compensation, benefits, and other forms of both tangible (bonuses) and intangible (recognition, appreciation) rewards.
- **Culture:** How it *feels* to work here. The everyday experience that either reinforces or erodes the promise we make. Think through tangibles and intangibles.

FROM MY JOURNEY

For many years, we had a strong employer reputation. We'd won multiple *Best Place to Work* awards and were well known in our industry for our talent. In fact, agency competitors and client-side companies regularly tried to recruit our people not just because they were talented, but because they knew anyone who came from our organization would be well-prepared and potentially a step ahead.

As we continued to grow, I realized something important: **having a great reputation isn't the same as being intentional about why someone would want to work in your company.**

Much of what made our work and culture special lived in my head. I could articulate it in conversation and feel it instinctively. But as we grew, hired more leaders, and needed consistency at scale, these thoughts residing in my head weren't enough. What was clear to me wasn't always clear to others, especially to candidates experiencing us for the first time.

That's when I understood the real work of an Employee Value Proposition. It required **stepping out of the leader's seat and into the employees' shoes** to ask why people joined, why they stayed, and what they told others about working with us. It meant listening to current employees, learning from alumni, and capturing the lived experience, not just the aspirational one. Getting what lived in my head onto paper was only the first step; involving others created shared language and ensured authenticity from the employee's perspective.

The lesson was clear: reputation may attract people, but articulation creates alignment. When you intentionally and collectively define and share why someone would want to work in your organization, you not only amplify your employer brand externally, but you also reinforce it internally. You strengthen your culture, clarify values, and align on both the tangible and intangible elements of your employee experience. And in the spirit of scale and succession, you are enabling others to carry the story forward both consistently and authentically.

GREAT PEOPLE: DEVELOP

OPEN WHEN: YOU'RE ONBOARDING NEW EMPLOYEES

Dear Leader,

The offer has been signed, and your new hire is walking through the door (or signing in to their laptop) for their first day. It's tempting to exhale and think the hard work is done, but really, it's just beginning.

The reality is that **great recruiting gets someone in the door; great onboarding gives them a reason to stay.** Without a clear, thoughtful onboarding process, even the best hire can go sideways. In addition, first impressions matter; for them and for you. A bumpy start sends the message that disorganization is the norm. A strong start signals that they've joined something intentional, supportive, and worth investing in.

It also sends another important message: *We value you and have high expectations for our work together.* And just as importantly: *We want to understand your expectations, too.*

Elevate onboarding to be more than administrative by framing it as an opportunity to weave people into your business and culture, clarify how work really gets done, and create shared ownership for success, from Day One.

A few guideposts to hold onto:

- **Make the process human, not just procedural.** Introduce them to people and stories that bring your culture to life.
- **Be explicit about expectations on both sides.** Clearly define what success looks like, how they can contribute, and what you'll hold them accountable for. At the same time, ask them to share their assumptions, expectations, and career hopes. Alignment early prevents frustration later.
- **Build a 30/60/90-day rhythm.** Adjust check-in frequency based on experience level, but go beyond task progress. Ask about the experience and what's surprising them. These moments are as much about listening as they are about guiding.
- **Pair them with a guide.** A mentor or peer can make the difference between feeling lost and feeling anchored.

- **Celebrate their arrival.** A warm welcome signals: *You matter here.*

Hiring people is expensive, and onboarding is an investment in your business and in another human. The return is quicker contribution, confidence, and momentum that can last for years.

With you in the welcome,

ACTIVATE THE FLYWHEEL: BUILD A TWO-WAY ONBOARDING RHYTHM

Thoughtful onboarding influences far more than the first day; establishing an onboarding rhythm reminds the entire organization that great people work here and that **we take shared success seriously.**

- **Before Day 1: Set the Tone.**
  - » Reach out personally with a welcome call or note.
  - » Share your purpose and values, and what matters most in how you work.
  - » Ask what drew them to the role, what they're most excited about, and what they're hoping to learn or contribute.
  - » Pre-plan their first few weeks, including manager touchpoints, training, early wins, and work assignments. Prepare the team, too, so that both sides are ready for each other.

- **Week 1: Build Connection and Context**

  » Beyond an introduction to the work, focus on relationships. Introduce them widely, share your story, and encourage them to share theirs.

  » Make explicit how decisions get made, how feedback flows, and what "good" looks like here.

  » Aim for them to leave the first week feeling seen, grounded, and connected, not just informed.

- **30/60/90-Day Check-ins: Align and Adjust Early**

  Use these check-ins to **reinforce onboarding as a two-way street.** Ask these questions consistently and listen carefully. Small adjustments made early prevent bigger issues later.

  » *What's going well for you right now?*

  » *What's harder than it should be?*

  » *Are your expectations of the role, and ours, lining up as imagined?*

FROM MY JOURNEY

We invested significant time and energy in recruiting great talent. Our people would rally around the process, carefully screening and selecting the right candidates. But then came the new employee's first day, and too often, it felt like an afterthought. We'd find ourselves scrambling the night before to set up a workstation, throwing together details that should have been ready long before. It was a jarring contrast to the care we'd shown during the hiring process.

It didn't take long to see the disconnect. If people truly were the lifeblood of our business, *why weren't we giving them the kind of start that reflected their value?* First impressions don't just influence how someone feels on day one; they also affect how long it takes them to trust, contribute, and believe they made the right choice.

So, we got intentional. We built an onboarding experience that extended far beyond paperwork and a first-day checklist. It looked out at least 60 days, balancing training, alignment on job responsibilities, and exposure to real work with meaningful connections to people and culture. The experience became a keystone of our employee journey, boosting confidence and satisfaction not only for the new hire but also for the teammates who welcomed them.

Eventually, we centralized onboarding ownership because we believed in it so deeply. In fact, we moved one of our talented, billable employees, someone with a clear passion and strength for training and development, into a full-time onboarding role. This was a significant investment for a services business. Still, we knew that how people begin sets the trajectory for everything that follows, and we believed it would pay off.

With dedicated stewardship, onboarding became smoother, more personal, and far more effective. Especially during periods of growth, it proved essential for helping new employees feel connected, confident, and able to contribute more quickly.

Onboarding stopped being an afterthought and became a pillar of our culture, a tangible way of reinforcing to everyone, new and tenured alike: You matter here.

OPEN WHEN: YOU REALIZE FEEDBACK ISN'T LEADING TO CHANGE

Dear Leader,

We've all been there, and it's frustrating. You give feedback, thinking you've been clear and constructive, only to realize later that nothing changes. Or worse, the person seems discouraged, confused, or even defensive. That's when it hits you: the feedback isn't getting through.

The problem isn't always *what* you said, it's often *how* and *when* you said it, and whether the other person was ready to receive it. If you're relying solely on annual reviews or one-off "tough conversations," they rarely deliver lasting change. I learned this slowly and not without missteps: leverage less judgment and more coaching.

Think of feedback as an ongoing exchange rather than a single event. Regular "coaching conversations" help normalize the process, making both positive and constructive feedback part of how you work together. When feedback is consistent, people stop bracing for it and start using it.

A few reminders when feedback misses the mark:

- **Shift from evaluating to coaching.** Reviews look backward; coaching looks forward. Anchor your feedback in growth and objective examples.
- **Make it timely.** Feedback weeks after the fact loses its impact. Offer it while the moment is still fresh and actionable.
- **Balance candor with care.** Honest feedback builds trust when paired with genuine respect. (See **Radical Candor** by Kim Scott.)
- **Check for understanding.** Don't assume they heard what you intended. Ask questions, listen to their perspective, and co-create next steps.
- **Create safety.** When people believe that feedback is meant to help, not diminish, they'll stay open and more likely to act on it.

Feedback, at its best, is a gift and one that honors someone's growth and signals your belief in their potential. When it lands, it feels like an investment in their future. Proof that you care enough to notice, and to help them move closer to their best.

With you in the coaching conversation,

ACTIVATE THE FLYWHEEL: TURNING FEEDBACK INTO COACHING

Feedback lands best when it feels like an investment in the individual's future. These small adjustments help turn feedback into a shared, forward-focused coaching dialogue.

- **Open and Share:** Briefly describe what you are seeing and then open the dialogue for them to share their perceptions: *This is what I see. How do you see it?*
- **Swap "You did/didn't" for "I noticed + impact."**
    - Instead of *"You missed the deadline."* Try: *"I noticed the report came in late, which created a scramble for the rest of the client team."*
- **Add "next time."**
    - Anchor feedback toward the future: *"Next time, let's align earlier so you have space to get ahead."*

- **Create space for dialogue.**
    - *How does that sit with you? or What do you think would help here? signals openness to dialogue and* collaboration, not monologue.
- **Illuminate the ripple effect.**
    - Help them see how their actions affect others, the work, or the broader team: *"Here's how this plays out downstream" or "Here's what others experienced as a result."*

FROM MY JOURNEY

I'm not sure I ever became completely comfortable giving constructive feedback, but I did get much more thoughtful about how to approach it - mostly thanks to feedback from those receiving it.

I remember one coaching conversation in particular. I'd spent hours preparing, determined to be calm, clear, and supportive. I outlined everything: what I'd noticed, why it mattered, and how I hoped we could move forward together. When the moment came, I delivered my talk track exactly as rehearsed.

When I finished, the person across from me looked at me with glassy eyes and was clearly upset, but not for the reason I expected. After a long pause, they asked softly, *Would you like to hear how I saw the situation?*

Oof. That was a wake-up call. I hadn't intended to dominate the conversation; I was trying to be helpful. But in my effort to get it right, I had forgotten that coaching isn't something you deliver, it's something you create together. If I had opened the conversation sooner, listened earlier, and asked for their perspective, it likely would've diffused my nerves and produced a far better outcome for us both.

It's a moment I'll never forget. **A humbling reminder that coaching is more than instruction; it begins with shared understanding. Feedback has the greatest impact when it becomes a joint exploration rather than a solo performance. A conversation, not a speech.**

OPEN WHEN: A TEAM MEMBER SHOWS UNTAPPED POTENTIAL

Dear Leader,

Few moments in leadership are as rewarding as spotting sparks of talent that even the individual might not yet see in themselves. It's a reminder that leadership isn't only about managing today's performance but equally about nurturing tomorrow's possibilities.

Untapped potential can manifest in many ways: curiosity, initiative, results, or glimpses of leadership behavior in unexpected moments. As you grow your business or team, a part of your responsibility is to spot this potential and nurture it in people. Don't think of it as handing them a roadmap; it is giving them opportunities to stretch; sometimes that means letting someone lead an initiative before they feel ready. But it's also about surrounding them with coaching and support and believing in them enough to let them try.

A few guideposts when you notice hidden potential:

- **Name what you see.** People often underestimate their own abilities. Be specific. Hearing you say, *"I see leadership in you,"* can be transformative.
- **Create stretch opportunities.** Assign projects that push them outside their comfort zone while still providing support. Growth happens when we are pushed to the edge of our capabilities.
- **Offer coaching and mentorship.** Help them build skills, confidence, and perspective as they grow into new responsibilities.
- **Balance challenge with safety.** Stretching is healthy, but do so with a parachute for safety, making sure stakes are appropriate for their stage of development and learning from missteps.
- **Celebrate progress.** Recognize not just the outcomes, but the courage it took to step up.

Years from now, the work people remember most may not be what they produced, but who believed in them early. The investment you make in someone today may unfold in ways you'll never fully see, yet its impact will be felt.

With you in spotting potential,

ACTIVATE THE FLYWHEEL: SPOTTING AND NURTURING POTENTIAL

Developing and nurturing potential depends on consistent observation. Not just noticing what's there today, but what someone could grow into next.

- **Watch for quiet signals.** *Who asks thoughtful questions, volunteers for stretch work, or naturally influences peers?* Pay attention to who grasps ideas beyond their current role and connects dots others may miss.
- **Point to it and create dialogue.** Don't assume people know you see their potential. Tell them what you're noticing, then invite their perspective. Ask how they see their own growth and where they're curious to stretch.
- **Pair challenge with coaching.** Offer assignments slightly beyond their current scope, then walk alongside them. Growth accelerates when stretch is matched and supported.
- **Reflect back progress and provide direction.** Regularly point out growth they may not yet recognize, while also offering constructive feedback to guide what's next.
- **Prioritize mindset and behavior alongside skillset.** In today's fast-changing environment, experience and current skills matter, but they're no longer enough. Increasingly, future success depends on a person's ability to learn, adapt, and grow. As highlighted in *Harvard Business Review: 21st Century Talent Spotting,* today's talent discovery is less about having the "right" skills and more about potential to learn new ones. Signals of a person's potential include curiosity, motivation, sense-making, resilience, and the ability to engage and influence others.

FROM MY JOURNEY

There was a point early in our business when growth was outpacing our ability to staff it. Client needs were expanding, expectations were high, and we couldn't hire great people quickly enough. The only option was to look within to spot hidden potential and accelerate people's growth.

We began scanning the organization for those who had already proven themselves with great work and strong client relationships. Living our values was the baseline. But what really set people apart was the "x" factor: curiosity, initiative, ownership of the work, critical thinking, and the willingness to go above and beyond independently.

We tapped those people, gave them opportunities to step into greater responsibility, and supported them as they stretched. Some of our strongest team members emerged from moments like that. Not because they were the most seasoned, but because they had shown us that they were ready to rise.

It was a lesson we never forgot: in times of growth, the future leaders you need are often already in the room just waiting for a chance to step up to the plate.

OPEN WHEN: YOU NEED TO GROW LEADERS, NOT JUST DOERS

Dear Leader,

The leap from individual contributor to leader is one of the biggest transitions in any career, and it is one of the most frequent challenges leaders face. In fact, **you** may still be feeling the growing pains on this one, personally. Many people excel at doing: executing with high quality, delivering results, and even exceeding expectations. But leadership requires a completely different set of muscles to be developed: setting clear expectations, guiding, inspiring, and perhaps most importantly, getting results *through others.*

It's not an easy shift, and not everyone can do it. New leaders often wrestle with delegation: "It's faster if I just do it myself," with influence: *How do I motivate without micromanaging? and with substantiation: What is my value if I'm not the one doing the work?* Without guidance, even your highest performers can flounder in this new role.

Your job is to help them build both confidence and leadership competence. That means:

- **First, teach the art of letting go.** Delegation isn't shirking responsibility, it's multiplying impact. Help them see it as empowerment, not abandonment.
- **Reframe success.** As doers, people are measured by their own output. As leaders, their success now lies in the growth and impact of their team. Ensure expectations are clear and that reward structures are in place to motivate the new behaviors and outcomes you are looking for.
- **Model inspiration.** When assigning tasks, create clarity, connect work to purpose, help others see their own potential - this is the work of leadership.
- **Coach doesn't rescue.** Resist the urge to swoop in when things get hard. Use mistakes as learning opportunities and build experience.

Just as Rome was not built in a day, leaders are not built in a day. With patience, coaching, and intentional development, your doers can grow into leaders. Growing leaders is key to developing your business because those leaders must grow in order for YOU to take on the increasingly complex responsibilities of your thriving business.

With you in the growing,

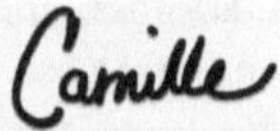

ACTIVATE THE FLYWHEEL: HELPING DOERS BECOME LEADERS

These actions help high-performing doers create the mindset shift, habits, and finesse needed to lead through others.

- **Practice delegation.** Ask them to pick one task to delegate each week and reflect on how it went. *What worked? What felt hard?*
- **Shift the scoreboard.** Together, redefine success metrics centered around team outcomes, not individual contributions.
- **Shadow and reflect.** Have them observe you leading. Then debrief the *why* behind your approach and decisions.
- **Create stretch assignments.** Give them responsibility for leading a project or initiative with coaching along the way.
- **Find the balance.** Help them hone their ability to find a balance between micromanaging and disappearing. Practice setting clear outcomes, empowering others to choose *how* to deliver, and checking in for alignment, without hovering or redoing the work.

FROM MY JOURNEY

When I was guiding others in leadership development, I often leaned on John C. Maxwell's book The Five Levels of Leadership, which describes how leaders grow from relying on position to earning influence through results and the development of others. It was a helpful reminder that leadership is a journey, not a single leap. But what mattered most wasn't the framework; it was watching it come alive in real people.

One team member stands out. Early on, her influence came mostly from title. She was used to excelling as a doer, and letting go was hard. But with coaching and encouragement, she began to shift. I observed her listening more, delegating with faith, and investing in her team's success. Over time, her credibility grew as she produced results *through others*.

The real turning point came when she realized leadership wasn't about being the smartest person in the room but rather helping others shine. Her confidence deepened, humility grew, and she became a pillar of our culture. I remember marveling at how many leaders eventually emerged from *her* influence.

The framework gave us language, but it was this lived experience that made leadership real. Watching someone move from doer to leader reminded me: leadership is a practice, perhaps introduced in training or through reading books, but grown daily through modeling, feedback, patience, and shared success.

OPEN WHEN: YOU NEED TO INVEST IN LEARNING TO FUEL THE FUTURE

Dear Leader,

I once came across a quote that made me stop and reflect:

CFO: *What happens if we invest in developing our people and they leave us?*

CEO: *What happens if we don't and they stay?*

I'm not sure who to credit, but it stuck with me.

Here's the thing: when business gets busy or budgets tighten, "learning" is often the first thing to fall off the calendar. It can feel optional—a *nice-to-have* that can wait until things slow down or purse strings loosen. But here's the paradox to reset your mindset: in times of growth and pressure, think of learning as a lifeline rather than a luxury. It strengthens your business, keeps your people adaptable, and fuels a culture of continuously becoming the next best version of themselves, staying relevant for clients and the market.

A culture of curiosity and continuous learning keeps your team sharp, engaged, and ready for what's next. It fuels innovation, prevents stagnation, and signals that you value not just what your people do today but who they're becoming for tomorrow. When investing intentionally, **learning is a strategic bet, not a side activity.**

A few reminders when deciding where to put your resources:

- **Learning isn't an expense, it's an investment.** The ROI shows up in stronger customer performance, more engaged employees, and higher retention.
- **Be a role model.** When leaders prioritize their own learning, they signal that growth is part of the job, not an extracurricular.
- **Bake it into the rhythm.** Learning shouldn't only happen at conferences or annual trainings. Create steady touchpoints: team discussions, skill swaps, shadowing, coaching circles, stretch projects.

- **Honor different styles.** Some learn best through courses, others through experimentation or reflection. Meet people where they are.
- **Link learning to purpose.** Connect new skills to the impact your business aims to create.
- **Look outward.** External learning brings in fresh thinking and expands networks, fueling innovation and potential partnerships.

Investing in learning says to your team: *We believe in you and your potential,* and that *people development is a contributing factor to company growth and evolution.*

With you in learning to build the future,

ACTIVATE THE FLYWHEEL: EMBEDDING LEARNING

Learning fuels the future when it's both embedded in daily work and intentionally invested in at key moments to support your vision and goals.

- **Share and discuss.** In team meetings, rotate who brings an article, podcast, or insight to spark conversation—consider monthly themes tied to your strategy.
- **Create peer learning.** Pair team members to teach one another a skill (technical or soft) that they've mastered.
- **Initiate and protect a 30-minute habit.** Encourage one half-hour block each week for personal learning (reading, reflection, or training). Guard it like client time.
- **Assign and reflect.** When delegating work, ask: *What will this person learn from this assignment?* Debrief afterward to make the learning explicit.

- **Invest deliberately and multiply it.** When learning is tied to strategy, invest intentionally, even when it's inconvenient. Prioritize group learning where possible, and cascade insights so individual growth is everyone's gain.

FROM MY JOURNEY

As we evolved into a customer-centricity consultancy, we came to an important realization: our future success depended on strengthening our team's business acumen. Many of our people came from deep research backgrounds. They were exceptional at designing research engagements, capturing consumer insight, and translating data into accurate graphics and summaries. What we needed to build next was the ability to translate those insights into *why a business should care and what to do about it.*

To make that shift, we decided to invest in outside, immersive training to develop a core group of account strategists – people who were on the front line of listening to and responding to client needs. It was not a small decision. This was a highly billable group, and the training we chose was both time-intensive and expensive. There was no "perfect" time to re-arrange workloads or make trade-offs with client work. Yet, we knew that postponing this investment would limit our ability to deliver higher-value, more consultative work in the future.

We made another intentional choice: this wouldn't be individual, one-off training. We wanted the group to learn together–to practice, challenge one another, and build shared practices and confidence. We dedicated time from May through August, knowing it would stretch us in the short term.

We knew the payoff wouldn't be immediate. There was no single moment when everything suddenly clicked. Instead, we began to see small but meaningful shifts. People started asking different, contextual questions at the start of client engagements. They were framing insights within the broader business context, not just the research objective. Conversations moved more naturally toward implications and recommendations. Over time, small changes compounded. What emerged wasn't just better output for our clients, but a different way of thinking; one that reflected the kind of consultative partnership we were trying to build.

The lesson was clear: investing in learning is rarely convenient, but it can be catalytic. When learning is tied to strategy, it is a purposeful way to build skills that accelerate transformation for both the business and the people who make it possible.

OPEN WHEN: IT FEELS EASIER OR MORE IMPORTANT TO "JUST DO IT YOURSELF"

Dear Leader,

It's an all too familiar trap. You look at the task in front of you and think, *it'll be quicker if I just do it myself.* Or you may also think, *I'm the only person who can do this and do it well.* Sometimes the task is literal, and sometimes it is about thinking, framing, or the story in your head. And in the moment, you may be right on one or both counts.

But in the long run, this instinct works against you and against the growth of your business, your people, and your own leadership capacity.

Consider this mindset shift: **delegation is not about offloading tasks, it's about developing people, multiplying capacity, and engendering trust.**

When you hold onto everything, including work and your thinking, you limit growth, yours and theirs. You stay busy, but not necessarily effective. And you unintentionally signal to your team that you don't believe in them or that they're not capable. Over time, this becomes a bottleneck, stifling both you and your organization's potential.

As your leadership responsibilities expand, it's also worth naming this truth: some of the tasks you were once great at may no longer be where you create the most value. That's not a loss; it's a win for you and for your company, because it means you're evolving as a leader *and* creating space for others to grow.

A few reminders when delegation feels like too much work:

- **Think long-term, not short-term.** Training someone may take longer now, but it will free you (and strengthen them) later.
- **Match task to growth.** Assign responsibilities that stretch people just enough to build skill without overwhelming them.
- **Share the "why" and the thinking.** Delegation isn't dumping; it's entrusting. Explain how their work connects to the bigger picture. Let people see how you're framing the problem, not just what needs to be done.

- **Resist the urge to rescue or micromanage.** Let people wrestle a little. Support them, but don't take the work back at the first sign of struggle.
- **Celebrate ownership.** When someone succeeds with delegated work, spotlight it. It reinforces confidence for them and for you.
- **Let go of your old strengths.** Passing on work you once owned creates room for others and allows you to focus on where your leadership is most needed now.

Delegation is one of the hardest habits for leaders to build because it requires patience, faith, and a willingness to be temporarily uncomfortable. But every time you choose to let go of tasks, decisions, or even unfinished thinking, you're not just lightening your load; you're multiplying your impact.

With you in the letting go,

ACTIVATE THE FLYWHEEL: BUILDING YOUR DELEGATION MUSCLE

Use these actions to strengthen your delegation muscle and multiply your impact through others.

- **Start small.** Pick one recurring task you normally hold onto. Train, delegate, and support someone else to own it.
- **Use the 80% rule.** If someone can do it 80% as well as you, delegate. That extra 20% will come with time and experience.
- **Shift your language.** Instead of *Can you help me with this?* try *"I'd like you to own this."* Being explicit about ownership matters, for you and for them.

- **Reflect weekly.** Ask yourself: *1) What do I need to accomplish this week that someone else could do? 2) What did I let go of this week that helped someone else grow?*

- **Do a clarity self-check.** *Where am I feeling frustrated because others don't seem to be keeping up? What's still living in my head that I need to make visible so others can move forward with me?*

FROM MY JOURNEY

During my tenure as CEO of Gongos, we were in continuous transformation mode. We had a clear vision and ambitious goals, but much of where we were headed was new terrain. We were, quite literally, building the plane while flying it.

Like many CEO's I talk to, the vision was clear in my head. I was comfortable making decisions without full information, adapting as we went, and holding several future steps at once. The problem was, my brain was often several months, if not years, ahead of everyone else's, and I didn't always realize how frustrating that was for the people trying to follow me.

I remember a moment when a trusted colleague and direct report said something that stopped me short. She told me she could see everything was clear in my head, but encouraged me to take what lived there and bring it out into the organization. Not just as direction, but as a more concrete story, the leadership team and, eventually, the broader organization could engage with and build upon.

I resisted at first. This task felt time-consuming. The picture wasn't finished. And frankly, it already made sense to me. But what I came to realize was this: committing the vision to paper in a more granular way—so others could understand it, too—actually gave me more clarity. The story didn't have to be perfect or complete. It could be a living document, evolving as we learned more and made progress. Also providing motivation to continue advancing the organization.

Once I made that shift for myself, my attitude toward others changed. What had felt like people "not keeping up" was really people not having enough context to fully join the journey. But putting definition around where we were going and why, even imperfectly, I moved from feeling frustrated to feeling understood. More importantly, I began to enlist others to help it take form.

This lesson stayed with me: When you slow down enough to share what's in your head, even before it is fully formed, you create space for others to contribute, commit, and grow alongside you. No matter how important the work, moving from solo effort to shared understanding increases ownership and turns vision into something more tangible.

OPEN WHEN: YOU NEED TO ADDRESS A DIFFICULT ISSUE DIRECTLY

Dear Leader,

Few things weigh heavier than knowing you need to have a difficult conversation. Whether it's addressing performance, delivering tough feedback, or navigating conflict, we often delay or soften it in hopes of not hurting feelings or of the problem resolving itself. But avoiding tough conversations corrodes trust and erodes culture. It signals that you'd rather avoid discomfort than treat the other person with honesty.

Hard conversations are not about being harsh. They're about being human. Respecting the other person means being honest and compassionate. This can be accomplished by clearly and objectively stating the issue, while honoring dignity and building trust.

Here are a few things to hold onto when you're preparing:

- **Don't delay.** Issues rarely shrink with time; they usually grow.
- **Lead with humanity.** You're talking to a person, not a problem. Begin by affirming their value, then move into the issue.
- **Be clear.** Vagueness creates confusion. Name the behavior or issue specifically, avoiding judgment and creating clarity.
- **Balance candor with compassion.** Deliver truth with kindness. Tone, body language, and intent matter as much as words.
- **Listen as much as you speak.** Often, the other person's perspective shifts the conversation from confrontation to coaching and collaboration.

Ironically, hard conversations can actually *strengthen* relationships when handled well, because they show you're willing to be honest and committed to the other person's growth.

With you in the courage,

ACTIVATE THE FLYWHEEL: FRAMEWORK FOR HARD CONVERSATIONS

This framework helps you approach hard conversations with confidence and care.

1. **Prepare with clarity.** Write down the core issue(s) in one sentence. If you can't name it clearly, you can't address it clearly.

2. **Start with value.** Affirm what you appreciate about the person or their contributions.

3. **Name the issue.** *"I've noticed..." or "What's concerning me is..."* Focus on behavior, not the person's identity.

4. **Explain the impact.** Connect the issue to team goals, client outcomes, or culture.

5. **Lean into dialogue.** Ask: *How do you see it?* or *What do you think is getting in the way?*

6. **End with a path forward.** Co-create next steps and check-in points.

FROM MY JOURNEY

Some of the toughest conversations I ever had were those in which a senior leader was out of alignment with our core values. This instance stands out because the individual was only behaving this way when I wasn't in the room. People came to me privately to share what they were experiencing and how it was affecting them. I always encouraged people to have a direct conversation first, but when those attempts failed or the behavior continued, I needed to step in. Because I hadn't witnessed the behavior myself, I had to communicate the issue through others' eyes and feelings, and I knew how hard that was going to be.

I tried to convince myself it would resolve on its own. It didn't. Complaints kept coming. Tension was building. And I knew I had to address it even though I dreaded it. I respected this person immensely; she had valuable business-world experience that I didn't, and I valued our relationship and the skills she brought. But ignoring the behaviors would've signaled that our core values were optional and the team was watching to see what I would choose.

When we finally sat down, I shared specific examples of how her behavior was being experienced by others and the ripple effects across the business. But I didn't stop there. I paired the feedback with the genuine sentiment that I cared about her, believed in her, and was invested in helping her shift these behaviors if she wanted to. I also pointed out the opportunity she had to create a meaningful, positive impact on others because of the unique strengths, background, and experience she brought.

The conversation wasn't easy to deliver, and it wasn't easy to hear. But once she could see both the impact and the opportunity to grow more clearly, the dynamic shifted from something I had to deliver to something we were committed to solving together.

While it took a few days, what happened next really surprised me. She asked thoughtful questions to understand the issues better and eventually enlisted me to gather and share future feedback from others so she could continue learning and growing. The conversation deepened our relationship and became the platform for one of the strongest leadership bonds of my career.

When candor is paired with care and with a belief in what someone can become, addressing a difficult issue doesn't break the relationship; often, the conversation offers the opportunity to strengthen it.

For additional guidance, see: *Great People, Open When: You Realize Feedback Isn't Leading to Change.*

OPEN WHEN: YOU WANT TO FUTURE-PROOF YOUR TEAM

Dear Leader,

The phrase *"succession planning"* often makes us think of top-level executives and their exit or transition strategies, but it's time to reframe that thinking. While that aspect is important, succession planning isn't only for the C-suite or founders nearing an exit. In a healthy, sustainable organization, it's about preparing for *beyond today* by identifying key roles and ensuring that:

- The skills, behaviors, and capabilities for success in those roles are clearly defined.
- Leaders and the organization are actively developing others to step into their roles over time.

Healthy organizations don't start succession planning when someone announces they're leaving; they weave it into the everyday rhythm of people development and leadership mindset. In many ways, it's an act of stewardship: of preparing people, systems, and culture to sustain success beyond any one individual.

- **As an individual leader:** True succession planning begins the moment you step into a role, not when you step out of it. If you want to grow, develop, and take on new responsibilities yourself, you must consistently coach and develop others. When you invest in someone to fill your shoes, you're not just developing *their* future, you're freeing yourself for *what's next.*
- **At the organizational level:** Succession planning starts with deliberately identifying the key roles across your business, defining the competencies and behavioral attributes needed to succeed, and mapping where that talent may come from, whether it's developed internally or acquired from the outside.

Succession planning, in both mindset and action, is the hallmark of enduring organizations. Every leader should be developing someone (or *someone's*) ready to carry forward. Whether you're leading a department, a project, or a team, the question remains: **If not you, then who? And if not now, when?**

At its core, succession planning is a commitment to building a stronger organization through learning, development, and continuity. It's the discipline of taking stock of what *is* today while preparing for what *will* be (and needs to be) tomorrow.

With you in preparing for the future,

ACTIVATE THE FLYWHEEL: BUILDING SUCCESSION PLANNING INTO YOUR CULTURE

Succession planning is an ongoing leadership discipline. This simple framework will help jump-start how it applies to your team or organization. Setting the tone for succession planning may initially make people feel vulnerable. To counteract this, remind people, *this isn't about replacement, it's about readiness.* The more we prepare others to step up, the more we set ourselves up for growth and a stronger future.

One practice that makes this far easier and far more consistent is creating a **Talent Map** (or succession map). Think of it as a living snapshot for your future-oriented critical roles and the people who could grow into them. Use the steps below as inputs to the map by documenting what you learn and revisiting it regularly as your business evolves. This ensures that it is documented and not held in someone's head.

1. Identify Essentials

- *What are the* ***roles*** *or* ***capabilities*** *most essential to your organization's future success?*
- *Which positions, if left vacant, would cause the greatest disruption?*
- *What skills, mindsets, and behaviors are truly differentiating versus merely functional?*

- *What skills, mindsets, and behaviors might we need more of/less of in the future?*

2. Assess Current: Who's Ready (and Who Could Be)

- *Who on your team shows potential to grow into these roles?*
- *What experiences, training, or coaching would accelerate their readiness?*
- *Where might you need to* ***look outside*** *for fresh perspectives or skills not yet present internally?*

3. Develop Deliberately

- Build development plans that stretch people into new responsibilities *before* they're ready.
- Create visibility and shared ownership; make succession part of your team conversations, not a closed-door process.
- Balance structure with flexibility. Plans evolve as people and the business evolve.

4. Revisit Regularly

- Reassess your talent and succession map **at least annually** or anytime your strategy shifts.
- Ask questions like: *Do we still have the right roles for where we're headed? Are the right people still in the right seats for where we're going next?*

FROM MY JOURNEY

Preparing your successor was a philosophy I was exposed to fairly early in my leadership tenure. Our first HR director used to say, *What if you got hit by a banana truck tomorrow? It was her way of injecting levity into a serious topic: what if something unexpected happened? Who would be ready to step into your role?*

And she wasn't just talking about me, then the Chief Operating Officer of the organization. She was speaking broadly, inviting all of us to embrace a mindset of **continual development and readiness**; to always be preparing others, not out of fear, but out of care for the organization and its people.

That perspective became even more real when we faced our own moments of sudden change. The ultimate unexpected situation came when John passed, but even years before, one of our partners suffered a debilitating stroke that left him unable to return to work. Each experience underscored a hard truth: *none of us is guaranteed tomorrow,* and our responsibility as leaders is to make sure the mission and the people can carry on.

Over time, this reframed how I viewed my role. Succession planning isn't morbid or transactional; it's an act of stewardship, taking responsibility to protect what you've built and to both invest in and empower others to continue building.

The simple act of sitting down to review your talent map and succession plan is as strategic as reviewing your financials. It forces you to assess *today* and prepare for *what's next*.

OPEN WHEN: YOU'RE NAVIGATING CHANGE

Dear Leader,

Change is one of the few guarantees in business, and yet it never feels routine. For you, it might signal opportunity, evolution, or necessity. For your people, it often feels like disruption, uncertainty... even loss. Whether it's a major transformation or a small shift in process, change triggers resistance because humans are wired to prefer the familiar.

This letter sits in the **Develop** section because change isn't simply something to *manage*. It's an opportunity to **grow people through**. Your role isn't just to get people to accept and move forward with the change; it's an opportunity to build confidence, capability, and resilience that lasts long beyond a single shift. When leaders do that well, they both develop people and set the stage for retention as a natural outcome.

Here's the truth at the heart of all change leadership:

People don't resist change as much as they resist being changed without clarity, context, or care.

Your job is not to make change painless. It's to make it navigable. It's to show people they won't go through it alone and to instill confidence not just in the destination, but in the journey itself. And when you invite people to help design the path, not just follow it, you tap into a different kind of energy: ownership instead of resistance. Consider these guideposts:

- **Start with why.** Even if the full path isn't clear yet, explain the purpose behind the change. People can handle uncertainty better when they understand what's behind it.
- **Acknowledge the human.** Change is emotional. Create space for questions, frustration, and processing without rushing people to "get on board."
- **Understand the impact.** Change feels different depending on the role. Meet people where they are. Understand the implications for different people, teams, and responsibilities, both the benefits and consequences. Leverage empathy in communications to acknowledge, *What's in it for me?* from their perspective.

- **Be honest before you're perfect.** Share what you know, name what you don't, and commit to updating people as you learn more. Transparency builds more trust than polished certainty.
- **Hold both fear and hope.** Let people express their worries without shame, and then help them imagine what could be possible on the other side.
- **Model steadiness.** Your energy sets the tone. Your calm confidence signals safety, even when the future is still unfolding.
- **Incite agency.** Involve people to help activate the change. Enlist their ideas and questions, and create opportunities for them to pilot pieces of the transition so ownership builds alongside momentum.

Because at its core, change doesn't happen to organizations; it happens **through people**. It is not just a behavioral shift; it's a mindset shift, and the tools, strategies, and plans matter, but what sticks with people long after and determines whether they are advocates of the change or merely comply is how they felt during the transition. *Did they feel informed? Included? Seen? Supported?*

Lead with clarity, empathy, and presence, and change moves from something to survive into something that strengthens culture and confidence. Change can even bring out the best in people who believe in you to guide them through.

With you in changing and the possibilities ahead,

ACTIVATE THE FLYWHEEL: CREATING A SENSE OF AGENCY FOR YOUR PEOPLE

Once you've clarified the intended change, enlist your people to help create the path forward and own the outcomes.

- ***Ask What do you need/What can you give?*** Give people a voice in developing the transition by inviting both support needs and contributions.
- **Co-create the change.** Form small teams to design and execute pieces of the change: communications, process, training, client messaging, etc.
- **Develop the narrative together.** Ask the team: *What story are we telling ourselves about this change? Is this the right story? Fast forward...What story do we want to be sharing six months, a year from now?*
- **Identify and celebrate progress.** At a regular cadence, ask the team to highlight learnings, improvements, and the courage to try new things. Even small, regular updates sustain belief and bolster hope. These are key elements in winning people over.

FROM MY JOURNEY

We decided to move offices after many years in a space that had served us well. Logically, the reasons were clear: our current location was isolated in an industrial park, far from the airport, and no longer aligned with who we were becoming. The new space was central, located in a vibrant downtown area, better for recruiting, and a better reflection of our evolving capabilities and culture.

But for many on our team, logic wasn't the issue. The old space held history. It was built when our founder was still alive. Some people lived closer to it. The move would mean longer commutes for some, parking garages instead of on-site parking, and a more open, collaborative layout. It was a lot of change, all at once.

Once we announced the move, we shifted our focus from managing the transition to inviting people into it. We started with listening sessions to understand concerns and hopes. Then we enlisted people to help co-create the change. From office design decisions and expanded remote-work flexibility, to rituals for closing one chapter and opening the next, to making communications engaging. Framing the move as more than a relocation, we positioned it as a symbol of who we were becoming as a company.

Not everyone loved every aspect of the change. Definite frustrations remained. But people felt heard and included. They could see how deeply we valued their role in the future we were building. And even when they didn't like every outcome, they understood why the change mattered to the business.

Two lessons stayed with me: You can't please everyone during change, AND you don't need to. What you do need is to work toward making people feel included and respected. When people are enlisted to help bring the change to life, inclusion emerges as a form of people development–strengthening problem-solving, resilience, and shared ownership that lasts long after the change itself.

For additional guidance, see: *When Things Get Hard, Open When: You're Leading Through Uncertainty* and *Beyond the Flywheel, Open When: You're Ready to Build Adaptability into Your Culture.*

GREAT PEOPLE: RETAIN AND GROW

OPEN WHEN: YOUR BEST PEOPLE ARE BURNING OUT

Dear Leader,

You can feel it when it happens. The people you rely on most, the ones who consistently go above and beyond, start to lose their spark. They're stretched thin, maybe running on fumes. And because they're wired to deliver, they're often the least likely to raise their hand until it's almost too late. They live in a double bind: they're rewarded for the very behaviors that eventually wear them down.

Burnout is usually about more than workload. It's the feeling of being consumed by work with no control, no visible relief, and no light at the end of the tunnel. And because every employee is a whole human with responsibilities and pressures beyond work, well-being must be considered in full context, which requires leaders to lead with empathy, flexibility, and intention.

Left unaddressed, burnout drains not just the individual but the culture, the team, and the future of the business.

A few things to remember when you see the signs of burnout:

- **Protect well-being as fiercely as productivity.** A burned-out high performer isn't an asset; they're at risk of disengagement, diminished performance, unintended influence on others, or leaving.
- **Remember, "some" is better than "none."** Don't let your best people reach a breaking point. Reduce workload, reduce hours, or grant short-term leave if needed. The goal is to keep people *sustainably* engaged. High achievers might need a gentle reminder: *your career is a marathon, not a sprint.*
- **Flip the script on control.** The work does not control us; we control the work. Model boundaries. Normalize saying no, reprioritizing, and adjusting timelines when quality or well-being are at risk.
- **Check in, don't check up.** Ask how they *really* are and listen without judgment. Sometimes the greatest antidote to burnout is feeling seen and supported so that you realize you aren't alone.

- **Redistribute intentionally.** Lighten their load by giving meaningful opportunities to others–not by handing off tasks indiscriminately.
- **Provide both relief and hope.** Short-term boosts (PTO, time away, monetary rewards) can help someone get through a period, but they are not a fix. True burnout recovery requires systemic change to workload, expectations, support, or structure.

Burnout doesn't mean someone is weak. It means they've been strong for too long without enough balance, support, or renewal. Protecting your best people is one of the most important responsibilities you hold as a leader. It preserves their health and the long-term health of your organization.

With you in preserving your most precious resource,

ACTIVATE THE FLYWHEEL: GUARDRAILS AGAINST BURNOUT

Preventing burnout requires intentional guardrails that protect energy before people reach a breaking point.

- **Regular pulse checks.** Add one simple question to your check-ins: *How's your energy this week?* Track patterns, over time, not just answers in the moment. Don't settle for, *I'm fine.* Dig deeper to reveal their true state of well-being and what's behind it.
- **Model boundaries.** Don't send late-night emails or praise unsustainable heroics. People follow what you do and notice what you value, more than what you say.
- **Prioritize ruthlessly.** Ask: *What really needs to be done now, and what can wait?* Clarity reduces overwhelm.

- **Proactively manage clients.** Too often, we take clients' words at face value rather than understanding what is truly important and why. Teaching the skills of open dialogue to diagnose clients' needs and timelines is a valuable skill that will serve people throughout their careers.
- **Celebrate balance.** When someone manages workload well: delegates, says no appropriately, or takes time off, recognize it as success, not weakness.

FROM MY JOURNEY

Early in my leadership journey, I'll admit I had a hard time spotting (and accepting) burnout in others. I was passionate about the work and about building something meaningful, and that passion fueled my own stamina. At times, it clouded my ability to see just how much effort and energy others were investing.

Thankfully, I had people around me who were willing to challenge my perspective and help me recognize the important truth: not everyone is wired to work the way I do, and that isn't a weakness. It's not only okay, but also necessary if you want to keep great talent engaged, healthy, and able to do their best work over the long haul.

One moment that reinforced that lesson came when one of our top performers became a new parent. She was juggling client travel, a demanding workload, and the realities of life at home. Slowly, the spark that had always defined her started to fade. Her energy and enthusiasm were replaced with overwhelm and fatigue. When she came to say she needed to leave for a job that offered more balance, I was caught off guard. She had been with us since the beginning, and I knew how much what we were building meant to her.

Instead of simply accepting her resignation, we had an honest conversation. I asked what she truly needed and why. What emerged was clear: she loved the work and the team, but the way her role was structured was no longer sustainable for this season of her life.

That's when it hit me: *some of this employee was better than none of this employee.* Long before flexible schedules were common, we worked together to create a reduced-hours arrangement, one that allowed her to contribute high value to the business *and* create space for her family.

The point wasn't the reduced hours schedule. It was the willingness to get creative in pursuit of a **win-win**. She stayed. She delivered meaningful work. She regained balance and energy. And the organization retained someone whose presence mattered–not just for the work she did, but for the spirit she infused into the business.

This taught me that protecting people from burn-out requires designing work in ways that allow great people to contribute sustainably by honoring the whole person over time.

OPEN WHEN: TURNOVER CREEPS UP

Dear Leader,

Few things are as unsettling as watching good people walk out the door. Some turnover is normal, even healthy. But when the number begins to creep up, it's a signal worth paying attention to. High turnover doesn't just cost in recruiting and training; it can chip away at morale, disrupt client relationships, and weaken culture. Sometimes, leaving those who remain to wonder, *Is there something wrong here?*

It's easiest to look at the surface reasons people give for leaving: better pay, a new opportunity, a shorter commute. But beneath those reasons, turnover usually points to something deeper: a lack of connection, growth, recognition, and, potentially, even trust in the organization and its future.

Here are a few things to consider when turnover ticks up:

- **Look beyond exit interviews.** The most valuable insights come from stay conversations: asking current employees what keeps them here and what might tempt them to leave.
- **Do an employee pulse check.** *Are people still connected to the work and finding it meaningful? Do they feel valued and have a sense of belonging?*
- **Examine growth pathways.** *Do employees see a growth pathway?* If employees can't see a future with you, they'll find one elsewhere. Clear development plans signal a future and reduce flight risk.
- **Audit workload and wellbeing.** Burnout and imbalance often precede resignations. Protecting energy is just as important as providing opportunity.
- **Don't overlook managers.** People don't just leave companies; they leave bosses. Equip your leaders to listen, coach, and support.

As a people-centered leader, the creeping up of turnover can feel personal. But viewed objectively, you can see it as a warning light rather than a failure. Respond with curiosity, humility, and action. This is an opportunity to strengthen your culture and recommit to your people.

With you in the listening,

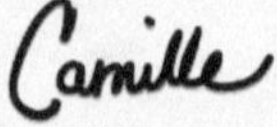

ACTIVATE THE FLYWHEEL: STAY CONVERSATIONS

Don't wait for exit interviews to learn what matters most to your people. Schedule "stay conversations" with a cross-section of employees **regularly**. Focus on questions like:

- *What do you enjoy most about working here?*
- *What frustrates or drains you?*
- *What would make this a place you'd want to stay long-term?*

Listen without defensiveness. Look for patterns and keep a running summary of insights over time. Pay attention not only to the answers, but also to the *questions they ask you*—those often reveal just as much. And remember: even small shifts made in response to these conversations can have a meaningful impact on retention.

For a deeper view of your organization's health, combine themes from stay conversations with insights from exit interviews and employee engagement surveys. Together, they give you a holistic picture of what's fueling people, what's draining them, and where small investments can create a big impact.

FROM MY JOURNEY

There was a stretch when we noticed a pattern that didn't show up as a crisis on paper, but it sure felt like one. Several people in the two-to-three-year of experience range were leaving within a relatively short period of time.

It was a bummer anytime someone left, but this group in particular was precarious. There were people we had hired early in their careers and invested heavily in training, mentorship, and building depth of experience. This two- to three-year mark is when many of them are just beginning to spread their wings and contribute more independently. Losing them meant losing future value, not just past investment.

Individually, their reasons for leaving made sense. A new opportunity. Promised career advancement. More competitive pay. But collectively, something felt off. The exits were too clustered to be ignored.

Instead of waiting for more people to leave, we started having intentional stay conversations with others at that same level of experience. We wanted to understand what they were experiencing *before* they made a decision.

What we learned was nuanced, not dramatic. People talked about uncertainty around growth paths and acknowledged a few missteps on our part regarding compensation. They wanted clearer signals about what came next and wondered whether staying would truly pay off in the long term. None of it felt urgent in isolation, but together it told an important story. And if we expected this group to be a pipeline for future growth, we knew we had to take it seriously.

We still lost more people than we would have liked, but those insights allowed us to act thoughtfully rather than reactively. We clarified development pathways, made expectations and opportunities more visible, and invested more intentionally in managers at that layer of the organization. We also took a harder look at our compensation structure. Just as importantly, we signaled we were paying attention, and that people didn't need to leave to be heard.

What's important here is that turnover often starts quietly, especially at career inflection points. If all you do is benchmark your turnover rate against industry averages, you risk missing the real signals. Leaders who tune into patterns, not just to statistics and reasons, and respond before exits accelerate, can shift retention from reactive to intentional.

OPEN WHEN: YOU'RE QUESTIONING IF PAY MATCHES VALUE

Dear Leader,

Maybe you're wondering whether compensation truly reflects the value your people bring or maybe you're starting to hear rumblings from the team on this topic. Either way, if you're questioning it, your people are likely wondering too. Money isn't everything, but it matters because it shapes how people interpret their worth, their contributions, and their place in the organization.

Compensation isn't just base salary, and it isn't just numbers. It includes benefits, bonus structures, paid time off -- all pieces of the value exchange between the company and the individual. But psychologically, it's about fairness, perception, transparency, and the narrative your organization tells about how people are rewarded for their contributions. Even a strong culture can't compensate for a rewards system that lags too far behind the market or feels inconsistent across the company.

A few guideposts to consider when these questions surface:

- **Know your market.** Invest in regular benchmarking so you have real data on where you stand. Guessing (or hoping) is not a strategy, and it's easy to get caught on your back foot.
- **Balance external and internal equity.** Pay should be competitive with the market *and* feel fair among colleagues. Disparities erode trust quickly.
- **Look beyond salary.** Benefits: healthcare, flexibility, wellness, learning support, career advancement, recognition, time off, bonuses, all of these things meaningfully influence the employee experience, especially long-term.
- **Be transparent.** People don't expect perfection, but they do expect you to be clear. Share how compensation decisions are made and what factors matter most.
- **Align rewards with values.** If you say people are your greatest asset, ensure pay and benefits reflect that belief.

Most research on compensation shows that salary increases provide only a temporary boost in motivation. Your job as a leader isn't to chase a moving target; it's to ensure compensation is fair. It's one lever among several that influence engagement and retention, and if you or your people are questioning it, it's a signal to pause, assess, and make sure your rewards reflect both the market and the organization you're trying to build.

With you in ensuring people feel valued,

ACTIVATE THE FLYWHEEL: COMPENSATION THAT BUILDS TRUST

People don't need perfection in compensation; they need fairness they can understand and trust.

- **Benchmark regularly.**
  Invest in and review market data at least once a year to understand where your roles sit relative to current salary norms, especially during periods of growth or shifting talent needs.

- **Check internal equity.**
  Audit compensation across comparable roles and levels. Look for gaps that don't make logical sense. If you can't explain the disparity, it's a signal to correct it.

- **Share your philosophy, transparently.**
  Be transparent about how compensation decisions are made: the why behind decisions, what matters most, how performance is evaluated, and how bonuses are determined.

- **Separate performance conversations from compensation surprises.**
  Offer regular feedback, recognition, and growth coaching throughout the year. Separating compensation conversations and performance conversations makes each more meaningful.

- **Make variable compensation meaningful, not corrective.**
  Bonuses should reward strong contributions and reinforce desired behaviors, not compensate for weak base pay. First, ensure foundational pay feels fair; then amplify motivation with performance-based rewards.

- **Listen for signal questions.**
  When employees start asking about titles, ranges, bonuses, or market norms, don't dismiss it as mere curiosity. It's often the first sign they're wondering about fairness.

FROM MY JOURNEY

At one point in our company's growth, we realized our fixed-pay model wasn't serving our people or us well. As the business became more complex, we needed a way to align individual performance with company performance, while also keeping fixed costs manageable in an unpredictable market.

That's when we introduced a variable compensation structure, with bonuses tied to both company results and individual contributions. It wasn't about rewarding effort alone; it was about reinforcing the connection between the health of the business and each person's success on the team. We provided quarterly financial updates so people could anticipate baseline bonus expectations and feel more closely connected to the business's performance.

Over time, we saw the shift. People began to think more like owners. Accountability expanded beyond individual tasks to the overall success of the business. And we were able to reward strong contributors without overcommitting to higher fixed salaries when markets fluctuated.

But here's the part that mattered just as much: **variable compensation never replaced the need for a fair base salary.** It wasn't designed to discount foundational pay; it was designed to *enhance* it. The base needed to feel fair and competitive first; only then could variable compensation feel motivating rather than compensatory.

We also structured the system so that the higher your title, the more leveraged your compensation became. Leaders shared more directly in the risk and the reward of the business.

Here's what I learned: Variable compensation isn't a cure-all, but for us, it became a meaningful way to financially recognize strong performance, share the monetary value being created, and strengthen the connection between personal contribution and the company's success.

Bonus Section: Four Questions Before Introducing Variable Compensation

When designed thoughtfully, variable compensation can deepen ownership and partnership between employees and the organization. When designed poorly, it can erode trust. These questions help you get it right.

1. **What behaviors do we want to reinforce?**
   Variable pay only works if it's tied to outcomes that matter. Be explicit about whether you're rewarding revenue growth, client satisfaction, innovation, teamwork or a combination. Each may have a different weight.

2. **How do we balance company and individual performance?**
   A healthy system recognizes both. Consider tying bonuses to a mix of company results (shared accountability) and individual contributions (personal ownership).

3. **How much variability is right at each level?**
   The higher up in the organization, the more leveraged compensation should be against company performance. For frontline roles, keep base pay stability higher; for leadership, align more closely with company outcomes.

4. **Can we explain it simply?**
   If employees can't easily understand how the system works, it will create confusion and decrease credibility. Transparency in both design and communication is essential.

OPEN WHEN: YOU NEED TO RE-INSPIRE YOUR TEAM

Dear Leader,

Every organization goes through cycles: periods where momentum feels unstoppable and periods where everything slows, stalls, or feels harder than it should. When energy dips, your team will look to you for direction, yes, but just as important, **they will look to you for belief.**

Re-inspiring a team is about more than cheerleading and pep talks. It's about reigniting conviction. Conviction in the purpose of the work, in the progress you're making, and in the collective strength of the team. It's also about ensuring people feel that they're not just passengers in the journey. Their contributions are essential; their ideas, effort, enthusiasm, and trust are critical to a successful future.

People want to be part of a winning team. And *winning* isn't just measured in revenue or market share; it's measured in client and employee satisfaction, in developing new offers or capabilities to ignite new growth; it's measured in people's growth and development, in feelings of contribution and belonging to something that feels **alive** and **worth giving their best to**.

Here are a few approaches that can breathe momentum back into the room:

- **Tell the story.** Remind people where you've come from as a business, why the work matters, and what you're building toward. Story fuels belief.
- **Offer reasons to believe.** Share proof points: customer wins, improvements, indicators, and stories of past challenges successfully overcome.
- **Create rituals.** Establish rhythms that spark connection and energy: kickoffs, debriefs, reflections, celebrations, or traditions that reinforce belonging.
- **Enlist the team in the lift.** Momentum grows when people feel ownership. Empower your team to help generate energy and progress.

- **Recognize and celebrate.** Shine a light on big and small wins. Celebration reinforces movement and reminds people they're part of something that's succeeding.
- **Be visible and bring energy.** Inspiration is contagious. Show up with clarity, conviction, and steadiness. If you don't model belief in the path forward, it's unreasonable to expect others to feel it.

When the cycle you're in feels flat, your job is to do more than diagnose and cheerlead. It's to help people see both possibility *and* progress. That combination has the potential to boost morale and get your team back in motion.

With you in the rally,

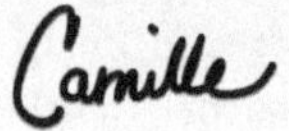

ACTIVATE THE FLYWHEEL: TEAM RE-INSPIRATION TOOLKIT

When momentum dips, leaders can re-ignite energy by making progress, purpose, and possibility visible again.

- **Wins Wall:** Create a visible space (physical or digital) where people can post wins: client feedback, personal milestones, project breakthroughs.
- **Ritual Reset:** Introduce a new ritual to mark progress—Friday "cheers and learnings," monthly celebration lunches, or quarterly reflection sessions.
- **Energy Audit:** Ask your team: *What's giving you energy right now? What's draining it?* Use the answers to make immediate, visible shifts.
- **Fundamentals Reset:** Periodically, retell the company's origin story and reemphasize the company's fundamentals and their importance. Make it real by tying in to recent client or people successes.

FROM MY JOURNEY

After more than 30 years of building a company, I learned that every business moves through cycles: growth, slowdown, and sometimes decline. Each season tests leadership in different ways, but some of the hardest moments come when energy dips and belief begins to waver.

One such period stands out for me. We had just lost one of our largest clients and were simultaneously hit by an unexpected downturn in a key sector. The mood across the company was heavy and low. Many people had only ever known "good times" in our business, and the sudden shift created uncertainty and declining morale.

We knew reassurance alone wouldn't be enough. To move forward, we needed to enlist people's help to create a sense of agency and shared ownership in what came next.

We brought everyone together for a half-day immersion focused on re-solidifying belief. At the center was our "fight story." Resilience wasn't new to us; it was part of who we were. This wasn't a failure; it was a cycle, and we had navigated cycles before.

But belief without agency fades quickly. So, we paired inspiration with ownership. We collaborated to outline ways everyone could contribute, from new-client outreach to competitive intelligence, to process improvements, to new capability ideas, and invited them to add their own ideas. We weren't looking for passive optimism; we wanted active participation.

Knowing momentum from big moments can dwindle away, we created a monthly rhythm to keep it alive: sharing what people were trying, what was working, what wasn't, and what we were learning along the way.

Unfortunately, that gathering didn't magically solve our challenges. But it began to shift something important. It reminded people, including me, that restoring belief and confidence comes from offering agency and helping people see themselves as co-authors of the next chapter.

OPEN WHEN: FIXING WEAKNESSES ISN'T WORKING (MANAGING TO STRENGTHS)

Dear Leader,

If you're reading this, chances are you've been pouring time and energy into helping someone improve. Despite everyone's best intentions, the performance still isn't shifting. You've coached, you've trained, you've clarified expectations, you've discussed consequences... and yet the same missteps keep resurfacing. They're trying. You're trying. And still... the breakthrough isn't coming.

This is one of the most frustrating leadership moments because it isn't about effort or attitude. It's a signal that you may be trying to coach someone through their weaknesses instead of identifying and unleashing their strengths.

Here's a truth I learned:

You can usually move a weakness minimally, but you can move a strength *maximally.*

CliftonStrengths (formerly StrengthsFinder 2.0 from Gallup, Tom Rath) introduced me to something simple and profound: people don't grow exceptional by fixing their weaknesses; they grow exceptional by operating in their areas of strength. When someone is stuck, it's rarely because they're not capable; it's because the role isn't aligned with what they naturally do best.

When you feel yourself hitting a wall in developing people, keep these reminders close:

- **Start by looking for what's right.** Before you zoom in on what's missing, ask: *Where does this person produce their best work? When do they light up? Where do results come naturally?*
- **Stop trying to "fix" people into fit.** Skills can be developed, but strengths are innate. Forcing someone to spend most of their time in an area of weakness drains energy from them, from you, and eventually from the team.
- **Design roles around strengths when possible.** Shift responsibilities toward what someone does exceptionally well and away from what chronically trips them up.

- **Pair complementary strengths.** Sometimes the answer isn't redistributing the workload, it's pairing the right people so strengths multiply instead of frustration accumulating.
- **Help people name their strengths.** When individuals understand what they're uniquely good at (and why it matters), ownership, confidence, and performance accelerate.

After several attempts and continued stalled performance, be open to this lesson: people don't thrive when they're managed to improve weaknesses. They thrive when they're energized. When they're empowered to do what they're great at. Not what they're merely tolerating.

Strengths-based leadership is both empathetic and strategic. It unlocks potential, nurtures engagement, and, when practiced across a team or organization, can elevate everyone.

With you in unleashing strengths,

ACTIVATE THE FLYWHEEL: MANAGING TO STRENGTHS AND PASSIONS

Managing to strengths and passions isn't a switch to flip—it's a stepped approach. Use these actions to test, learn, and build momentum in a way that fits your team.

1. **Strengths Snapshot**
   Have each team member take a strengths assessment, such as Gallup's CliftonStrengths (formerly StrengthsFinder 2.0), and share their top strengths with the team. Capture them in a shared space to give managers and teammates a common language for setting people up to succeed.

2. **Energizing vs. Draining Audit**
   Ask each person to list the tasks that energize them and the ones that consistently drain them. Energy is often a better indicator of fit than performance. Where energy is low, performance usually follows.

3. **Role Fit Experiments**
   For someone who's stuck, reassign 10–20% of their time for 60–90 days to work aligned to their strengths. Watch for shifts in confidence, momentum, and results. Don't redesign a role permanently. **Test and learn first.**

4. **Strengths Pairing**
   Pair people whose strengths complement each other so each can stay in their zone of excellence rather than compensating for weakness. Define clear "lanes" so no one is left repeatedly doing tasks that drain them.

5. **Two-Way Development Planning**
   In 1:1s, shift FROM: *What do you need to improve?* TO:
   Based on your strengths and passions, what do you want to grow into next?
   Then align training, stretch assignments, and mentorship to that answer, not just to the org chart.

FROM MY JOURNEY

I was well into my leadership journey when I first encountered the concept of managing to strengths. A facilitator in a workshop said something that stopped me in my tracks: *"Stop trying to improve people's weaknesses."* At first, it felt counterintuitive. *Wasn't growth about helping people get better where they struggled?* But the more I listened, and the more I heard from leaders who had put strengths-based leadership into practice, the more it clicked. It aligned with the empathetic, people-first kind of leadership I believed in.

When I returned to the office, I couldn't unsee the opportunities. We introduced CliftonStrengths company-wide and eventually had every new employee take it before joining so we could set them up for success on day one. We trained our managers on the philosophy and began using strengths as a core lens for development.

Two moments sealed it for me. We had a project manager who was always trying hard but constantly tripped over details and organization. We'd coached the weaknesses for years. Nothing stuck. CliftonStrengths revealed the real story: conceptual thinking, vision, pattern recognition, and strategy. We shifted the role toward innovation and capability development, and he flourished. The energy, confidence, and performance shift was unmistakable.

Another employee started as a researcher. Technically solid and procedural, but had a passion for design, and CliftonStrengths revealed communication and creativity as defining strengths. We took a risk and assigned her the task of bringing our client's deliverables to life visually. She became our first graphic designer and transformed our storytelling as a company.

Here's what I learned: improving weaknesses isn't irrelevant, but it shouldn't be the center of development. Mitigate weaknesses + Amplify strengths. And when strengths are paired with passions as a core principle of career development, retention, engagement, and performance all lift. People didn't just stay longer, they stayed happier, more confident, and more alive in their work.

OPEN WHEN: YOU NEED TO LET SOMEONE GO

Dear Leader,

No matter how much you invest in attracting, developing, and retaining people, there will come a moment when it's time to part ways. Sometimes the decision is theirs. Sometimes it's yours. Either way, endings can be hard, especially for human-centric leaders and cultures.

But how you handle goodbyes says as much about your culture as how you handle welcomes. Done poorly, departures can leave scars on the person leaving, on the people who remain, and quite frankly, on your credibility as a leader. Done thoughtfully and with grace, they can preserve dignity, reinforce values, and even create ambassadors for your business long after someone has moved on.

Here are a few guideposts when it's time to say goodbye:

- **Lead with humanity.** Whether the departure is voluntary or involuntary, treat people with respect and compassion. People will forget the words. They will remember how you made them feel.
- **Be clear, candid, and compassionate.** Ambiguity creates more pain than clarity. If you're letting someone go, explain the why with honesty, even when the truth is difficult.
- **Honor contributions.** Reflect the value they've added and the impact they've had. When someone chooses to leave, be genuinely happy for them.
- **Support the transition.** Provide notice, resources, or assistance where possible. Helping someone accomplish a soft landing demonstrates care, and people talk about how they were treated on the way out.
- **Mind the ripple.** Your remaining team is watching. How you handle this goodbye sets a tone for psychological safety, accountability, and trust in leadership.

- **Remember: letting go can also be an act of care.** If someone is struggling or the role isn't a fit, holding on can prolong the pain for everyone. Releasing them can open space for both them and the team to thrive again.

Most goodbyes are bittersweet. But when handled with honesty and dignity, they close one chapter with integrity and open the door to new beginnings on both sides.

With you in the letting go,

ACTIVATE THE FLYWHEEL: SAYING GOODBYE WITH GRACE

How you handle goodbyes reinforces your values just as clearly as how you welcome people in.

- **Prepare your words.** Write down what you want to say so your message is clear, respectful, and balanced between candor and compassion.
- **Hold space.** Allow time for the other person to respond, ask questions, or simply process. Don't rush the conversation.
- **Close with gratitude.** Name a specific contribution or quality they brought. Recognition matters, even at the end.
- **Signal continuity.** Communicate thoughtfully with the rest of the team and clients where appropriate. While people will want to be informed of the departure, equally important will be workload coverage and "what does it mean for them." Have a plan and express confidence in the path ahead.

FROM MY JOURNEY

One of our star team members had decided to leave for a client-side position that offered new growth opportunities. To say it stung to lose them was an understatement, and, of course, we tried briefly to entice them to stay. But once it became clear this next chapter mattered deeply to them, I knew the goodbye itself would matter, too.

We collaborated closely to ensure a smooth handoff. They inventoried their work, documented everything thoroughly, and did beautiful, thoughtful transitions to the teammates who would be taking over their responsibilities. Watching this process unfold filled me with pride because even in their departure, they were living our values. They weren't just leaving; they were ensuring the continued success of the work, their teammates, and the clients they cared about.

That experience influenced how I think about goodbyes. Earlier in my career, I often took departures, especially voluntary ones, too personally, as if they were a failure of leadership or culture. Over time, I came to see something different: helping people grow sometimes means letting them go.

When leaders handle exits with respect and care, the relationship doesn't end; it evolves. People carry your values, lessons, and culture into the world. And in doing so, they extend your impact far beyond the walls of your organization.

The lesson that stayed with me: how you say goodbye is part of how you lead. When you do it well, even endings can be a reflection of who you are...and who you've helped others grow into.

GREAT WORK

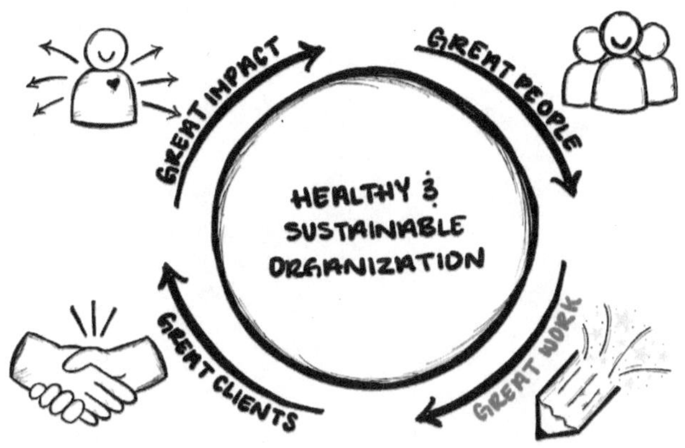

In this section, you will find letters to ***Open When*** you're striving to deliver excellence consistently, thoughtfully, and with pride.

Open When:

- You Want Your Client Experience to Become an Advantage
- The Work Feels Transactional
- The Work is Good but Not Evolving (Innovation Feels Stuck)
- Mistakes Happen
- Growth Strains Quality
- Excellence Feels Out of Reach
- You Need to Move from Working In the Business to Leading the Business

BEFORE YOU BEGIN

Great Work is the glue that forges Great People and Great Clients together, creating something valuable in partnership. It's where your brand promise is delivered, through both your client experience and the tangible quality of your work product.

Meaningful, high-quality work fuels pride within your organization and market performance. It inspires your people, proves your value to clients, and sets the stage for trust and growth. For many service businesses, great work is the single biggest driver of repeat business and organic business development.

In this section, we meet in the moments that define the heartbeat and rhythm of great work. The times when you are doing the foundational work of defining or sharpening your client experience. When growth creates the pressures of the work feeling transactional, or when you wonder if quality can keep pace with the excellence you've defined when you're in growth mode. We'll explore the very real tensions of innovation feeling stuck and the importance of adapting the work to changing market needs. We'll explore the realization that as your business evolves, your attention must shift from being in the work to leading and charting the path to the future.

An important note:

Quality vs. Excellence

As you read the letters in this section, it's worth pausing to recognize the distinction between **quality** and **excellence**.

- **Quality is the floor.** It's about the basics: delivering on time, on budget, and to the standards your clients expect. Quality is defined externally by your customers, and it earns you the right to play. Without it, trust is nonexistent.
- **Excellence is the horizon.** It's about moving beyond the basics to create work that inspires pride, craftsmanship, and differentiation. Excellence is defined internally by your culture and your aspirations, and it pushes you to grow.

The two are linked: **quality builds trust, and excellence wins hearts and minds.** As a leader, your job is to safeguard both—ensuring you never slip on the essentials while never settling for good enough.

Dear Leader,

Great work is a gateway to growth—not just for your business, but for your people and your clients. It's where trust is earned and confidence is built. Through great work, your brand is something others can *feel*, not just describe.

The work you choose to take on—and the work you choose to say no to—paves the path forward just as much as any strategic plan. And there's a duality to this. Great work develops your people just as they develop it. Over time, when the work stretches them, teaches them, and reminds them that what they do matters, it becomes part of who they are, just as their spirit, their passion, and pride live in the work.

And it selects your clients, too. Great work attracts clients who align with the value you create because it shapes their impact and sometimes even the trajectory of their careers. The consistent delivery of great work keeps them coming back, taking you with them when they move to new organizations, referring others, and inviting you into bigger conversations.

From the outside, great work looks like outputs: case studies, results, proof points, and awards. But you and I both know the real magic is in the experience: how you deliver, not just what you deliver. The intelligence is balanced with empathy and care in the way you show up. The responsiveness and undeniable investment you make in the success of the client's business. The courage to challenge the status quo when you know it will lead to a better outcome. These things aren't peripheral; they are the work.

If you ever want to see how far your business has come, look at the work. It will show you your evolutionary path -- how you've adapted to changing needs, raised standards, pushed and polished your craft, and grown into the company you are now.

So, as you step into the moments of this chapter, remember great work isn't something you produce. It's something you practice—choice by choice and client by client.

I'm cheering you on as you keep choosing the kind of work that grows you, your people, and your business.

With respect,

OPEN WHEN: YOU WANT YOUR CLIENT EXPERIENCE TO BECOME AN ADVANTAGE

Dear Leader,

In the early days of a business, client experience often feels effortless. You are there on the front line of delivery, and everyone works closely together and can almost read each other's minds. But as growth happens, what once felt natural is harder to sustain. Without intention, the consistency of your client experience begins to fray, and along with it, your brand promise.

Defining your client (or customer) experience is about more than process. It's about clarifying the **behaviors, outcomes, and feelings** you want every client to walk away with. It's about aligning your people to a shared expectation of how to deliver. Not just the *what* of the work, but the *how*. Done well, your client experience is a living expression of your purpose and values, a market differentiator, and a source of pride for your team.

Here are a few guideposts to consider as you define (or re-define) your client experience:

- **Start with your Why.** Anchor the experience in your purpose. *What do you want clients to consistently feel because of working with you?*
- **Make it tangible.** Translate lofty ideas into specific behaviors. For example: *How quickly do you respond? How do you handle mistakes? What does going above and beyond look like in practice? What does being invested in a client's success look like in practice?*
- **Empower your people. Especially in a service business, employees are the living, breathing representation of your brand promise.** Give them clear expectations, but also the trust and autonomy to deliver in ways that feel authentic.
- **Build for consistency, not scripts.** The goal isn't robotic sameness, but a reliably positive experience, no matter who on your team the client interacts with.

- **Check for erosion.** As you grow, regularly ask clients and the team: *Are we delivering what we promised? Is the experience consistent across teams and projects? Where are cracks showing up? Do we need to evolve our experience to better match today's needs and market conditions?*

When you're intentional about defining your client experience, you safeguard your brand promise. When you are consistently delivering positive client experiences and outcomes, growth follows. Because great work, delivered consistently, creates the engine for repeat business, referrals, long-term partnerships, and your brand equity in the market.

With you in making and keeping your brand promise strong,

ACTIVATE THE FLYWHEEL: THE CLIENT EXPERIENCE ALIGNMENT MAP

At its best, your client experience is the translation of your Fundamentals into meaningful interactions. Consider these simple alignment prompts to develop and hone your client experience.

- **Ground in Purpose**
    - » *What's the bigger* why *behind your business?*
    - » *Does your client experience reflect and reinforce that?*
- **Define Signature Behaviors**
    - » *What do you want clients to see, hear, and feel in every interaction?*
    - » These should be observable, repeatable actions—not just words on a wall or in a training document.

- **Name Outcomes**
    - » *What consistent results do clients walk away with? (e.g., clarity, solutions, speed, confidence?)*
    - » *Are those outcomes tied to your brand promise? Is your value proposition reinforced?*
- **Evoke Feelings**
    - » *How should clients feel after working with you?* (e.g., respected, understood, inspired, supported?)
    - » *Are those feelings happening consistently across teams?*
- **Gain Feedback and Evolve**
    - » Through one-on-one conversations or short surveys, regularly ask clients: *How are we doing on these important behaviors and outcomes? Are these behaviors and outcomes still meeting your needs?*
    - » Leverage feedback to continuously improve the team's ability to deliver and to assess changing client needs over time.

FROM MY JOURNEY

When we opened our doors, we didn't have a defined client experience, far from it. Every client was important, and we wanted them to feel well-served so they would come back. We obsessed over every detail together, every day. We were vigilant about sticking to timelines and budgets. We triple checked our data to ensure accuracy. We debated everything, down to the best font for our reports. The time invested in alignment was important—and manageable—because there were so few of us, and our passion united us for success—both ours and our clients'.

It worked for a while. Clients were happy, and we were proud of the care we were putting into the work. But as we gained more experience, we realized that we were devoting a lot of effort to tasks and behaviors that our competitors were also doing. That level of effort didn't make us unique. Those behaviors kept us *in the game*; they were table stakes, but they didn't necessarily set us up to *win*.

As our Flywheel spun faster, pressures increased. New projects. New teams. New types of clients to serve. And those of us who began the business together were no longer interacting at the same frequency as we once did. We couldn't; we were busy with work, growing the business. When we did meet, we compared feedback, and that's when cracks started to appear. The basics were still mostly holding true, but the way the work *felt* across clients was inconsistent. While one client raved about the usability of our deliverables, another overtly questioned the difficulty in the path to get there. It didn't matter how strong the final product was. If the journey to get there didn't feel easy, consistent, trusted, and confident, the relationship was at risk.

Two things became painfully clear:

1. We had grown big enough and diversified enough that without an intentional client experience, we risked inconsistent delivery across teams and erosion of trust.

2. If we could define and operationalize an experience that was rooted in serving client needs and aligned with our strengths, it could be a real differentiator.

So, we got intentional. We talked to clients to uncover what they most deeply valued beyond the basics, and we dug into what they already saw as our strengths and sources of uniqueness. We engaged our people to understand the behaviors and outcomes they believed made the biggest impact. Out of this process came our **brand promise**—anchored in our clients' needs, delivered through our people, and reinforced by clear expectations.

That shift turned our client experience from something **assumed** into something **intentional**, and it became one of our greatest competitive advantages.

And here's an important truth: some of the best brands in the world don't keep you coming back because of the product alone, but because of the consistently positive experience you trust they will deliver. Service businesses are no different. If you don't define your client experience, it will define itself, and it rarely defines itself in ways that enhance your brand, your growth, or your relationships.

For additional guidance, see: *Establishing (or Re-setting) Your Foundation, Open When: You're Defining Your Fundamentals.*

OPEN WHEN: THE WORK FEELS TRANSACTIONAL

Dear Leader,

I remember that feeling when the work starts to feel like a set of tasks rather than the meaningful work you are used to. Another deliverable. Another meeting. Another deadline. Nothing is technically wrong, but your enthusiasm has dimmed. When this happens, either to you, your team, or both, you can start to lose sight of why you fell in love with the work in the first place.

Transactional work might get things done, but it rarely leaves you feeling truly satisfied and inspired to stick with it and do more.

That's when it helps to step back and remember: **great work is never just about output, it's about meaning.** Your work is the channel through which your purpose comes alive for your people and your clients. It's the pride in your craft, the thoughtfulness, the going above and beyond, that tells someone, *"We cared enough to make this great."* It's also in the outcomes that you create through your work—the meaningful results, the positive influence, and the change that your work inspires.

When work starts to feel transactional, try these approaches to re-center:

- **Reconnect to Purpose.** Remind your team (and yourself) why this work exists in the first place. *Who benefits? What difference does it make?* Tie the day-to-day tasks back to the larger mission. This feeling of transactionality particularly plagues more mundane tasks, but these are often the most important for ensuring quality.
- **Stay Close to the Client.** Sometimes the most powerful antidote is simply hearing the client's voice. Bring in feedback: their goals, their gratitude, their success stories. It reminds people that their work matters to someone on the other side.
- **Re-inspire Craftsmanship.** Encourage people to take pride in the details, the excellence, and the extra 5% that elevates work from adequate to memorable. It's important to celebrate outcomes, but the craft it took to get there is equally valuable, and spelling out the mechanics can help others learn.

- **Refresh the Story.** Teams need rituals, recognition, and stories that remind them they're part of something meaningful. Share examples of how the work creates value, including client testimonials or interviews. Make the impact come to life for your team and help people see the difference their work creates over time.

Every team and every leader go through stretches when the work feels routine. But if you leave that feeling unattended for too long, it can dull your culture, your performance, and your brand. Great work is more than the sum of the deliverables. It's a reflection of your brand, your team's pride and enthusiasm, and ultimately the differentiated value you create for clients.

With you in keeping the work meaningful,

ACTIVATE THE FLYWHEEL: COMMODITY VS. CRAFT

A feeling that the work has become more transactional could be a signal that you've slipped into commodity mode. Often, stepping back to reignite your craft is the antidote to restoring meaning. The goal isn't to choose between commodity and craft; it's to recognize when your work has drifted into commodity-only mode and pull it back into craft. Then, where possible, systematize that craft so it scales without losing its soul. That's when your organization steps into true differentiation.

Commodity Work	Craft Work	Craft at Scale
Prioritizes speed, efficiency, and consistency	Prioritizes meaning, impact, and differentiation	Brings efficiency and impact together
Get it done mindset	*Make it matter* mindset	*Make it matter consistently* mindset
Meets basic or baseline expectations	Elevates expectations with excellence	Delivers excellence in a way that can be repeated across people and teams

Commodity Work	Craft Work	Craft at Scale
Often interchangeable with competitors	Unique, harder to replicate	Unique *and* sustainable
Keeps you in the game	Helps you win	Builds long-term competitive advantage

FROM MY JOURNEY

There were times in my career when the work felt routine – even a bit hollow. I remember a point mid-career when I actually pondered, *Have I chosen the right path? Is it time for a change?* I liked my work and my team, but I questioned whether what I was doing truly mattered. I found myself craving something deeper.

At that time, our purpose statement was something like: *We help leading brands create products and services people will love.* I remember spending time with that statement one day and deciding to test it against reality. I went backward, reviewing the projects I had recently worked on. Messaging that made people feel more understood, productive improvements that solved real frustrations, new ideas brought to life, and, just as importantly, ideas we helped clients not launch, saving them time, cost, and brand image erosion. When I zoomed out, I saw it clearly; we were helping companies make better decisions for real humans. We were creating impact. I had just lost sight of it in the day-to-day managing of the work.

If I was feeling this way, I knew others in my team must face these same moments. So, I was determined to introduce a new habit. Not only bringing our work and our impact to life, but bringing clients into our organization to tell the story of impact themselves. Hearing firsthand how our work influenced decisions, created meaningful outcomes for their organizations, and often for them, personally reminded us why we existed. It gave a powerful voice to our purpose, and even though the tasks of the work didn't change, it was the inspiration we needed to regularly reconnect to it.

When work begins to feel *meh*, don't assume the impact isn't there. Instead, step back, reconnect to purpose, and let the voices of the people you serve remind you what your work really does in the world.

OPEN WHEN: THE WORK IS GOOD BUT NOT EVOLVING (INNOVATION FEELS STUCK)

Dear Leader,

When the work is good but it's not evolving, it's confusing, even frustrating, because nothing is wrong, yet something in you knows clients are hungry for fresh ideas, and the business needs to stay relevant to continue growing. Innovation can be one of the trickiest levers to pull in business. For some leaders, it feels daunting: *"We don't have time for this."* For others, it feels unnecessary: *"We're already at the top of our game."* And sometimes it feels like a luxury: *"We can't afford to innovate right now."* But here's the hard truth: failing to innovate erodes value, often faster than you realize.

Innovation doesn't have to mean big, radical reinventions. More often, it's about building a culture of continuous improvement where people at every level remain curious, keep listening, and stay tuned in to your purpose, your customers, and your people. It's not about changing for the sake of change or about chasing novelty. It's about relentless focus on making things better, step by step.

Sometimes innovation points outward: improving products, services, experiences, or partnerships. Sometimes it points inward: streamlining processes, strengthening communication, or rethinking business models. Either way, the spark usually comes from paying attention to today's pain points and not dismissing them as *"just the way things are,"* but seeing them as springboards for something better.

When innovation feels stuck, don't pressure yourself to leap to the next "big idea." Instead, create an environment where ideas can flow:

- **Stay Close to Your Customers.** Their frustrations, dreams, and evolving needs are the raw material for innovation.
- **Empower Your People.** Encourage your people to spot areas for improvement and voice ideas for larger shifts. Your job as a leader is to create alignment on the future direction, then enable autonomy to experiment for improvement. A safe-to-try and safe-to-suggest mindset unlocks more than any brainstorming session.

- **Look for the Everyday Friction.** The best ideas often come from solving the little inefficiencies that everyone has learned to "work around."
- **Balance Outward and Inward.** Both customer-facing improvements and behind-the-scenes refinements can move the needle.

Above all, don't wait for urgency to force change. Start small, stay curious, and let continuous improvement be your fuel. That's how good work transforms into new value for your clients, your people, and your business.

With you in creating new value,

ACTIVATE THE FLYWHEEL: SOURCES OF INNOVATION

Innovation is fueled by rhythm and intention. The strongest ideas often sit at the intersection of client needs, your core competencies, and purpose. When you drift outside that triangle, innovation can be expensive or distracting unless you're deliberate about partnerships.

Make innovation a continual focal point for your organization by building a cadence that routinely taps into these sources:

1. Customer Voice

- *What pain points, desires, or unmet needs are clients expressing—directly or indirectly?*
- *What shifts are happening in your clients' industry that may signal emerging needs?*
- *Do I have clients who are willing to provide input on new product or service ideas or participate in co-creation?*

Innovations often start with listening and observing differently.

2. Employee Voice

- *Where is friction slowing people down or causing re-work?*
- *What challenges or ideas are frontline teams raising again and again?*
- *Can we pilot new ideas with a subset of employees to experiment and iterate?*

The people closest to the work often see opportunities first.

3. Market Shifts

- *What shifts are happening in your industry, competitor landscape, adjacent categories, or technology?*
- *Who is experimenting even small, or imperfectly, in ways worth watching?*

Breakthroughs often come from looking sideways, not just forward.

4. Process Friction

- *What's clunky, inefficient, manual, or like a workaround?*
- *Where does energy drain instead of flow?*

Small improvements can unlock big energy.

5. Patterns & Anomalies

- What's happening more often than it used to?
- What's not happening that used to be automatic?
- Has anything surprised you recently? Good or bad?

Innovation often hides inside *"that's odd..."* moments.

6. Strategic Partnerships

- *Could partnering help build on our strengths or create differentiation without full ownership?*

Sometimes the smartest innovation is shared—not built alone.

7. AI & Emerging Technology

- *How can AI help detect patterns faster or prototype ideas more quickly?*
- *Where could automation elevate quality rather than speed alone?*
- *What emerging tools could remove friction or unlock new client value?*

AI isn't innovation in itself, but it can accelerate or amplify other sources when used intentionally.

And across all sources, scan for **Purpose Alignment:** *Does this idea reinforce our "why" or pull energy away from it?* Purpose-anchored innovation resonates more deeply with stakeholders and increases the odds of adoption and sustained success.

FROM MY JOURNEY

Innovation has been a constant topic throughout my career, both in the companies I led as CEO and in the many client organizations with whom we worked. Nearly everyone had the same aspiration: to be innovative, customer-centric, and more agile to accomplish both. And nearly everyone struggled to make that aspiration real.

Over time, a pattern became clear. Most organizations, including my own at times, were still operating with control, predictability, and risk aversion as their primary guideposts alongside organizational structures and decision hierarchies designed to uphold them. Those safeguards exist for good reason. They protect quality, mitigate risk, and create stability. But they also make experimentation difficult and leave little room for learning from failure. And in a world changing faster than our structures and business norms were designed to handle, that tension surfaces quickly.

What struck me is that innovation rarely stalls because of a lack of ideas. It stalls because of **how work is organized and how decisions are made.** Traditional organizational hierarchies slow learning. Centralized decision-making often limited responsiveness. And the further insights sit from action, the harder it is to evolve.

I saw this idea articulated powerfully in *The Octopus Organization: A Guide to Thriving in A World of Continuous Transformation.* Leveraging the octopus metaphor, the authors describe organizations designed to manage complexity by operating in multiple modes at once with distributed autonomy (the tentacles), all connected by a shared purpose, clear goals, and strong alignment (the head). In this model, innovation isn't owned by a department. It's embedded in how the organization works.

Leading this way changes the role of the leader. Plans become more dynamic, and leadership becomes more immersive. It requires staying close, paying attention to what's emerging, making continual course corrections, and communicating often to keep the organization aligned.

Here's the lesson that stayed with me: Innovation builds on what we've learned about structure and control while asking us to reconsider where control belongs. When leaders create clarity around goals and what's required for future success, and then distribute decision-making closer to the work, innovation becomes part of the operating rhythm rather than an occasional event.

When the work is good but not evolving, the answer is rarely another strategy session. More often, it's a recalibration of trust, autonomy, and responsibility for the future to the people closest to the work, and a deeper investment in alignment and communication across the organization.

For additional guidance, see: *Beyond the Flywheel, Open When: You Realize the Customer is No Longer the Center,* and *Beyond the Flywheel, Open When: Growth Requires More Than What's Inside Your Walls.*

OPEN WHEN: MISTAKES HAPPEN

Dear Leader,

No matter how much you train, prepare, how strong your systems are, or how talented your people may be, mistakes will happen. They're an unavoidable part of doing business. **What matters most is how you respond.**

When mistakes occur, your instinct might be to minimize, deflect, or quietly fix them. But here's the truth: clients and teams don't expect perfection, but they do expect honesty, accountability, and a commitment to making things right. Owning a mistake transparently, and without defensiveness, can actually *strengthen* trust rather than weaken it.

A healthy mindset for mistakes reframes them as growth moments:

- **For Clients:** Mistakes can be opportunities to demonstrate responsiveness, care, and partnership. *We see it, we own it, here's what we're doing about it.*
- **For Teams:** Mistakes should not be a cause for shame. Instead, they should be treated as raw material for improvement. *What can we learn? How do we prevent this in the future?*
- **For You:** Mistakes test your leadership. *Do you show up with empathy? Do you stay calm under pressure? Do you use the moment to reinforce values and brand promise?*

How to Lead Through Mistakes:

- **Acknowledge Quickly.** Once a mistake is identified, inform quickly, accompanied by steps to correct and prevent recurrence.
- **Apologize Clearly.** A simple, direct apology goes further than over-explaining. The simple words *"I'm sorry"* convey ownership and humility.
- **Act Decisively.** Share what steps you'll take to correct the issue and prevent recurrence.
- **Debrief with the Team.** Take time to talk about what happened and why. This isn't a blame session; it's a learning session.

- **Re-center through Learning.** Turn the mistake into an input for stronger systems, smarter processes, or sharper communication. Empower the team to help implement new measures.

Mistakes sting, but they also humanize. Handled with transparency and integrity, they show your people and your clients that trust, humility, and resilience ride alongside great work.

With you in learning and growing from mistakes,

ACTIVATE THE FLYWHEEL: THE 4 A'S OF MISTAKE RECOVERY

Mistakes related to client work often require calm yet swift action, especially when the work product affects client decision-making. Internalizing this simple framework serves as a go-to triage for addressing mistakes with care, professionalism, and expediency.

1. **Acknowledge:** Call it out honestly and without delay.
2. **Apologize:** Own your role, without excuses.
3. **Act:** Correct the issue and communicate the fix.
4. **Adapt:** Capture lessons learned to strengthen the system for next time.

FROM MY JOURNEY

With long-standing, high-volume client relationships, mistakes are bound to happen simply because of the sheer number of at-bats. One that still sticks with me happened with a client we'd partnered with for nearly two decades. We had a strong reputation across their organization - years of accurate data and trusted delivery had earned us that confidence.

Then came the miss. The numbers we provided weren't just slightly off. They were wrong enough that decisions could have gone in the wrong direction. And by the time we caught the error, the data had already been distributed to key stakeholders, including a newly arrived, highly influential executive we hadn't yet built a relationship with.

Our direct client was a longtime champion of ours and was understandably upset. And it wasn't just because of the mistake itself. It was because **her credibility was on the line.** The work didn't just let *us* down; it put *her* at risk at a critical moment.

We did everything we knew to do. We owned it immediately. We corrected the numbers. We laid out the process changes to prevent it from happening again. Normally, that would have been enough. But this time, it wasn't. The stakes were higher, and the damage extended beyond the deliverable.

So, we reached for something deeper: the strength of our history. The consistency we had built. The partnership we had proven. We reminded her of the years of high-quality work and trust on both sides. Not as justification, but as context. As truth.

There was a pause on both ends, a moment to consider whether the relationship, and the value it had created, was still worth continuing. Thankfully, the equity we had built over the years carried us through. We came out the other side intact, humbled and sharper for it.

Mistakes don't erase history, but they will test it. The trust you build over time determines whether a mistake forms a permanent fracture or a moment you recover from, together.

OPEN WHEN: GROWTH STRAINS QUALITY

Dear Leader,

Growth is exciting, but it can also quietly threaten what made you successful in the first place: high-quality work. When client demand is high, teams are stretched, systems feel strained, and the careful consistency you built in the early days can start to slip. If clients notice, trust can erode faster than it took to build.

First, let's make an assumption: you know how quality is defined in your world. It's different than excellence. **It's about delivering flawlessly on the basics, every time.** In fact, quality is typically defined externally by your customers: their standards, their expectations, their tolerance for error. If you don't meet those, nothing else matters.

Think of it like a car. At a minimum, the car needs to start reliably and get you from point A to point B. If it can't do that, no amount of heated seats, sunroofs, or smart tech will convince someone buy it. The same is true for your business. **Quality is the permission slip that allows you to serve higher-level needs, to innovate, and to continue to grow.**

As growth accelerates, keeping quality intact means getting intentional:

- **Codify Standards.** Document what "quality" means in measurable terms, so consistency isn't left to interpretation.
- **Build Scalable Systems.** Invest in processes, tools, and training that scale as volume increases. Heroics don't scale; systems do.
- **Inspect What You Expect.** Don't just assume quality is happening; audit it, review it, and measure it regularly.
- **Empower Ownership.** Quality can't rest on a single team or function. Everyone needs to feel responsible for delivering the brand promise.
- **Listen Closely.** Client feedback is your early warning system. Build mechanisms to hear, act on, and quickly loop back learnings.

Every growing company faces this test. The key is to prepare for it. Growth doesn't have to cost you quality, but quality will cost you growth if you don't protect it.

With you in growing without compromise,

ACTIVATE THE FLYWHEEL: PROTECTING QUALITY AS YOU GROW

The market defines "quality"—not you.

What once set you apart eventually becomes expected. As clients' needs evolve, the baseline for *good enough* rises. If your quality doesn't rise with it, what was once a differentiator risks becoming a liability.

To grow without compromising quality, think of quality as a foundation with four cornerstones. If even one is weak, the whole structure is compromised. When growth puts pressure on your business, strengthen your foundation first, then build from there.

Cornerstone	Purpose	Risk if Unprotected
1. Standards	Define what quality looks like and make it clear, measurable, and non-negotiable Re-define as client needs evolve	Inconsistency, rework Irrelevance
2. Systems	Enable quality to scale through processes, tools, and training	Reliance on heroics that burn people out
3. Ownership	Make quality everyone's responsibility	Gaps in accountability, finger-pointing
4. Feedback	Use client and employee voices as an early warning system for quality concerns and shifting expectations	Problems surface too late Reactive fixes rather than proactive solutions

FROM MY JOURNEY

During a period of fast growth, we were onboarding more people than we could reasonably support. Through the lens of supply and demand, client demand was rising fast, but our supply of experienced, well-trained people couldn't keep pace. The same people who were busiest serving clients were also the ones we relied on to ramp up new team members. It became a vicious cycle: the more we grew, the less capacity we had to protect the quality that earned us that growth in the first place.

Occasional errors were normal—that happens in business. And we had a process for understanding how the slip-ups happened and how to rectify the situation with the client. But when the slip-ups became more frequent and made their way onto our weekly Operations meeting agenda, we knew this was a signal of something bigger. While we were keeping up with growth, we were treading water, not swimming gracefully and certainly not performing proudly. That was our wake-up call.

We did everything we could in the moment. Hands-on triage to help diagnose root causes, experienced leaders staying as close to the work as possible, talking about it weekly to ensure we were on top of not only the quality concerns but also any resulting client feedback. I'll just say it wasn't one of our finest eras, and, regrettably, it shouldn't have been, given that we were experiencing record growth.

Once the immediate busy stretch subsided, we were able to pause and retrench. We reviewed, revised, and recommitted to our standards, invested in additional training, and built more detailed and user-friendly training materials and processes so that we would be better prepared next time.

As leaders, the equation can feel deceptively simple: we're overwhelmed → let's hire more people → growth problem solved. But there's a delay that often goes unaccounted for, and it's felt hardest by your frontline team.

What that season taught me is that adding people is only half the equation. Preparing the organization to scale well is what completes it. It protects your team and the quality on which your growth was built. Growth only sustains when quality can scale with it.

For additional guidance, see: *Great Work, Open When: Excellence Feels Out of Reach* and *Great Work, Open When: Mistakes Happen.*

OPEN WHEN: EXCELLENCE FEELS OUT OF REACH

Dear Leader,

Excellence is yours to define, but the key is to define it clearly, set expectations around it, and hold your team accountable. Great work and excellence go hand in hand, together fulfilling your brand promise.

There will be times when excellence feels like a mirage. Always close, never quite attainable. Sometimes it's like playing whack-a-mole: fix one issue, and another pops up. Other times it feels far off because you've raised expectations, adopted new systems, or stretched to meet evolving client needs. It can feel frustrating and even exhausting.

But here's the perspective: **excellence is not a finish line.** Because the market shifts, your clients' needs shift, and your capabilities evolve, what "excellence" looks like evolves too. Even when it's yours to define, the market eventually catches up. That's why excellence isn't a one-time achievement; **it's a discipline**, generated in the everyday performance of the organization, not a single milestone.

This is where cultivating a mindset of restless *dissatisfaction* becomes your advantage.

Restless dissatisfaction isn't about nitpicking or never being satisfied. It's the belief in **progress over perfection**. Those small, steady improvements compound into transformational change. It's pride in what you do, paired with the conviction that you can keep elevating it.

When excellence feels out of reach, resist the urge to lower the bar. Instead, redirect your energy into building systems and habits that make both delivering on today's standards and continuous improvement part of the everyday fabric of your business:

When Excellence Feels Out of Reach, Focus On:

- **Clarify the Standard.** Define what excellence looks like in your context and how it goes beyond delivering "quality." Be explicit about expectations so the team knows what they're aiming for.

- **Reinforce Accountability.** Hold yourself and others to those standards. Excellence isn't aspirational unless it's tied to clear ownership and follow-through.
- **Build Feedback Loops.** Regularly gather input from clients, peers, and employees to identify gaps and opportunities for improvement.
- **Embed Restless Dissatisfaction.** Celebrate what's working *and* ask, *How can we make this stronger?* Progress over perfection is the path to sustainable excellence.
- **Balance Efficiency and Craft.** Create systems that ensure consistency at scale while preserving pride, care, and meaning in the work.

Excellence doesn't come from chasing perfection. It comes from refusing to settle. Over time, this combination of clarity, accountability, and a healthy dissatisfaction with the status quo will not only elevate your work but also inspire pride across your team.

With you in pursuing progress over perfection,

ACTIVATE THE FLYWHEEL: PROTECT THE MOMENTS THAT MATTER

Excellence isn't about slowing everything down. It's about knowing *when* to slow down. Identify the moments in your client experience that produce the highest value for your clients and/or the biggest opportunity to differentiate your offerings, where craft and care have the greatest impact. These moments are the leverage points that transform good work into great work.

1. **Define your Moments that Matter:** Pinpoint 3-5 inflection points where excellence is most visible to clients and most essential to outcomes. Examples: discovery conversations, data sense-making, workshopping, insights and outcome generation, and final deliverable review.

2. **Slow Down with Intention:** Not every step deserves the same depth of thinking or polish. In the moments that matter, pause to engage critical thinking, ask questions, refine, and elevate.

3. **Build in Checkpoints:** Beyond your standard quality expectations, create simple, intentional checkpoints: a second set of eyes to elevate a final deliverable, a quick alignment huddle before key client conversations, a dry-run before a major presentation.

4. **Eliminate Noise Around the Moments:** Cluttered processes, unnecessary meetings, and busy work steal energy from deep thinking. Critical thinking and elevation should feel supported, not burdened by hoops to jump through.

5. **Celebrate Craft:** Point to it when someone elevates a moment that matters. Honoring great work reinforces the behaviors that create excellence and inspires others to rise to the occasion.

FROM MY JOURNEY

In our industry, the final deliverable, the report or presentation, was the ultimate *moment that mattered*. It was the capstone of every project, the place where craft was on full display. Our clients repeatedly told us that our deliverables stood apart. They were willing to pay a premium for them because of the storytelling, the visuals, and the strategic framing that helped their organizations take action.

But over time, the competition's elevated deliverables and our restless dissatisfaction kicked in. We realized that if the final deliverable was where excellence *showed up*, the real opportunity was much farther upstream—in a moment many companies treated as transactional: **the proposal phase**.

A few people on our team were naturals at it. They didn't just respond to what clients *asked* for; they helped clients discover what they truly *needed*. They asked different questions, listened for clues, and reframed the brief in ways that expanded thinking. Clients often said, *"I hadn't considered that,"* or *"This helps me articulate what I've been struggling to put into words."*

Those interactions changed our client experience. Clients didn't just choose us because we were reliable. They chose us because they'd already felt our strategic partnership before any *real* work began.

That early upstream conversation became a moment that mattered just as much as the final deliverable. Maybe more. But only a handful of people were doing it consistently. Scaling it across the organization felt like a mountain. Still, we knew that if we could replicate that excellence, we'd differentiate not only what we delivered, but *how* we began.

So, we built a flexible framework. A set of questions, a discovery rhythm, a mindset shift that helped teams uncover the real "why" behind a client's request before jumping to the "what" or "how."

Then we taught it—slowly and deliberately.

We coached our senior people first, enlisted them to train others, created follow-up checkpoints, and reinforced wins. It wasn't fast, and at times it was frustrating. But it was transformational.

Over time, this one upstream shift cascaded into everything else: stronger alignment, more strategic work, improved storytelling, and yes, even better deliverables.

The goal is not to elevate everything. Excellence begins to emerge when you identify the moments that matter most in the client experience and commit to the slow, deliberate work of scaling them. When consistency forms around the right moments, excellence moves from aspiration to the norm.

OPEN WHEN: YOU NEED TO MOVE FROM WORKING IN THE BUSINESS TO LEADING THE BUSINESS

Dear Leader,

If you were on the frontlines of building the business in the early days, chances are you did it because you love the work. You were good at it. You thrived on client interactions. You knew no one could deliver quite like you. In the beginning, that was your superpower—your fingerprints on every engagement, your presence in every client meeting.

You built the business by being in the work. You will scale it by learning to let go of the work.

But as the business grows, that same superpower can be your kryptonite. What once fueled momentum now risks stalling it. You can't scale if everything depends on you being in the room. At some point, your role must shift: from working **in** the business to working **on** the business.

How do you know when it's time?

- You're the bottleneck. Projects and decisions wait on you.
- You're exhausted. There aren't enough hours to serve clients *and* run the company.
- Growth feels fragile. Too much depends on your personal involvement.
- People stagnate. The team stops asking for more responsibility because you're slow to give it.
- You feel resentful. *Why am I the only one working this hard? Does anyone else work evenings and weekends?*

The risks of not making the leap are real for both you and the team. Burnout. Lost opportunities. A fragile team or company that struggles without you now and may be in a real deficit without you.

Letting go doesn't mean abandoning what you love. It means purposefully redefining your role. It's about investing in leaders who can carry the work forward, trusting your people to step into the spotlight, and reserving your energy for focusing on strategy, culture, and the future. At first, this may look like dividing your time between client delivery and business-building. But as you grow, your client work should gradually give way to leading the organization.

And what if you discover you're better at being in the work than in the business? That's not failure, it's clarity. Some founders thrive as visionaries and rainmakers but aren't wired to run operations. In those cases, the strongest move is to bring in a leader who loves running the business as much as you love building it.

Growth demands courage. The courage to loosen your grip, empower others, and step fully into leadership. It's not about doing less. It's about doing what only you can do: creating the conditions for your people, your clients, and your business to thrive.

With you on leading forward,

ACTIVATE THE FLYWHEEL: IN THE BUSINESS VS. ON THE BUSINESS

Use the columns below to help diagnose your current orientation. Being honest about how you spend your time is the first step toward shifting your focus.

The shift won't happen overnight. It's a gradual reallocation of your time and energy. Early on, you'll live in both columns. But over time, more of your focus belongs *to* the business, where only you can lead. Your calendar is the truth-teller. The more your hours reflect the right column, the more time you are investing *in* the business. Sometimes it helps to enlist an accountability partner to keep you honest to the shift you're making.

When You're Working IN the Business	When You're Working ON the Business
Deeply immersed in delivering client work	Designing systems, frameworks, etc. that enable work without you; Developing leaders who multiply capacity
Troubleshooting and firefighting	Anticipating problems and reducing future friction
Being the "go-to" for most decisions	Creating clarity so others can decide without you
Driving growth through personal effort and your output	Leading growth through strategy, brand, and vision Building external relationships (boards, investors, partners, industry peers, strategic clients)
Success = personal success	Success = team capability and scalability; nurturing the long-term health of the company

FROM MY JOURNEY

Letting go of the work wasn't easy for me. It wasn't because I didn't trust my team. I did. I was proud of the capable, invested people I had surrounded myself with. My challenge was twofold:

1. **Staying Relevant:** I worried that if I wasn't directly in client work, I'd lose touch with what was happening on the ground. *How could I chart the company's future if I weren't fully aware of today?* And since we were frequently experimenting with new offerings, I wanted to be in the thick of it.

2. **Questioning My Value:** Client work offered tangible proof of contribution—immediate input and output. Shifting away from that made me wonder: *Would others still see my value? Would I?*

I leaned heavily on advice from my mentor and external peers who had walked this path. With their guidance, I gradually redefined my role with intention. I carved out space to keep some client work, but with qualifiers: it had to be strategic, it had to be an area where I could bring unique value, and someone else had to be along for the ride as a mentee to grow from the experience.

I also found new ways to stay close to the frontlines—reviewing key proposals, weighing in on critical deliverables, and scheduling regular strategic check-ins with clients. Those conversations not only kept me connected to the market, fueling continuous improvement opportunities, but also positioned me in an advisor role by enabling me to offer perspective on industry trends, strategic leadership, and even coaching and encouragement to clients.

I'll admit, I wasn't great at letting go of decisions or stepping out of the work. And who knows, perhaps we would have scaled more quickly, more effectively if I had released my grip sooner. But I can say this: I got better.

As we transformed the company, I discovered that my greatest contribution wasn't in doing the work myself. Instead, it was in charting the future and designing the conditions for our people and the work to thrive. Creating clarity for myself and trusting others freed me to lead forward, and it gave my team room to step into their own strengths so they, too, could thrive.

GREAT CLIENTS

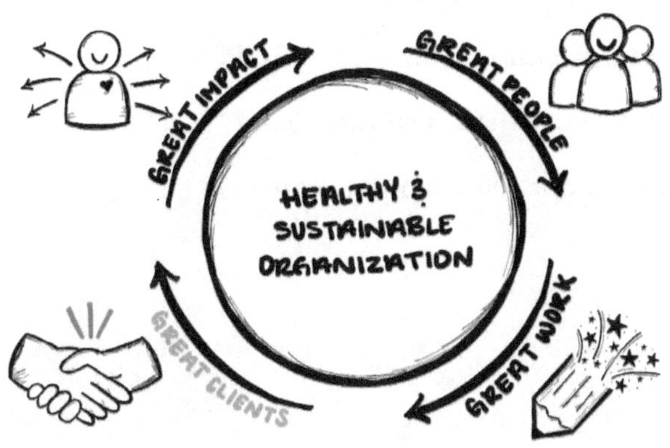

In this section, you will find letters to ***Open When*** you're attracting, growing, and sustaining client relationships built on trust and shared value creation.

Open When: (Attract)

- You Are Defining Your Target Customer(s) and Value Proposition
- You Are Going After (or Working With) Your First Client
- You Realize You Can't Scale Without a System
- You Are Tempted to Say Yes to Every Opportunity
- Your Proposals Aren't Winning the Way They Should
- Marketing and Business Development are Out of Sync

Open When: (Develop)

- You Want to Become a Partner, Not Just a Vendor
- You've Earned Trust and Want Greater Access
- You Want to Understand and Anticipate Client Needs
- The Client Wants More Than You Agreed To

Open When: (Retain and Grow)

- You Lose a Client
- A Client is at Risk of Leaving (or a Long-Term Relationship Feels Stale)
- Too Much Depends on One Client or Sector
- You're Afraid to Lose Revenue, but You're Losing Something Bigger
- You Want to Deepen a Partnership
- You Sense Competitors are Gaining Momentum

BEFORE YOU BEGIN

This section meets you in the moments of leadership that don't surface in pitch decks or client growth plans, yet determine the health and longevity of your business. It's the thrill of landing the first client who believes in you. The knot in your stomach when a once-strong relationship starts to feel fragile. The hard decision to say **no** to a client that isn't aligned, even when revenue pressure whispers **yes**.

Attracting, developing, retaining, and growing great clients isn't just about sales; it's about building your brand -- what you stand for as a business. The clients you choose (and who choose you) shape your culture, your capabilities, your confidence, and your team's energy. The right clients fuel the Flywheel: they trust you, stretch you, advocate for you, and grow with you. The wrong ones can drain energy and distract you from your purpose and mission.

Through these letters, we'll navigate the defining inflection points of client stewardship. We'll (re)visit the early days of clarifying your value proposition and building a business development engine from scratch. We'll explore what it takes to evolve from vendor to partner, to listen more deeply than you speak, to diversify relationships for stability, and to strengthen connections when the ground gets unsteady. We'll also face the realities of client loss, knowing when to fight for the relationship and when to release it with grace.

Individually, these letters meet you in defining moments with intention. As a collection, they support a toolkit for building a portfolio of great clients. Not just big ones or recognizable ones, but **the right ones for your business**.

Dear Leader,

A signature may begin client work, but trust sustains it. Trust is formed by showing up with curiosity, by listening to what's said and what's not said; by understanding the pressures, challenges, and aspirations that affect their world, and by bringing your best people and ideas to the table again and again.

Yes, clients want results, but just as important, they want to feel understood. They want partners who take the time to "get them," who are courageous enough to challenge their thinking when needed, and who are invested in their success as if it were their own. The best relationships are the ones where both sides grow, where your expertise elevates their ambitions, and their ambitions stretch your capabilities.

Winning new clients is energizing. But long-term success isn't powered by client acquisition alone; it's powered by retention. Fueled by great people and great work, developing and retaining clients is often easier, more cost-effective, and more fulfilling than constantly chasing the next new logo. The healthiest businesses do both: they nurture and grow the clients who already trust them, and they attract a steady flow of new clients who align with their purpose and values.

I don't believe that loyalty happens by chance. It happens when clients feel the intention behind your actions. When you anticipate needs before they're spoken. When you bring fresh thinking rather than recycled frameworks. When you show up enthusiastically, make their life easier, and consistently deliver on your promises.

Client stewardship blends humility and confidence. The humility to meet clients where they are and listen more than you talk, and the confidence to offer bold guidance when they need it most. Holding both facilitates long-term value creation and a space where growth from real partnership—and real impact—can flourish.

With you in building client relationships that last,

GREAT CLIENTS: ATTRACT

OPEN WHEN: YOU ARE DEFINING YOUR TARGET CUSTOMER(S) AND VALUE PROPOSITION

Dear Leader,

If only having a great idea were enough. If only the market rewarded us for our passion, our experience, and our belief that our product or service can make a difference. But the truth is: the market doesn't reward potential, it rewards relevance.

And *relevance starts with clarity*.

Defining your target client requires moving beyond who could benefit to who truly needs and values your offer—and is willing to invest in it. Not "any company going through change" or "anyone who wants better insights." Broad categories aren't target clients. They're wishful thinking. The real work is narrowing your focus until you can describe your ideal client and pain point so clearly that you'd recognize them if they walked into a room.

When you start with that depth of understanding: their pressures, constraints, aspirations, KPIs, fears, and hopes, everything else becomes easier. This level of knowing enables you to **speak their language and to reframe from selling a product or service to fulfilling a need**. Needs such as relief, momentum, credibility, confidence, and growth. You are identifying things they already care deeply about.

And that leads to your value proposition: the reason they will choose you over someone else.

A powerful value proposition isn't about you and what you do. **It's about them and why they need you.** It reflects the outcomes they're trying to achieve, not the deliverables you're trying to sell. It clarifies not just the *what* of your offer, but the *why now* and *why you.*

When you know your client and the value you bring to them, things fall into place more smoothly. Without that clarity, you risk chasing opportunities that drain time and energy more than they deliver positive results.

Here's the encouragement in the work ahead: a sharp value proposition and a clear target don't shrink opportunity, they accelerate it. When you choose who you're really for, you stop chasing and start attracting. The right clients hear themselves in your story. The wrong clients self-select out. And your team gains the focus, confidence, and energy that come from knowing exactly who you serve and why they choose you.

With you in defining,

ACTIVATE THE FLYWHEEL: DEFINING YOUR TARGET CLIENTS AND VALUE PROPOSITION

Defining your target client and value proposition go hand in hand. Use these steps to jumpstart your process and be ready to iterate with input from current and prospective clients and the market.

1. **Start with needs, not ideas.**
   Before you develop what you want to sell, get grounded in what your ideal client needs. Identify the problems they are actually trying to solve, not the ones you hope they care about.
   Tip: Need fulfillment is far easier and more profitable than generating demand from scratch.

2. **Get specific, painfully specific.**
   If your target audience could apply to "everyone," it applies to no one. Define your best-fit client by industries, role(s), size, ambitions, pressures, buying triggers, and characteristics that matter.
   Ask: Who is most likely to value us regularly and deeply, not just hire us occasionally?

3. **Articulate your value proposition from their perspective and in customer language, not yours.**
   Your value proposition isn't what you do. It's the meaningful outcome customers get because of you. For more targeted resonance, identify and communicate how you want customers to *feel* working with you.
   Ask: Why do they choose you over other options? And can you prove it with evidence, examples, or outcomes?

4. **Stress-test your differentiation.**
   What makes you different isn't automatically what makes you valuable.
   Ask: Does this distinction matter to the customer or only to us? Would they pay for this difference? Would they defend it in a meeting without us in the room?

5. **Complete and refine your positioning with a simple framework like this:**
   - **For:** the specific audience you serve
   - **Enables:** the outcomes you deliver – **in their language**
   - **Best Because:** the reason(s) they should choose you over others

6. **Pressure-test with the market.**
   Share your positioning with a small group of trusted clients or prospects and listen without defending. If something doesn't resonate, be curious rather than defensive.
   Realize: Your goal isn't to be right; it's to be relevant

7. **Treat what follows as the validation stage, not the guessing stage.**
   Use early conversations, pitches, and proposals to validate and sharpen your positioning.
   Realize: The best value propositions are not invented. They're discovered conversations with prospective clients and truly understanding the market, its conditions, and the pain points you solve for.

FROM MY JOURNEY

One of the biggest mistakes that I have seen B2B businesses make (including my own) when creating or redefining their value proposition is becoming overly transactional in how they talk about their work. It's natural to default to what's easiest to articulate: depth of experience, breadth of offerings, features, benefits, pricing, response times. All useful information, but all centered on *us*, not the client.

We ran into this head-on as we were evolving our company from a traditional research agency into a customer-centric consultancy. Our ambition had grown. Our capabilities had expanded. But our language and framing hadn't caught up. Even though we were increasingly helping clients make better, more confident decisions to move their organizations forward, our value proposition kept swinging between too general to be meaningful and too specific to be resonant. We ended up with a list of capabilities rather than a reflection of client needs.

That's when a concept we already knew intellectually became incredibly practical: **The Hero's Journey** (Joseph Campbell)

Applied to value proposition work, the idea is simple but powerful. **Your client is the hero, not you.** They're facing a challenge, navigating a risk, making a decision, or leading a transformation. **Your role isn't to be the star of the story; it's to be the guide.** The mentor. The partner who provides experience, a plan, the tools, and the support to help them move forward with confidence.

This mindset shift significantly changed our frame of reference. It relieved the pressure of explaining what we do and replaced it with a more meaningful question: *What journey is our client on, and how do we help them succeed?* Our language began to change. We moved from features to outcomes. From "segmentation and persona development" to "helping teams stop spreading resources too thin and focus on the customers most likely to drive profitable growth," and from "advanced analytics and dashboards" to "faster, smarter decisions without drowning in data." Of course, we still needed to be clear about our offerings, but that articulation became secondary to meeting clients in the moment and making them feel understood.

And don't lose sight of this: **the Hero's Journey only works if you truly know your hero**. That meant doing the harder work of deeply understanding our target clients—their motivations, pressures, context, and goals—and using *their* language, not yours. Our first attempts at redesigning our value proposition were not perfect. The process was iterative. But as we made progress, resonance followed.

The lesson I learned in all of this: a strong value proposition isn't about proving how good you are. It's about helping clients feel understood, valued, and important in the work they're trying to lead. Enough so they trust you to walk alongside them as a guide.

OPEN WHEN: YOU ARE GOING AFTER (OR WORKING WITH) YOUR FIRST CLIENT

Dear Leader,

You will likely remember your first client for the rest of your career. Whether it's a small engagement that barely covers expenses or a big-name brand you've admired for years, that first "yes" lands with a special kind of energy. It feels like validation that what you are building has value in the world. It may be exciting, affirming, and terrifying... all at once!

This first denotes the moment you begin to **translate your vision, or at least your capabilities, into value for someone else.** It's where belief begins to become proof.

A few things to keep in mind as you step into this moment:

- **Focus on understanding, not proving.** Curiosity builds confidence. Listen more than you pitch. Show them you understand their world, their pressures, their goals. The goal isn't to talk about how great you are; it's to make *them* feel understood, supported, and confident in choosing you.
- **Clarify your value, together.** Be specific about what problem you solve and what success will look like for *them*. Make sure you're aligned on the "why" and the end result they want to achieve, before you jump into the "how."
- **Start as you mean to go on.** You are establishing the expectations that will follow your brand: reliability, clear communication, thoughtful work, and follow-through. A first client relationship has the power to influence your norms. Select those norms intentionally.
- **Think beyond the first project.** Every interaction builds your reputation. When you deliver meaningful impact, even on a modest scope, you create advocates who can open doors you never saw coming.

Your first client is more than your first transaction. It is the beginning of fulfilling your promise to the world. The promise of *who you are, how you operate,* and *what working with you feels like.* Treat it with care and intention. There will be many clients ahead, but there will be no other "first," and this is the foundation that others will build upon.

With you in winning,

ACTIVATE THE FLYWHEEL: PRACTICES THAT BUILD TRUST EARLY

These practices focus on how it *feels* to work with you. They'll help you earn trust quickly and lay a foundation for everything that follows.

- **Promise with precision.** Commit to what you can execute flawlessly and then do it. Trust compounds faster than ambition. **There's no faster way to disappoint than overpromising and underdelivering.**
- **Stay close to the work.** In these early days, your presence matters. Not only does it give clients confidence, but it also gives you invaluable insight into what works and what needs to evolve. You'll scale soon enough. Soak in the invaluable insights from being on the front line, now.
- **Deliver seamlessly.** You are delivering more than a product or service - you are delivering an experience. **Small friction points in the experience can overshadow great thinking and great deliverables.** Build a process that feels easy to work with for your clients and for you.
- **Show up like a partner.** Invest time in understanding their business context and what they care most about. Ask meaningful questions. Signal you're there to support their success beyond this initial contract.

- **Gather Feedback, Express Gratitude.** Seek out constructive feedback for continuous improvement. Send a note, make a call. Express personalized, genuine thanks for doing business together.

It's important to note that while the stakes may feel highest with your very first client, the principles apply every time you begin working with a new one.

FROM MY JOURNEY

When we opened the doors of Gongos, our very first client was a marquee brand that had worked with us at our former organization. On paper, it looked like a sure thing. It was an existing relationship and provided built-in familiarity. But in reality, this time felt very different. The stakes were higher on both sides.

We were no longer part of an established company; we were a start-up with a new name, a new structure, and something very real to prove. And while the relationship carried forward, the risk equation had changed. For our client, choosing us now required trust without the safety net of a larger brand. For us, this wasn't just a project; it was a test of who we would become.

This awareness guided every decision we made.

With that first project, we were intentional about what we promised, resisting the temptation to overextend just to impress. Because there were only a handful of us, we were on the front lines of the work, which was good because it signaled commitment and accountability. And we paid just as much attention to *how* working with us felt as we did to the work itself because we understood that early impressions would define far more than this single engagement.

Honestly, we treated this first project like a case study in motion-capture dos and don'ts that would begin to define the future of our business and how we wanted to deliver for every client who followed.

I'm happy to say the project was successful. But more importantly, the relationship endured. In fact, that organization didn't just become our first client; they became our longest-standing one. Both our company and theirs underwent many changes, but we were still working together 30 years later.

Looking back, what I realize is: Winning the first project gets you started, but it's delivery that sets your Flywheel in motion.

OPEN WHEN: YOU REALIZE YOU CAN'T SCALE WITHOUT A SYSTEM

Dear Leader,

In the early days, business development often feels personal. You're leveraging your network and your reputation; you are hustling. But there comes a point where growth requires more than one person's energy. To scale, you need what I call a business development engine: a repeatable system that attracts, wins, nurtures, and grows clients consistently.

Building this engine isn't just about adding salespeople or cranking out proposals. It's about aligning sales goals and client experience with process and people. Done well, your business development system feels less like selling and more like inviting clients into a relationship where the value you create together is clear, and mutually beneficial results are the outcome.

A few guideposts as you build:

- **Define your funnel and client experience with clarity.** From awareness to engagement to proposal to close to winning the next project, know what each stage looks like and who owns it. Define what success looks like for each stage, and, just as importantly, how you want the client to *feel.*
- **Integrate marketing and business development.** Marketing generates awareness, consideration, and credibility; business development builds relationships and turns the brand promise into a scoped engagement. The two should feel coordinated and seamless to the client.
- **Embed an organizational mindset.** Everyone in the organization should understand how to articulate the value proposition clearly, compellingly, and succinctly. Embed an "everyone can help us grow" mindset from the get-go, showing people how their role connects to gaining and maintaining client relationships.

- **Track the right metrics.** Focus less on vanity numbers (like sheer leads) and more on conversion rates, relationship health, and lifetime value.
- **Stay human.** Systems matter, but people buy from people. Don't let the process strip away your company's authenticity and what makes it unique.

A business development engine isn't built overnight, and once in motion, it continues to take time, energy, consistent focus, and fine-tuning as client and market needs change. As the system becomes turnkey, your business development engine will free you from relying solely on referrals, chance introductions, or founder hustle. It creates sustainable momentum for growth and is a system that should be locked into the "always on" position.

With you in revving the engine,

ACTIVATE THE FLYWHEEL: THE BUSINESS DEVELOPMENT GROWTH LOOP

Business development is hard work and takes consistent effort, focus, and evolution as your business grows and changes. To get you started, use this high-level framework that steps you through the major stages.

1. Awareness: Signal credibility and clarity of your value and offer

Effective marketing grabs the attention of the right clients and makes them think: *"They get my challenges, and they might be exactly what we need."*

- Clear value proposition.
- Relevant and differentiated proof points specific to your offer.
- Thought leadership that demonstrates understanding, not self-promotion.

2. Engagement: Conversations that build interest, consideration, and connection, not pressure

The goal isn't necessarily to convince; it's to understand and begin to demonstrate value.

- Listen first, pitch second.
- Explore fit through understanding their goals, desired outcomes, and constraints.
- Demonstrate behaviors to show what it would *feel* like to work together.

3. Proposal: Designed for resonance, not information overload

Proposals should be a continuation of the conversation and an opportunity to demonstrate that you understand their needs and are uniquely capable of serving them.

- Demonstrate understanding of the *why* before digging into the *how.*
- Position the proposal as a pathway to achieving their desired outcomes, not a catalog of your services.
- Reinforce differentiation: *why you versus everyone else?*

4. Close & Grow: Deliver with intention, expand with purpose

The close is not the finish line; it's the starting line, with the mindset: *We're building something, not just completing it.*

- Deliver seamlessly and proactively. You're investing in this project as a steppingstone to the next.
- Through feedback, measure impact in their terms, not yours.
- Listen for new opportunities and capabilities connection points to grow the relationship.

FROM MY JOURNEY

We operated under a seller/doer model. The same people responsible for winning the work were also responsible for delivering it. Clients loved it, and so did we. But it created a predictable pattern: **the busier we were delivering, the less we sold.**

Whenever project load peaked, outreach slowed. Follow-ups were postponed, conversations were delayed, and proposals were rushed or deprioritized. We told ourselves we'd get back to business development "once things slowed down."

But by the time things slowed down, it was too late; often the funnel had dried up, and we were scrambling to refill it.

Looking back, some of our lowest troughs in revenue came immediately after some of our highest peaks. Nothing was wrong with the market. We simply hadn't been planting seeds while we were harvesting.

This isn't unique to our business. Now, as I mentor other leaders of professional services firms, I see the same pattern again and again. Brilliant teams land work, dive into delivery, and unintentionally turn off the engine that brought the work in the first place. Consistency in business development effort and focus separates organizations that grow from those that stall.

To break the cycle, we established standing business development meetings. Same time every week, no exceptions. We set goals, reviewed progress, shared ownership, and focused not only on expanding with current clients but on pursuing new logos. It didn't eliminate the tension of the seller-doer model, but it did build discipline. And discipline built momentum.

Growth comes from keeping business development "always on," no matter how busy you are.

For additional guidance, see: *Great Clients, Open When: Your Proposals Aren't Winning Like They Should.*

OPEN WHEN: YOU ARE TEMPTED TO SAY YES TO EVERY OPPORTUNITY

Dear Leader,

There's a paradox to growth that can take years to learn, so consider this letter a shortcut: **Too many yeses can stall your growth just as quickly as too many nos.**

In the early days, every opportunity feels like gold. A prospective client shows interest, and your instinct is to lean in: yes to the project, yes to the new industry or sector, yes to whatever keeps revenue flowing. It feels responsible. It feels necessary. And sometimes, it is.

But not every opportunity is an opportunity for you.

Some will pull you off your strategic course. Some will sit outside your strengths and force you into gray areas that drain time, confidence, and margin. Some will stretch your team so thin that even your best work suffers. And some will simply erode energy -- the most valuable currency you have.

Discernment is one of the most underrated skills in leadership. Knowing what to pursue matters but knowing what to walk away from matters just as much. When you have the courage to say no to the wrong opportunities, you protect the space, the focus, and the capacity to say yes to the right ones; the ones that align with your purpose, play to your strengths, and accelerate your Flywheel rather than slowing it down.

Here are a few guideposts to help you decide:

- **Check for alignment.** *Does this opportunity support your purpose, strategy, and target customer, or distract from it?*
- **Weigh capacity.** *Do you have the people and systems to deliver exceptional work without compromising what's already in motion?*
- **Protect culture.** *Will this client or project energize your team or deplete them?*
- **Think forward.** *Does this create momentum for future growth, or is it just a short-term fix?*

- **Consider your brand.** *Will this decision reinforce what you want to be known for, or blur it?*

Your job isn't to say yes to everything. Your job is to say yes to what matters so your team, your clients, and your business can thrive.

With you in the discernment,

ACTIVATE THE FLYWHEEL: CHOOSING THE RIGHT OPPORTUNITIES

Use these guidelines to help evaluate opportunities through a strategic lens, ensuring the opportunities you accept are ones you can deliver with excellence.

1. **Start with a Fit Scorecard.**
   Use a consistent rubric to evaluate opportunities and avoid relying solely on instinct. Consider alignment with strategy, ideal customer match, margin potential, team energy impact, and long-term relationship potential. A scorecard helps keep things objective and brings a clearer mindset.

2. **Check your *Why Yes?* and *Why Now?***
   Ask directly: *Are we saying yes because this is the right opportunity or because it showed up at the right moment?* Revenue pressure can disguise misalignment. A few extra questions up front protect confidence and delivery later.

3. **Confirm that you have the right people to deliver the intended value.**
   Every strong engagement depends on having *the right* talent in the right seats—not just available people, but the right people. Before saying yes, ask: *Do we have (or can we promptly put in place) the expertise, experience, and relational skills required for this client to feel well-served?* If you don't have the right people ready to show up fully, the opportunity isn't a yes; it's a risk.

4. **Be clear about what this yes is meant to advance.** Don't say yes simply to do more; say yes to do more of what matters. If the opportunity accelerates your strategy, deepens your expertise, strengthens your positioning, or opens a valuable door, it may be worth the stretch.

FROM MY JOURNEY

One of our large clients approached us with a project that was a bit of a diversion from our typical work. On the surface, it looked enticing: a new revenue stream within an existing client, the ability to build relationships with new contacts; a tempting opportunity. But there was a problem: the project was a misfit with our core competencies. We were also stretched thin, and taking it on would mean learning on the fly while risking quality.

Instead of forcing it, I had a conversation with the client and told them the truth. This work wasn't in our sweet spot, and we didn't have the capacity to deliver the high-quality work they expected. But I didn't leave them hanging. I recommended another firm in our industry that I knew could deliver the project well.

The client not only thanked me for being honest and transparent but pointed to this as a great example of our company's integrity. The owner of the other firm was both surprised and delighted to get our referral. It was a risk after all, they could have taken more business from us down the road, but the bigger risk was doing the project poorly and damaging our reputation.

A few years later, that same firm sent a large new client our way. Reciprocity realized.

Saying no protects your integrity. And sometimes, it opens new doors you couldn't have imagined.

Bonus Section:

When the client and the work are the right fit, but your team is at capacity, don't default to an automatic yes or no. Use the **"Yes, But"** approach to protect quality *and* preserve the relationship.

How it works:

- **Yes, but… on a delayed timeline**
  "We'd love to take this on, but to maintain the quality you expect, we'll need to begin x weeks later."

- **Yes, but… with a different team mix**
  "We'll assign a different set of experts than you've worked with before, and we're confident they'll deliver at the same high standard."

- **Yes, but… with refined deliverables**
  "We can take this on, but we'd recommend narrowing the scope to ensure depth and quality."

Why it works:

- Signals honesty and transparency.
- Positions you as a partner, not a vendor chasing revenue.
- Protects your team from burnout while maintaining client trust.

OPEN WHEN: YOUR PROPOSALS AREN'T WINNING LIKE THEY SHOULD

Dear Leader,

It grows frustrating when *"We really like you, but..."* is a common refrain. When clients show enthusiasm in the conversation, but something gets lost in the translation into a proposal, interest isn't converting into a win. This is especially frustrating when you are confident in your ability to deliver great work.

One truth to hold close: **proposals don't win on information alone; they win on resonance.**

If a proposal reads like a set of answers or a menu of your capabilities rather than a signal of partnership, it checks the boxes but doesn't build confidence or connection. It certainly doesn't set you apart.

Proposals are more than documents; they are opportunities.

Reframing proposals as opportunities to spark dialogue, not just to respond to a request, is a mindset shift. Proposals are a chance to explain what you do and demonstrate how you think, how you listen, and how you will show up when you win the work.

Before you write a single word, get curious and ask:

- *What outcomes are they truly trying to achieve?*
- *How will success be defined and by whom?*
- *Who else has influence over this decision?*
- *What do they value most: speed, innovation, certainty, partnership, efficiency, risk mitigation?*

The answers bring resonance to the proposal, and, more importantly, your **asking signals that you understand their world.**

Think of a proposal as a rehearsal: a chance for the client to experience what it might *feel* like to build something with you. Your job is to make them feel three things: **understood, confident, and eager to work with you.**

To do that, build every proposal around three anchors:

- **Relate.** Demonstrate that you "get" them, including their challenges, goals, pressures, context, and language.
- **Prove.** Substantiate your plan and related experience with examples, results, outcomes, case studies, and evidence.
- **Differentiate.** Make it obvious why you are the partner they can't replicate or replace.

And do all of this **in their story, not yours.**

Their business, their outcomes, and their language should be the narrative thread. Your capabilities should be the supporting cast. If they feel seen in the proposal, their desire to work with you naturally grows.

Whenever possible, don't just *send* a proposal; *walk it through live.* It transforms the experience from transactional to relational, giving both sides the chance to clarify assumptions, build connections, and co-create what success looks like.

When proposals relate, prove, and differentiate, they stop being paperwork and start resonating with clients' needs, creating the beginnings of a partnership.

With you in improving your win rate,

ACTIVATE THE FLYWHEEL: THE PROPOSAL EXPERIENCE

Proposals are a primary client experience touch point. When a client reads (or hears) your proposal, they're not just absorbing information—they're experiencing you. Run through these five checkpoints to improve your proposal delivery and win rate.

1. **Clarity.** *Is it easy to understand, free of jargon, and structured in a way that makes sense from the client's perspective?*

2. **Credibility.** *Does it build confidence through proof points, examples, and professionalism?*

3. **Connection.** *Would the client see themselves in the proposal: their language, their context, their goals, their timeline?*

4. **Conversation.** *Does it incite dialogue and interaction, rather than serve as a one-way pitch?*

5. **Conviction.** *Does your enthusiasm and passion for the engagement shine through in an authentic, contagious way?*

FROM MY JOURNEY

As I mentor business owners and entrepreneurs, I'm continually struck by the mindset many hold around proposals. For many professional services leaders, proposals feel like a necessary chore. Something we *have* to do to get the work. A hurdle to clear before the "real" relationship begins.

But when leaders treat proposals as paperwork, that's exactly how they show up.

I'm often asked to review strategic proposals from the outside. Not for technical accuracy, but for objectivity. And over and over, two patterns appear:

1. **The story is about the proposing company, not the client.**
   The proposal highlights expertise, capabilities, and accomplishments, but not the client's context, goals, pressures, or language.

2. **The enthusiasm and personality that make the company special never make it onto the page.**
   In person, these leaders are energized, distinct, and deeply passionate about the work. But in proposals, they become flat—technically correct, but emotionally passive.

The result? The client learns what the company can do, but doesn't feel what it would be like to do it together or why they are the right company for the challenge.

Understand that proposals aren't just a gateway to getting the work. **Proposals are an opportunity to get smarter about clients and to continuously tune your brand expression.** Every proposal is a chance to refine how you speak to the market, how you demonstrate understanding, and how you bring your unique way of thinking to life, increasing your chances from mere interest to conversion.

When you treat proposals as discovery, expression, and value creation in itself, not obligation, you don't just improve your win rate. You improve your clarity on the market, client needs, and your brand positioning.

OPEN WHEN: MARKETING AND BUSINESS DEVELOPMENT ARE OUT OF SYNC

Dear Leader,

In many organizations, marketing and business development run on parallel tracks, occasionally crossing paths but rarely moving in sync. Too often, they even clash: different goals, different mindsets, different timelines, and not enough communication. Marketing generates awareness and attracts customers, while business development builds relationships and pursues revenue. Both are doing valuable work but not always aligned on how the two efforts knit together.

When these functions operate separately, the system feels clunky. Leads go cold. Messages lack impact. Opportunities slip through the cracks. And the client experience turns inconsistent: what they hear from marketing doesn't always match what they experience in a sales conversation.

But when marketing and business development operate as one unified system, everything runs more smoothly and with greater power—for the team, for your business, *and* for the client.

Marketing fuels brand clarity, curiosity, and credibility - making business development's job easier. Business development converts that momentum into conversations, proposals, and growth - bringing client insights back to marketing to keep messaging relevant and resonant. It's a loop: interest → connection → opportunity → insight → refinement.

Done right, a client experiences one continuous story: one brand promise, one narrative, one transition from interest to engagement to partnership and eventually, to repeat business.

A few guideposts to optimize the relationship:

- **Clarify roles, handoffs, and goals**. Everyone should know where marketing ends, where business development begins, and where they overlap. Shared metrics and standing touchpoints increase alignment and speed.

- **Share a common narrative.** Your brand promise, value proposition, and differentiators should appear consistently across campaigns, conversations, proposals, and delivery. This not only sets expectations for clients but also strengthens your brand equity.
- **Collaborate on targeting.** Define ideal clients and sectors *together.* When marketing throws leads over the wall and hopes for the best, or business development chases prospects in isolation, nobody wins.
- **Measure what matters.** Don't stop at activity metrics. Track progress across the client journey: awareness → engagement → conversion → revenue → retention.
- **Keep it human.** Clients shouldn't feel the seams between departments. What they experience should feel like one brand, one team, one commitment to their success.

Optimizing the relationship between marketing and business development is about creating harmony. Each function has its own job to be done, but when they operate under one shared understanding of success, **brand strength turns into growth, consistently.**

With you in syncing up,

ACTIVATE THE FLYWHEEL: THE ALIGNMENT BRIDGE

To activate the full power of both marketing and business development, facilitate these bridges:

- **Message Bridge.** A clear value proposition, consistent story, and clear intent/call to action across every touchpoint. Clients should hear one narrative and be inspired to move to the next stage of the purchase funnel.

- **Process Bridge.** Clear roles, goals, handoffs, and communication loops. Everyone knows who owns what, when, and why.
- **Metrics Bridge.** Joint measures of success that reflect the whole client journey. When both functions win (or lose) together, the growth strategy solidifies and builds momentum.

To move from theory to reality, devote time to immersing in each other's shoes. Try shadowing. Have marketing attend a few client pitches and have business development weigh in on campaign planning. Mutual empathy is the fastest path to alignment.

FROM MY JOURNEY

As a business owner, I often worked closely with our marketing team to elevate our brand image. Sometimes we nailed it—our message resonated with clients and gave us an edge. But other times, we drifted into what I can only call "fluffy." The words were beautiful, even inspiring to us internally, but when the business development team held them up through the client lens, the reaction was sometimes: "Yes, but does it mean anything to clients? *"Can we actually sell this?"*

That reality check was invaluable. Marketing gave us aspiration; business development gave us practicality. The sweet spot was finding language that inspired both sides: it elevated our brand while also being rooted in what clients actually needed and valued.

At one point, I realized marketing didn't even know the business development team's revenue goals, yet they were responsible for forming the very first client impressions. That disconnect was costing us. So, we instituted weekly "growth strategy" meetings where marketing and business development sat at the same table to align goals, messaging, and client needs.

It wasn't always easy, but the shift was transformational. Instead of parallel tracks, we started moving in concert. Marketing sharpened its voice by listening to the client realities business development brought back, and business development benefited from a stronger, clearer brand story.

Marketing without the client's voice is art. Business development without marketing's voice misses its multiplier. Together, they have the potential to create magic: a stronger brand, clear expectations, and a driver of growth.

GREAT CLIENTS: DEVELOP

OPEN WHEN: YOU WANT TO BECOME A PARTNER, NOT JUST A VENDOR

Dear Leader,

Vendors fulfill requests. Partners create value. The difference may sound subtle, but to clients, it can make a world of difference.

When you're seen as a vendor, the relationship is transactional. You get asked to quote, respond, and deliver, often competing on speed, price, and availability. The work may be steady, but the position isn't one of strength. Vendors are easy to replace.

But when you're seen as a partner, the dynamic shifts. You're invited into the conversation earlier, asked to weigh in on strategy, and trusted with engagements and decisions that chart the client's future. You're harder to replace because you function as an extension of their team and are part of how they operate.

The shift is earned, and it doesn't happen by accident. It requires you to:

- **Listen for the unsaid.** Go beyond the brief and uncover the underlying business problem, not just the articulated one.
- **Bring fresh thinking.** Don't just meet expectations: offer insights, ideas, or approaches the client hasn't considered.
- **Show you are invested.** Understand their business as well as they do, even better. Develop a knowledge estate and be the connector among initiatives and people.
- **Take a long view.** Look beyond today's project to what will matter in six months or six years. Help them prepare.
- **Be courageous.** Partners don't always agree with clients. They challenge respectfully when it serves the bigger goal.
- **Make their job easy.** Anticipate needs, smooth obstacles, and be one step ahead.

The beauty of partnership is that it creates mutual investment: the client's success becomes your success, and vice versa. It transforms the relationship from one of service delivery to one of shared growth, both personally and professionally.

With you in elevating,

ACTIVATE THE FLYWHEEL: THE PARTNERSHIP CHECK-IN

Before client interactions: a meeting, an email, a presentation, or a proposal, ask yourself these questions. The more often you select the second part, the more you demonstrate and earn partnership.

- *Are we showing up to complete the work, or to elevate the work?*
- *Are we reacting to requests, or thinking about and anticipating needs?*
- *Are we talking about deliverables, or about what they are trying to achieve and the outcomes that matter most?*
- *Am I helping them get the work done, or helping them show up stronger?*
- *Am I protecting the relationship, or deepening and nurturing it?*

Remember: Partnership isn't always about doing more work; it's about creating more value.

FROM MY JOURNEY

For nearly a decade, we worked with a particular client on transactional, price-competitive projects. The relationship was steady but limited. We were seen as a reliable vendor. We delivered high quality, on time, and within budget, but we didn't have the access or visibility to show up as a strategic partner.

That changed the day we were told a new senior executive would be joining an upcoming meeting. We knew this was our opening to show up differently. Instead of walking in with a proposal response, we walked in with perspective. Years of knowledge about their business, awareness of industry forces, and ideas for how they could move from where they were to where they needed to be.

The executive noticed. Within minutes, t*he conversation shifted from: Can you do this project?* to: *What else do you see?* What followed was a large cross-company engagement, our first opportunity to play a strategic role with this client. It transformed how we were viewed inside the organization. Suddenly, we weren't just executing; we were advising leaders, opening doors to new audiences, and providing input to strategy.

But the real lesson wasn't about getting into the room. It was about **staying** there. To remain a partner, we had to keep earning that position. That meant consistently showing up with more than technical expertise: we had to demonstrate a grasp of the client's business, industry, pressures, and ambitions. We became their objective outsider, valued not only for delivering but also for connecting the dots, anticipating needs, and offering candid guidance. We saw this pattern repeat across many relationships over time; it was the blueprint for how we approached client relationships.

Partnership is earned and re-earned. You aren't granted partnership merely by working harder or doing more work, but by showing up with perspective, courage, and contribution that is additive to what the client organization could achieve on its own.

OPEN WHEN: YOU'VE EARNED TRUST AND WANT GREATER ACCESS

Dear Leader,

It's easy to feel secure when you have a strong relationship with a client. But if that relationship lives with just one stakeholder, one project, or one department, you're walking on fragile ground. A single leadership change, budget shift, or reorganization can wipe out years of effort and business building, not because of performance, but because access was concentrated rather than distributed.

Diversifying within a client isn't just about selling more; it's about building resilience and creating broader value. Multiple entry points create stability for you and add value for the client. When multiple teams, leaders, or functions see the benefit of working with you, your presence embeds itself rather than being optional. You are woven into their operating system. At that point, switching costs rise not because of contract terms, but because of the impact you create across the organization. Often, you're in a unique position to connect the dots between teams and initiatives in ways that are difficult for internal groups that operate in silos.

A few ways to diversify with intention:

- **Look beyond the immediate buyer.** Ask: *Who else in the organization faces similar challenges, goals, or opportunities?*
- **Leverage your champions.** Happy stakeholders often open doors when you ask them.
- **Tailor your value.** Don't assume what resonates in one business unit will resonate in another. Customize your story to the needs, challenges, and aspirations of the prospective stakeholders.
- **Be patient.** Expanding takes time. Each new relationship should be cultivated with the same care as the first.
- **Protect your base.** Diversification only works if your original stakeholder continues to feel well-served. Don't stretch so far that you weaken the original relationship.

Diversification is a form of stewardship. You've already invested in understanding your client's business and context. Expanding within the organization allows that understanding to have a win/win effect: greater impact for them, and greater stability for you.

You're moving past becoming indispensable to one person, and you're trying to create more value for the whole.

With you in the expanding,

ACTIVATE THE FLYWHEEL: EXPANDING WITHIN AN EXISTING CLIENT

To diversify within a client's business, don't start with a "selling" mindset. Start by mapping the organization to better understand where value can be added. Having a client org chart is invaluable, but even if you don't have one, these tips are still effective.

- **Map the Value Footprint.** After every project or milestone, ask yourself: *Who else in the organization could benefit from what we've just created or unlocked?*
- **Socialize Success, Not Offerings.** Share outcomes, don't sell your capabilities at this stage. A short impact summary, a replay of insights, or a "what we learned" moment often attracts new stakeholders more organically than a pitch will.
- **Ask for Connections, Not Referrals.** Your existing champions don't need the pressure of trying to sell you–just ask them to introduce you. Use simple questions like: *Who else might be able to benefit from what we've done here?* Or *is there someone else this work affects that we should include in the conversation?*

FROM MY JOURNEY

One of the best ways we diversified within a client was simply by letting our work speak for itself. Many of our client teams had opportunities to present results to cross-functional audiences, often a mix of departments, levels, and decision-makers.

Two things often happened:

1. **Curiosity sparked.** Someone in the room would approach us afterward, intrigued by the work, asking if we could help with challenges in their part of the business. Exposure led to new invitations.

2. **Creation of warm entry points.** We didn't just present and walk away. We collected names and contact information from attendees. That gave us a warm reason to follow up: *We saw you in the session last week. Can we set up some time to get to know each other better? Or wondered if you'd like to chat further about your priorities.*

Those simple but intentional steps created opportunity. The work wo did for one team often became the calling card that helped open doors for others. Over time, we weren't dependent on a single relationship or budget. We had built a presence across the system.

What I learned is that every presentation is more than a deliverable. It's an opportunity to plant seeds across the client organization. Visibility leads to access, access opens conversations, and conversations create opportunity for expansion.

This topic is so important to growing your business in a healthy, sustainable way that I'm including additional perspective from a different angle.

 FROM MY JOURNEY (X2)

Diversifying within a client isn't always about expanding reach. It can also mean expanding your offerings. That's where things get tricky. Clients come to know you for *one* thing, and even if you've added new capabilities, they may not automatically believe you can deliver with the same level of excellence.

We faced this when we introduced new service offerings. Our clients trusted us deeply in our core area, but when we tried to introduce something new, the response was often cautious. *We love you for this, but are you really as good at that?*

The reality is, believability is critical when diversifying offerings. It takes time, patience, and persistence to earn trust in a new space. We had to listen more carefully, tailor our pitches more thoughtfully, and sometimes even pilot small projects to prove our credibility.

Over time, those seeds began to grow, but the process was slower and more difficult than diversifying through exposure to our existing work. It required perseverance, creativity, and a willingness to keep showing up, even when the "yes" didn't come right away.

What we learned is that expanding offerings is possible and important, but don't underestimate the hurdles of awareness and credibility. Lag time between launch and sales may be greater than you anticipate, and you may need to prove yourself all over again.

OPEN WHEN: YOU WANT TO UNDERSTAND AND ANTICIPATE CLIENT NEEDS

Dear Leader,

Understanding what clients need today is essential, but anticipating what they'll need tomorrow is where a strong future for your client and your business really begins to take shape.

Clients will tell you what they need, but you have to be ready to listen and act. The challenge goes beyond hearing their words; it entails building effective systems to capture, interpret, and act on their feedback. Without structure, input and insights get lost in inboxes, one-off conversations, and meeting notes. With structure, feedback is fuel: guiding decisions, shaping the client experience, and even sparking reinvention. Beyond this, it sends a signal to the client that the relationship is important to you and that your business cares about continuous improvement.

A true client centric business does more than collect feedback. It creates intentional mechanisms to:

- **Gather input consistently.** Surveys, One-on-one check-ins, advisory boards, or even informal debriefs are all effective methods for gathering input.
- **Spot the signals.** Separating isolated frustrations from systemic issues and uncovering emerging needs is critical to understand the signal rather than the noise.
- **Close the loop.** Letting clients know how their feedback influenced change builds trust and loyalty.
- **Look ahead.** Using feedback not only to fix today's issues but to anticipate tomorrow's opportunities.
- **Express gratitude.** Too often, client relationships are taken for granted, especially longstanding ones. Leverage feedback time not only to listen, but to express gratitude for the partnership.

Over time, these listening systems create a dynamic cycle: you meet current needs more effectively while positioning yourself to evolve alongside your clients. This is where reinvention often begins, not in a boardroom brainstorming session, but in the voices of the clients you serve.

With you in listening deeply and acting with intention,

ACTIVATE THE FLYWHEEL: PROACTIVE LISTENING IN PRACTICE

Don't wait for clients to *volunteer* feedback. Treat listening as a strategic practice and rhythm for your business using this three-part framework:

- **Create a Cadence of Listening Opportunities:** Don't leave feedback to chance. Build touchpoints into the client experience: post-engagement debriefs, quarterly business reviews, midpoint check-ins, or informal "pulse" conversations. Assign an owner to each type of touchpoint and curate the insights received from the combination of touchpoints. Summaries by client can be used by the teams serving the client, while a holistic summary looking across clients can serve as input for strategic planning and your innovation pipeline.

- **Ask Questions that Surface Unspoken Needs:** Clients may not volunteer critical feedback if it feels uncomfortable. Try prompts like: *What would make working together even easier? What one thing should we change going forward? What's becoming more important inside your organization?*

- **Reflect & Close the Loop:** Show clients their input mattered by circling back with *"Here's what we heard." "Here's what we're changing."* or *"Here's what that means for you going forward."* Clients are more likely to continue providing input when they can see the impact of their voice.

FROM MY JOURNEY

Because we were a marketing research company at our roots, one of our signature deliverables was a findings report—rich with data, analysis, charts, and recommendations. For years, that was the standard. And honestly, we were proud of the rigor.

But along came some feedback that changed everything.

After delivering a large project, a longtime client asked for a candid debrief. He told us, *"Your reports are good... but I need to challenge you to make them great."*

He explained that he was sharing our reports with extremely busy executives who needed to make high-stakes decisions fast. Even our "executive summary" was too dense, too data-heavy, and used "research-speak" rather than "business-speak." They didn't need a story that was clear, memorable, easy to digest, and translated understanding into action.

Then he said the line that stayed with me for decades:

"Give me one hard-hitting, action-oriented slide. The rest should live in a story. I need something simple enough that anyone can understand and act on it, and with the right balance of succinct and compelling to hold their attention to the end."

It was uncomfortable feedback—because he was right.

We took the challenge seriously. We rebuilt our format around story, clarity, and action. Instead of reporting everything we learned, we elevated what mattered most. And we didn't stop with that client. We began tailoring that narrative-driven approach across our portfolio.

Some clients preferred the traditional format. Others loved the shift. But over time, that **"signal through the noise" storytelling style became our differentiator**—something competitors struggled to replicate because they were still anchored to data volume rather than its meaning.

One moment of honest feedback from a client who cared enough to say it out loud reimagined not only a deliverable but, over time, redefined our brand.

Listening may feel passive, but it can be truly transformative. Sometimes, the most meaningful innovations come from clients who use your work and are willing to collaborate on improving it to help *them* succeed.

For additional guidance, see: *Great Work, Open When: The Work is Good but Not Evolving (Innovation Feels Stuck)* and *Beyond the Flywheel, Open When: You Realize the Customer is No Longer the Center.*

OPEN WHEN: THE CLIENT WANTS MORE THAN YOU AGREED TO

Dear Leader,

Here you are...you've won the work, you're immersed in the engagement, and the client asks for *more*. Could be a bigger scope. Expanded deliverables. Faster outcomes. You name it. More than your team can realistically provide within the original timeline, budget, or staffing.

And it's tempting, so tempting, to say yes immediately.

You want to strengthen and protect the relationship and prove your value. There may even be an adrenaline rush from being the hero.

But here's the risk: **saying yes too quickly can do more damage to the relationship than pausing and then responding with consideration for the changes at hand.**

A reactive yes can lead to:

- Overpromising and underdelivering
- Rework and confusion
- Team fatigue and burnout
- Margin erosion
- And ironically, weakened trust

Scope change is normal. Client needs evolve and priorities shift. That's not a problem, that's real life. The problem isn't the change request; the problem is when leaders respond impulsively rather than intentionally.

Proactive client management is defined by **stepping into a partnership and it can sound like this:**

"I hear you. Let's look at what this change means for timeline, resources, and budget so we can make the right call together."

That single pause, that moment of reflection, is often what separates a transactional relationship from a strategic one.

Because when you pause to assess the following, you are protecting not just the health of your business, but your client's outcome:

- What the request truly requires
- What tradeoffs may need to exist
- What new value may be unlocked
- What risks it introduces
- What support you need to do it well

Leaders often fear that setting boundaries will weaken the relationship. But the opposite is true. When you are clear about what you can and cannot deliver without compromising value creation, **you strengthen trust**. You demonstrate reliability, professionalism, and genuine commitment to great work.

A client who experiences that kind of stewardship wants to work with you again. Not because you say yes to everything, but because when you say yes, you mean it.

With you in the thoughtful response,

ACTIVATE THE FLYWHEEL: LANGUAGE THAT PROTECTS VALUE AND THE RELATIONSHIP

When a client asks for more than what you've scoped, pause the impulse to immediately say yes and open up a dialogue. These simple scripts make the pause feel proactive and natural—bringing confidence to both sides.

- **Acknowledge the request and build a connection before setting boundaries:** *Thanks for raising that – I can see why it would be valuable.*

- **Create the evaluation pause to position the solution as a joint decision, not a direct yes or no:** *Let's take a minute to look at what this change means for the timeline, scope, and budget so that we can make the right call together.*

- **Explore the "why now" to uncover the true urgency and context:** *Help me understand what's driving the change: is it a shift in priority, stakeholder expectations, or did something new happen internally?*

- **Define options – not obstacles to reduce pressure and invite collaboration:**

  » *There are a couple of ways we could approach this...*

  » *We can expand the scope and timeline.*

  » *We can swap X for Y without increasing overall cost.*

  » *While the overall engagement price increases, the deliverables increase value by...*

- **Affirm partnership to reinforce the boundaries that serve their success, not just yours:** *Our goal is the same: great outcomes and a great experience. If we align on a path forward, we'll deliver both.*

FROM MY JOURNEY

A wake-up call about proactive client management and business management in general came early in my career on a large project for a loyal client. It was important work and, for us, a bit of a stretch. We were using a new methodology that hadn't yet been fully battle-tested. The client was engaged and excited, and as the work progressed, more was asked of us. Additional thinking, expanded deliverables, deeper analysis, and leveraging our top talent to achieve what we needed to with this work.

And I kept saying yes.

At the time, it felt like the right thing to do. My top priorities were accomplishing great work and pleasing the client. I wanted to prove our value. And, in many ways, I was succeeding. Loyalty was deepening, trust was growing, and the client was thrilled. What I wasn't doing was pausing to consider the *full* picture: the additional value we were creating, the strain on our resources, and the opportunity cost for the business.

John, our CEO at the time, pulled me aside and helped me see what I couldn't yet see for myself.

He acknowledged my intent first, and this mattered to me. *It's great that you want to take care of the client and prove out a new method. You're building real loyalty.* Then he gently named the other side of the equation: *We're not charging appropriately for the value we're creating, or considering the opportunity cost to the company of having so many of our people dedicated to this one project.*

That conversation stuck with me.

This wasn't about pulling back on delivering excellence or saying no to clients. It was about learning to pause long enough to consider the full business equation. To recognize that value creation matters and that leadership means shepherding value for the client *and* the business. That moment reframed how I thought about scope, pricing, and the importance of proactive client conversations about value creation throughout a project's life. Over time, it also influenced how I coached others, helping teams move from instinctively pleasing clients to confidently managing work in a way that protected outcomes, people, and the long-term health of the company.

Our team was wired first and foremost for delivering excellence to clients, so even years later, conversations about pricing and value creation remained a muscle we were strengthening. **But that early lesson stayed with me: Client stewardship means considering the full equation: what creates real value for the client *and* what sustains the business that delivers it. Saying yes without pause may feel accommodating in the moment, but can be short-sighted over time. Teaching teams to pause, assess, and honor both sides of the equation deepens client relationships, and the business strengthens because of it.**

GREAT CLIENTS: RETAIN AND GROW

OPEN WHEN: YOU LOSE A CLIENT

Dear Leader,

No matter how strong your business or how committed you are to your clients, at some point, you will lose one. Various reasons exist; it might be due to budget cuts, leadership changes, a competitive switch, a misstep with deliverables, or simply because their needs evolved beyond what you could provide. No matter the reason, it usually stings. After all, relationships are personal, and losing one can feel like failure.

But here's some perspective: client loss is part of the business cycle. The key is what you do with the loss and how you respond to it.

Here are a few guideposts to navigate client loss with integrity and while also gaining insight:

- **Exit with grace.** How you say goodbye matters. Make it respectful and supportive, not defensive. Leave the door open by showing appreciation. Never burn a bridge.
- **Seek feedback.** Ask directly: *What drove the decision? What could we have done differently?* Sometimes the answer is outside your control, but sometimes it's not.
- **Learn and adapt.** Take the lessons forward and look for patterns. *Was there a gap in communication, quality, capability, or relevance that you can address for future clients?* Take responsibility where it is yours and release what isn't.
- **Stay in touch.** Clients who leave may circle back. I've seen it happen often. They move roles, their new supplier disappoints, or circumstances change. A respectful goodbye leaves room for future hellos.

The reality is, losing a client doesn't always mean you did something wrong. Sometimes it means you helped them grow beyond where they were. Sometimes it means you outgrew each other. Sometimes it means your next best opportunity is waiting somewhere else.

What defines you is not whether a client leaves, but how you respond to the loss. Leave every client with integrity and use the experience as a platform for continued evolution. In time, those endings often plant the seeds for new beginnings. And remember, when a relationship ends, your business development engine is more than a safety net, it's a reminder that you are built to keep going!

With you in turning endings into openings,

ACTIVATE THE FLYWHEEL: TURNING LOSS INTO LEADERSHIP

As much as it stings, client loss is a business reality. Reframe loss from a stall in momentum to an opportunity to advance by responding systemically rather than emotionally.

This high-level sequence is a starting point for moving through loss with confidence:

1. **Pause the Story.** Before reacting, ask: *What assumptions or stories am I making about why we lost this client?* It's easy to create emotional narratives in the heat of the moment. Don't stew in speculation. Get clarity to fuel objective, forward movement.

2. **Go to the Source.** Seek clarity directly from the client. Accept the feedback without defensiveness and remember that the simple act of asking is a signal of grace and care for client relationships and for the team.

3. **Debrief with Intent to Learn.** Host a short, structured post-loss review with the team. Make it constructive so that it feels safe. The goal is learning, not blaming. Ask things like: *What were the facts? What signals did we miss? What did we do well? What would we do differently next time? How do we help other teams prevent this?*

4. **Reassure the Team.** Acknowledge their effort and reinforce their value. Address job security concerns openly and transparently.

5. **Close the Loop with the Client.** One last touchpoint to offer gratitude, support during transition, and a door left open for future opportunities, when appropriate.

6. **Reinvest the Energy.** Leverage the learnings to level up other account relationships or improve processes. Accelerate business development to fill revenue gaps. Redeploy the talent to new opportunities as soon as possible to reinforce your belief in them and their ability to grow from this experience.

FROM MY JOURNEY

Over the years, of course, we broke ties with some clients. Sometimes it was anticipated, sometimes it blindsided us; I can tell you it rarely felt good. Each loss carried its own weight and its own lessons.

One goodbye is worth sharing. It was a large engagement, with recurring revenue, so highly valuable for us and deeply embedded in the client organization. When we lost it to a competitor, the team felt like it came out of left field. But when we debriefed, we realized the warning signs had been there all along. The client had raised concerns in subtle ways, and while nothing was ever "on fire," nothing was fully right either. When the program came up for renewal, it shouldn't have been such a surprise that they explored other options.

We chose to exit with grace. I personally spoke openly with the client to understand the decision; we helped transition the project to the new supplier and remained available afterward in case the transition needed support. Our team handled it professionally. Internally, though, the loss took a toll. There was bitterness, disappointment, and a creeping fear: this project had been the full-time work of several people. What did it mean for their future?

In some respects, that's where the real leadership work began. This was a talented team that just happened to take a misstep. We reassured the team that their jobs were secure and that they would be redeployed to new opportunities. (Thank goodness our business development engine was always running.) More importantly, we turned the pain into progress. We dissected the loss together, without blame, identified root causes, and baked the learnings into our account management playbook, identifying cues to minimize the chances of future repeats.

Time heals all wounds, and these same people leveraged a growth mindset to prove their value to other clients. This original setback became a catalyst for personal growth, organizational resilience, and a stronger client experience across the board.

Grace is a strategy, not a softness. Grace in the goodbye to the client and grace in the way you lead the team forward after the breakup. Both moments can define you far more than the loss itself.

OPEN WHEN: A CLIENT IS AT RISK OF LEAVING (OR A LONG-TERM RELATIONSHIP FEELS STALE)

Dear Leader,

Sometimes client relationships start to drift. The signals vary: a slow fade that makes a long-term partnership feel stale, or more urgent shifts like shrinking scope, fewer strategic conversations, slower replies, or a new decision-maker at the table. Whatever the scenario, the feeling underneath is the same: **the relationship is vulnerable, and you can feel it.**

When you sense the shift, the instinct is to hold on tightly, push harder, sell more, and prove your value. And yes, recommitting matters. But too much intensity can backfire. The path back to stability starts with deep listening and a curious mindset.

If the relationship is still alive, it often needs fresh energy, not pressure. Lean in, gain understanding, and show up with new energy. Re-energize the relationship with fresh ideas, new voices from your team, or a reframing of value that reminds them why your partnership is strong. Long-term clients especially need these sparks to stay engaged.

But here's the other truth: not every relationship is meant to last forever. Sometimes clients outgrow your offerings, the business context shifts, or they simply want to try something new. Forcing the relationship to continue can create more harm than good. Letting a client go with grace preserves integrity and often keeps the door open for a future return.

The art of leadership is knowing which path you're on. *Is this a relationship ready for recommitment, or is this the moment to let go?* Either way, the key is to approach it with openness, professionalism, and respect.

With you in navigating the crossroads,

ACTIVATE THE FLYWHEEL: DIAGNOSE THE PATH - REIGNITE OR RELEASE

When a relationship feels vulnerable, take time to reflect and consider next best actions. Use the prompts below to **diagnose whether to reignite the relationship or release it with grace when the time is right.**

Reignite if most of these are true:

- Their goals have evolved, and there is an openness for you to evolve with them.
- Concerns are fixable without compromising your team or values.
- Internal advocacy exists.
- You have fresh thinking, talent, capability, or perspective that matches the needs they have surfaced.

Release with grace when most of these are true:

- Their needs have shifted beyond your strengths or no longer align with your business strategy.
- Continuing would compromise your people's growth path or erode quality.
- The work has become more effort than energy for both sides.
- The value you offer and the budget available are no longer aligned, despite goodwill on both sides.

An important caveat exists here. Letting go is not always immediate or binary. You may need to sustain the partnership while you build replacement revenue, since protecting your company's health comes first. Releasing with grace can look like:

- Reducing scope gradually
- Focusing on projects where the value equation is healthy for both sides
- Transitioning responsibility over time, not all at once

FROM MY JOURNEY

We used to joke, but also seriously observe, that client relationships often hit a "seven-year itch." Much like in a marriage, around the five-to-seven-year mark, some clients started to get restless. They'd look around at other vendors, not necessarily because we were doing anything wrong, but because the natural business cycle made them curious about what else was out there.

Once we recognized the pattern, we began treating it with the leadership responsibility it deserved. We built it into our account management playbook to keep a special pulse on long-term clients, especially those that still felt strong. We scheduled key conversations not only to monitor satisfaction but to stay attuned to evolving needs and shifting priorities. These interactions helped us gain insight into *whether we are still fresh. Are we still relevant? Are we still making them feel like they matter?*

Above all, we made one conscious shift that sharpened our mindset and behaviors: **We treat existing clients with the same "special-ness" as we do in a very first engagement.** Don't make assumptions. Don't short-cut. Bring passion, intelligence, and pride... every single time.

By taking this approach, many of our long-term relationships didn't just survive the seven-year itch; they grew stronger. Clients felt we were investing in them with the same enthusiasm as day one, and that effort often paid off with decades-long partnerships.

Retention requires as much intentionality as acquisition. Long-term clients should feel the privilege of loyalty and the commitment of a partnership that is still fresh and evolving.

This topic deserves perspective from another angle

FROM MY JOURNEY (X2)

Not every client relationship is meant to last forever. We had a large engagement with one client that spanned more than 15 years. Over time, their needs shifted in a direction that no longer aligned with our business strategy.

We explored options for how we might continue supporting them: tweaks to our offerings, new approaches, creative partnerships with other vendors, but none of it fully created a win/win for the client and for us. We could have tried to "finagle" a solution, but doing so would have distracted us from building new capabilities, confused our people, and ultimately compromised both our future direction and our team's satisfaction with the work.

In the end, the client chose another supplier who was better positioned to deliver what they needed. It was a hard pill to swallow. But it was also a clear example of a relationship that had run its course. By letting go gracefully, we preserved mutual respect and freed ourselves to focus on where we could add the most value for clients and our people.

Sometimes, keeping a client means losing yourself. The more courageous choice is to part ways with the integrity that protects your people, your strategy, and your future.

OPEN WHEN: TOO MUCH DEPENDS ON ONE CLIENT OR SECTOR

Dear Leader,

Many businesses have a "hero client" at some point(s): the one whose projects fuel revenue, growth, momentum, and mindshare. It feels great... until it doesn't. Because when too much of your business relies on one client, one sector, or one type of work, you're vulnerable. A leadership change, budget cut, or market downturn can turn a strong year into a shaky one in a matter of days.

An unbalanced client portfolio doesn't just create financial risk; it creates reputational risk. It also affects behavior inside your company. Teams begin catering to one client's needs at the expense of others. Innovation may narrow if this client does only one type of work. Even if the client is profitable for the company, morale can suffer when people feel they're working **for** a client rather than **with** them.

Diversifying is one of the most intentional strategies you can pursue as a company. A healthy portfolio has variety: a mix of industries, client logos, client sizes, capabilities utilized, and relationship maturities. While diversification doesn't eliminate risk, it does reduce the chance that a single event can destabilize your business.

Steps for Building Balance:

- **Audit your portfolio.** Map revenue concentration by client logo, sector, and capability, including how much of your talent is tied to each.
- **Set guardrails.** Define what percentage of revenue any one client or industry should represent; do the same for new business versus clients that have been with you for enough time that you would consider them existing/returning clients.
- **Pursue adjacencies.** Grow into areas close to your current strength areas, where credibility naturally transfers. This could include industries, service offerings, stakeholders, or geography.

- **Invest in breadth and depth.** Pursue new client companies while also growing into new areas and deepening relationships within existing client organizations.
- **Keep a future lens.** Anticipate where growth may come from three to five years out, not just today.

When your client portfolio is balanced, you gain more than stability; you set the stage for a healthy and sustainable organization. A diversified portfolio also provides more permission to say no when needed, invest with foresight, and lead from strategy rather than fear.

With you in the balancing act,

ACTIVATE THE FLYWHEEL: THE PORTFOLIO HEALTH CHECK

This diagnostic will help you understand whether your client portfolio is supporting sustainability or creating risk.

Ask yourself:

1. **Revenue Concentration.** Is *more than 25–30% of revenue tied to one client or brand (or a very small number of clients)?*
2. **Talent Concentration.** *Would losing a single client impact the workload of more than 10-15% of our team?*
3. **Sector & Use Case Diversity.** *Are we too concentrated in one industry or one type of work?*
4. **Range of Relationship Maturity.** *Do we have a mix of new business, mid-stage, and long-term clients?*

5. **Pipeline Reality Check.** *Are we actively cultivating opportunities to rebalance the future, or are we doubling down on what we already have?*

If the answers reveal an imbalance, develop a strategy to rebalance over time, not overnight. You will need to protect the work you have while building the work you need. **Add before you subtract.**

Make the portfolio health check an annual ritual and discuss it openly with your team. Explain how diversification protects the business and the people. When everyone understands why balance matters, they can help build it.

FROM MY JOURNEY

When we first opened our doors, we were 100% reliant on one large automotive client. That relationship kept us alive, but it also made us vulnerable. Not only were we dependent on a single client's budget, but we were also tied to one industry known for its economic swings. We knew that if we didn't diversify, our future was at risk.

Our first step toward diversification was small, but important. We targeted adjacent industries: durable goods with motors, where our credibility transferred. Our very first non-automotive client was in the boating category. Not exactly a huge leap, but it was proof we could expand our expertise and our brand reputation beyond where we started. That one foothold became a story we proudly told, and it gave us the confidence to keep going.

But the real turning point came when two large opportunities emerged. These opportunities spanned the consumer goods and retail industries, providing us with a much greater range. But we had a small staff, already stretched thin, and serving these new clients well would require putting some of our best people on these engagements. People who were deeply embedded in our automotive work. It was a risky trade-off. But in the spirit of diversification and the long-term health of the company, we knew what we had to do. We reassigned talent, delivered on the new opportunities, and in doing so, laid the foundation for a healthier, more balanced portfolio.

Over time, and with intentional effort, that diversification took hold. We expanded across multiple sectors, earned the trust of a wide range of Fortune 500 clients, and even set internal metrics to track our year-over-year progress, ensuring we never drifted back into overreliance on any single client or industry.

Diversification isn't just a strategy; it's a discipline. Sometimes it means making tough trade-offs in the short term to build stability and resilience for the long term.

OPEN WHEN: YOU'RE AFRAID TO LOSE THE REVENUE, BUT YOU'RE LOSING SOMETHING BIGGER

Dear Leader,

Being a client-centric organization doesn't mean the client is always right. In fact, that phrase can be dangerous if taken literally. Sometimes the cost of keeping a client: on your culture, your people, or your future strategy, outweighs the revenue they bring in. That's when the most courageous decision you can make is to walk away.

Walking away from a client is rarely a black-and-white decision. But if you aim to create true win/wins between clients and your people, you'll recognize when the scale has tipped too far in the wrong direction. Protecting what matters most: your values, your team's wellbeing, and your company's long-term health, must take priority. Because toxic clients don't just drain resources; they weaken morale, skew your strategy, and ultimately take more than they give.

Signs It May Be Time to Walk Away:

- The client consistently disrespects your team or operates against your core values.
- The account consumes disproportionate energy relative to the value it creates.
- Revenue reliance on the client is a risk rather than a stabilizer.
- Every interaction feels like a compromise rather than a collaboration.
- Their demands stretch you outside your core strengths in ways that misalign with your future direction.

Walking away is rarely a quick call. It requires forethought, professionalism, and grace. Be clear with the client, be respectful, and if possible, help transition the work elsewhere. How you end relationships becomes part of your reputation just as much as how you begin them.

Equally important is how you communicate internally. Your team needs to understand the reasons behind the decision, and that this isn't a shortcut for handling every difficult client. When done well, they'll see it as evidence that you are willing to protect them, the culture, and the company's integrity.

The short-term sting of lost revenue is real. But the long-term payoff: reclaimed energy, a stronger culture, and sharper alignment with your true direction, almost always outweighs it.

With you in choosing courage over compromise,

ACTIVATE THE FLYWHEEL: COURAGEOUS CLIENT DECISION-MAKING

These guideposts help you slow down, face the full equation, and make decisions that protect your people, your strategy, and your future.

1. **Assess the Cost of Staying.** Ask: *If this relationship continues exactly as it is today for the next 12 months, what will it cost us in terms of culture, morale, strategy, leadership energy, profitability, and opportunity?*

2. **Voice the Truth.** Sometimes clarity precedes courage. Voicing out loud to yourself or your leadership team: *We are keeping this client for the revenue, not because the relationship is healthy.*

3. **Prepare.** Walking away requires forethought, not impulse. Consider in advance: Transition plan, timing, internal implications of staff, replacement revenue, and communication approach.

4. **Communicate.** With the client: Be respectfully transparent and support the transition; With the team: Honor their efforts and reinforce the *why*.

5. **Reinvest the Energy.** Redeploy free capacity and renewed energy with intention—business development, key clients, creation of new offerings/innovation opportunities.

FROM MY JOURNEY

When a well-known brand signed on with us, it felt like a big win. One of those names any company would be proud to have on its roster. We celebrated the win, feeling a rush of validation and possibility. But honestly, even in the excitement, the early signs of misfit were there.

During scoping, the client seemed stressed, disorganized, and overwhelmed, and despite best efforts to calm, that energy immediately transferred to the team. What should have been a collaborative kick-off became a scramble. Expectations shifted constantly. Deadlines compressed without discussion. The tone was transactional, not respectful. We weren't being asked to bring our expertise; we were being asked to react.

At first, we did what many teams do: we tried harder. We worked late, jumped through hoops, and absorbed the chaos in the hopes that things would get better. But as the project went on, the cost became more obvious: people were no longer energized; in fact, they were burning out, and morale was slipping fast. Even pride in the work was beginning to diminish—a clear sign that the cultural mismatch was present.

We rallied and delivered the project to the quality level we promised. We cared about the impact of the work, and we weren't going to abandon the engagement. But alongside the push to the finish line, we had another responsibility: to protect the team. I stayed close to them, acknowledged how difficult the engagement was, and made it clear that this was not normal and it would not become our norm.

When the project wrapped, we made the intentional (and difficult) choice not to pursue further work with this client. We exited with professionalism. We thanked them for the opportunity and had an honest exchange about the relationship and its learnings.

On paper, it may have looked like we were turning away revenue and prestige. In reality, we were protecting something more valuable: our people, our culture, and the way we wanted to feel when we are achieving great work.

Not every dream client is worth the cost. Sometimes the most important win is the courage to choose your people over adding the prestigious logo to your portfolio.

OPEN WHEN: YOU WANT TO DEEPEN A PARTNERSHIP

Dear Leader,

Not every client relationship offers the privilege of true partnership—the kind that goes beyond transactional exchanges. But when it does, that's where the most meaningful impact lives. And I don't just mean financial impact. I mean human impact, strategic impact. The kind of work that would be hard to imagine without the unique combination of your expertise with theirs. At this point, you've moved beyond collaborating to **co-creating value that neither could achieve alone.**

Deep partnerships emerge when both sides invest in each other's success. You share goals, co-design solutions, and build a mutually reinforcing collaboration rhythm. Contracts and proposals still exist, but the frame is different. The contract is there to ensure alignment on the work you've envisioned together and to achieve shared purpose.

The starting point is always the same: **excellence in the basics**. Follow through on commitments, communicate clearly, and consistently deliver great work. Without this foundation, you haven't earned the right to grow deeper.

Once you do, try these methods for building deeper partnerships:

- **Listen Differently.** Go beyond tactical needs. Ask about future priorities, pressure points, and aspirations. Listen for what's said and what's not.
- **Co-Create.** Build something new together: solutions, frameworks, or pilots. Always bring your expertise, but leave space for their ideas.
- **Share Wins and Risks.** Celebrate milestones as joint victories. When challenges arise, face them side by side, not as supplier and buyer, but as partners.
- **Build Multiple Bridges.** Expand connections across functions, levels, and business units. The deeper the web of relationships, the stronger the partnership.

- **Align Purpose.** Connect your work to their larger mission. Loyalty strengthens when clients see you invested in what matters most to them.

Deepening a partnership takes time, courage, generosity, and a willingness to **give and take**. The goal is **mutual advancement**. These are the types of partnerships you look back on with pride because you didn't just deliver great work, **you built something meaningful together.**

With you in deepening partnerships that last and grow,

ACTIVATE THE FLYWHEEL: THE PARTNERSHIP SPECTRUM

Every client relationship lives somewhere on a spectrum. The deeper the relationship, the greater the trust, collaboration, and shared value. It's difficult to leapfrog stages; you earn your way forward through how you consistently show up.

As you review the stages, ask yourself: *Where do we sit on the spectrum with our top five (or ten) clients, and what would we need to do to move to the next stage?*

1. Vendor: Reliable Execution

- *What it looks like*: You provide what's asked, reliably and on time.
- *What to watch*: The relationship is transactional, easily compared on price, speed, and availability.

2. Preferred Partner: Trusted Capability

- *What it looks like*: Clients proactively seek you out for important projects because of consistency, quality, and expertise.
- *What to watch*: Without new thinking, you risk being replaced by a competitor who feels fresher or more innovative.

3. Strategic Partner: Integrated Influence

- *What it looks like*: You're part of the bigger picture. Clients ask for you to join conversations about strategy and direction, not just execution.
- *Risks*: If you stop listening or bringing new ideas, the relationship can plateau or decline.

4. Co-Creator: Shared Value

- *What it looks like*: You and the client build something together: new solutions, frameworks, playbooks, or innovations neither could achieve alone.
- *Upside*: Reciprocal value exchange. Loyalty grows naturally because the value is mutual.

FROM MY JOURNEY

One of our long-time clients approached us about something that instantly felt different. They wanted to hire us for another project, but this time it was a project to build something new together. The solution they envisioned wasn't just innovative to them; it was cutting-edge for the entire consumer insights industry. There were already competitors operating in the space, and the client could have gone to any of them. But they came to us because of our strong delivery track record, our ability to pair deep consumer understanding with custom technology, and our long-standing knowledge of their business. This wasn't simply new work. It was an invitation to evolve our relationship.

Neither side knew exactly what the solution would look like at the start. Instead of rushing into the software specs, we began by defining the outcomes we each needed. What followed was more than a year of building side by side. It was more of developing, experimenting, iterating, challenging, and championing for one another. It was demanding and energizing at the same time.

The result was a breakthrough: we launched a minimum viable product and the service that would surround it. Together, we refined it until it became the consumer input platform for almost every audience the client cared about, domestically and globally. The pride in what we had created was palpable. For them, it unlocked new strategic capability. For us, it became a new differentiated offering we could scale across our client base. The work didn't just deepen the partnership; **it reset our growth trajectory.**

Looking back, that opportunity didn't come by chance. It came about because our team had consistently delivered great work, listened deeply, understood the client's business, stayed ahead of industry shifts, and showed up not only as problem solvers but also as strategic thinkers. When the client had a need, they couldn't trust anyone else; we were already in their consideration set.

The invitation to co-create didn't happen in that moment. It was earned through the many actions that preceded it. Deepening a partnership is about the way you show up day after day.

OPEN WHEN: YOU SENSE COMPETITORS ARE GAINING MOMENTUM

Dear Leader,

In long-term relationships, it's natural for new companies to try to gain the client's attention: reaching out, pitching fresh ideas, and showing up with tempting offers. Sometimes your client may even work with you and competitors simultaneously on adjacent initiatives. It can stir anxiety and even defensiveness. After years of building the business, it's natural to let frustration lead you to question: *Why are they entertaining someone else?*

But if you step back, you will realize that competition is a natural part of a long-term partnership, and it's not a sign that you are failing. You cannot prevent competitors from showing up, **but you can ensure that when they do, your value speaks louder than they do.**

Retention in a competitive environment requires you to be at your *A game* every single day. A meaningful and consistently delivered brand promise, fresh thinking, and a trusted relationship that runs deeper than the next proposal.

Ultimately, it's important to realize that competition isn't always a threat. It can be an important catalyst—a reason to sharpen your differentiation and bring renewed energy to the relationship. Clients want partners who are focused on continuous improvement, not those who grow complacent. Your job is to listen, evolve, and add new value even after the relationship is well into its mature phase.

When competition is circling, keep these guideposts in mind:

- **Reinforce the Basics.** Clear communication, honoring commitments, and delivering with excellence are table stakes. Small cracks in the foundation give clients an easy reason to explore other options.
- **Be Present.** Relationships matter and are nurtured through contact and care. Consistently demonstrate that you are as invested in their success.

- **Differentiate in the Doing.** Saying what makes you unique isn't nearly as important as demonstrating it through how you deliver. Every interaction is a brand expression. *What proven value can you offer that competitors can't replicate?*
- **Regularly Share What's New.** It's only natural for clients to explore new partners. Instead of focusing energy on defending your position, regularly share new ideas, insights, and solutions. Innovation doesn't have to be big to be meaningful. Small improvements signal to clients that you are continuously evolving and improving your offer.

Competition is healthy. The real win is when you're spending less time on defense and more time on offense, showing up as the strategic partner who consistently delivers, consistently evolves, and consistently cares about the client's business as much as their own.

With you in growing stronger through competition,

ACTIVATE THE FLYWHEEL: STAY COMPETITION-AWARE, NOT COMPETITION-REACTIVE

Staying attuned to the competitive landscape keeps you on the offense. Understanding who is emerging in your space, how their capabilities compare with yours, and where they fill gaps you'd compete in makes you a more strategic partner to clients and enables you to evolve smartly, not impulsively.

- **Build a Competitive Awareness Rhythm.** Identify channels: conferences, industry newsletters, networking groups, analyst reports, even social platforms, to track new entrants and evolving players. Look for patterns in offerings, language, technology, and pricing. Get to know leaders in adjacent firms. You're gathering signals to get smarter, not to stress you out.

- **Scan the Market Through Your Client's Eyes.** Ask: *If I were our client, what trends, capabilities, or vendors would catch my attention right now?* If the relationship allows, ask them directly. Clients often appreciate the conversation. Curiosity builds empathy and helps you stay relevant without needing to be first.

- **Anchor in Your Strengths and Reinforce Them.** Internally, stay grounded in your purpose and value proposition; they are your compass for evaluating shifts in the landscape. Externally, don't assume clients remember your differentiation and full capabilities just because they once heard them. Reinforce through how you deliver, not just what you say.

- **Evolve Through Curiosity, Not Fear.** Often, you don't have to reinvent offerings to stay competitive. Sometimes the spark is small: a new technique, a reframed offering, a more intuitive client experience, a refreshed deliverable format, or updated pricing and timelines. Small renewals help clients continue to see you as *current*, as *relevant*.

- **Be Open to Unlikely Allies.** Clients know that most firms can't do everything. Strategic partnerships, whether initiated by you or requested by the client, can fill value chain gaps without forcing you to become something you're not. Collaboration can be a competitive edge.

FROM MY JOURNEY

In our early days, as we diversified our business beyond automotive, we earned favored partner status with a major client—our largest at the time. We weren't just getting work; we were authoring it. We were invited to the table as thought partners, designing and beginning initiatives before proposals were even written, a true extension of their team. We were co-creating new research approaches, helping the client get closer to their customer at the exact moments that informed decision-making. We offered a range of options, adaptability, and a deep understanding of their business. It felt like we had earned the highest level of partnership.

Then a new decision-maker arrived. He brought with him a preferred vendor from his previous organization.

At first, we weren't worried. We were proven. We had advocates. We had history and trust. We knew the client's business inside and out. But the competitor brought something we didn't: **a niche capability tailored specifically to that industry.** They were specialists, not generalists. And when we reviewed their work, we had to admit, they were excellent at their craft and highly attuned to the industry and this client's needs.

It wasn't that we had grown complacent. But we had made a quiet, unconscious strategic decision over time: to be versatile problem-solvers who could design around a client's needs rather than hang our hat on one specialized method. That choice had served us well... until it didn't.

This moment didn't force us to pivot our strategy, but it *did* force us to get clear about it. We stepped back and asked ourselves hard questions:

- *Where does our generalist model serve the client best?*
- *Where do specialists provide differentiated value that we don't need to replicate?*
- *And where might we benefit from having niche offerings of our own?*

It wasn't comfortable. But it was necessary because, as we continued to build the business, we would frequently come up against the generalist-versus-specialist tension. It sharpened our thinking about who we were **and** who we weren't. It pushed us to articulate our strengths more clearly and to make conscious strategic choices about where to go deep and where to remain broad.

Sometimes, the gift of a competitor is clarity about the value and relevance of your own client offerings.

GREAT IMPACT

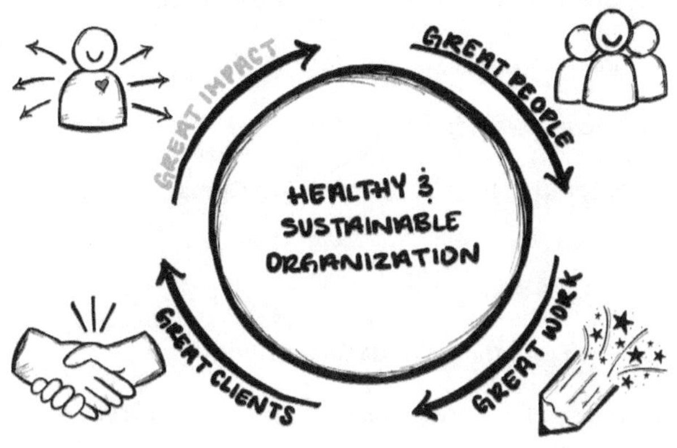

People, work, and client relationships fuel impact every day. Over time, their combined force adds up to something larger. In this section, you'll find ***Open When*** letters for moments when you're shaping what that impact becomes both inside your organization and beyond it.

Open When:

- You Wonder if What You're Doing Really Matters
- The Weight of the World Makes Your Work Feel Small
- You Need to Inspire Hope
- You're Tempted to Prioritize Short-Term Gains over Long-Term Value Creation
- It's Time to Give Back
- You Achieve Something Worth Celebrating
- You Need a Strategic Plan to Align Your Vision and Your Team
- You Are Ready to Shape Your Legacy - Intentionally

BEFORE YOU BEGIN

Impact is where purpose becomes visible.

It's the space where effort and execution begin to shape lives through the work you do, the values you practice, and the way you share success. Impact is measured by more than scale or results alone. Impact lives in the *substance* of your influence: what your organization stands for, how it shows up, and the imprint it leaves on people, clients, the broader community, and the future.

Even the most purpose-driven leaders can find themselves wondering: *Does what I'm doing really matter?* Especially in a world full of distractions, speed, constant change, and pressure to prioritize profit over principle. Yet this is also where leadership deepens: when you reconnect to your purpose, to the lives you're affecting, and to the possibility that business can be both a vehicle for prosperity and a force for good.

This section meets you in those moments.

When you question whether your work truly matters, when you're called to inspire hope, balance long-term value over short-term gain, pause to celebrate progress, or extend impact beyond your walls. And when you begin to look ahead, aligning vision with the team's day-to-day, giving back, and shaping the legacy you want to leave behind.

Impact isn't just what you create.

It's what you leave behind, and who you lift along the way.

Dear Leader,

It may not feel like it in the moment, but many of the decisions you make as a leader have a ripple effect far beyond your immediate reach. The example you set, the culture you build, the people you develop, and the work you choose to pursue...all of it leaves a lasting imprint. I suppose impact can happen by chance, but if you're reading this letter, you likely lead with intention, and you know that impact isn't something you tack on at the end of success; it's what gives success its meaning.

When the Flywheel is turning, great people doing great work for great clients, you start to feel it. Your people are thriving, your clients are benefiting, the business is growing, and somehow, fulfillment begins to find you and your business's stakeholders. Don't get me wrong. It takes constant effort and being one step ahead of the game to keep that Flywheel spinning. But when it does, the rewards reach well beyond financial growth. There's pride, belonging, and a shared sense of accomplishment that fuels everyone involved.

The true mark of impact is that it outlives the moment. It shows up in how your people describe their work and how your clients describe partnering with you. Their stories go beyond outcomes achieved. The stories embody the personal growth they experienced and the feelings of community and camaraderie while achieving it.

Even when people move on, they carry pieces of what they learned with them. The philosophies, values, behaviors, and habits formed inside your walls. That's the quiet legacy of a leader who leads with purpose: impact that spreads.

And it doesn't stop with your company or team. Meaningful impact radiates outward to your industry, your partners, your community, and even your competitors. It's reflected in how you give back: through thought leadership that elevates others, partnerships that raise standards, and acts of generosity or kindness that remind us that business, at its best, can be a force for good.

Leadership has a shelf life. Impact doesn't. When you lead with purpose and invest in people, you create more than results; you create possibilities that extend far beyond what any single key performance indicator can measure.

With you in making ripples that last,

Camille

OPEN WHEN: YOU WONDER IF WHAT YOU'RE DOING REALLY MATTERS

Dear Leader,

There will be days when you question whether all the effort, all the sacrifice, all the heart you pour into leading is really making a difference. You'll look at the numbers, hear the noise, feel the pressure of the endless to-do lists, and stay vigilant about the competition and wonder if any of it truly matters. *Is it all worth it?*

Yes, and it does. More than you can see in this moment.

Impact doesn't always announce itself in quarterly reports or awards, though it's nice when it does. More often, it reveals itself quietly, when you pause long enough to read between the lines. And sometimes, it speaks at full volume in the stories your people and clients enthusiastically share, bringing your work and your culture to life.

You'll see it when a client you once guided reaches out years later to say, *"You helped me think differently,"* or *"You changed the trajectory of my career."*

You'll feel it when an employee who moved on returns as a customer because they unquestionably trust your work, or when an advocate returns because the experience they had under your leadership carries forward in how they lead now. And you'll know it when your company's reputation precedes you -- not just for what you do, but for how you do it.

When you invest in building great people and great clients through meaningful work, you create impact that compounds. It lives in the culture you've built, the values and examples your people carry with them long after they leave. It lives in the work that raises the bar for your industry. It lives in the trust that fuels long-term relationships and opens new doors when clients bring you along into their next chapters.

You may never fully see the reach of your positive influence. But the people you've inspired will feel it. The clients you've helped grow will know it. The communities you've touched will be better for it.

So, when doubt creeps in, remember: your leadership travels farther than you'll ever know. Every act of courage, every moment of hope you inspire, every decision to do right by your people and clients, all accumulate into something deeply human and enduring.

Keep showing up. Keep leading with courage and purpose. Because what you're doing really does matter.

With gratitude and belief in you,

ACTIVATE THE FLYWHEEL: KEEPING IMPACT STORIES ALIVE

Even the most purpose-driven organizations can lose sight of their positive influence amid day-to-day pressures. Making impact stories visible (and routine) reminds your people, clients, and community that what you're doing together matters. Having these stories to lean into can be the inspiration YOU need to keep going.

1. Build a Rhythm of Reflection

Establish a regular cadence (monthly, quarterly, annually) to surface and share stories of **impact**. Rotate focus around the Flywheel:

- **Great People:** Celebrate examples of core values in action.
- **Great Work:** Showcase projects that embody exceptional work, new capabilities, and your brand promise.
- **Great Clients:** Highlight client partnerships and outcomes achieved. If the client shares the story in their own words, via quotes, video, or a live interview—even better.

- **Great Influence:** Capture stories of giving back: thought leadership, meaningful impact you've made to contribute to your industry, mentoring, or community give back initiatives.

2. Make Storytelling a Shared Practice

Encourage everyone to contribute. Any team member can submit examples of proud moments, lessons learned, or recognition from clients or peers. Create a simple process to collect and spotlight these regularly.

3. Close the Loop

When you share an impact story, connect it explicitly to your purpose, mission, and values. Draw the through-line between *why you exist* and *how the work shows up in the world.*

4. Keep a Living Archive

Capture these stories through an internal newsletter, a town hall segment, a visual wall, or a digital library. Over time, it translates into your organization's evidence of meaning, a record that says, *we made a difference.*

FROM MY JOURNEY

When a core part of your value proposition is to help clients bring their work to life through insights, design, strategy, or innovation, it's only right that you live by the same principle. That was our philosophy. If we were responsible for helping clients to feel and see their impact, we needed to make ours visible, too.

As a leadership team, we became intentional about it. One of our longest-standing practices emerged from our **quarterly strategy sessions**. Alongside reviewing financial performance and business goals, we made space to **reflect on our impact.**

This reflection time served two purposes:

First, it forced us to lift our heads from the day-to-day hustle to acknowledge what we had actually accomplished together. It was a chance to see the forest, not just the trees, and to appreciate the momentum that sometimes gets lost in the noise of employee concerns, deadlines, and deliverables.

Second, it reminded our people and us that success wasn't defined only by the numbers. After each session, we shared highlights with the entire company. Stories of impact that reflected both *what* we achieved and *how* we achieved it.

Eventually, we took it a step further. Each quarter, we introduced **Impact Heroes**: team members recognized for living our core values, creating outstanding client experiences, or strengthening our culture in visible ways. These stories became as anticipated as the quarterly financial updates because they connected the dots between *effort and meaning.*

By embedding these reflections and recognitions into our business rhythm, we kept our "why" front and center. It was a reminder that our goals went beyond growth and profitability; we valued people, progress, and the positive effects we created together.

OPEN WHEN: THE WEIGHT OF THE WORLD MAKES YOUR WORK FEEL SMALL

Dear Leader,

There will be days when the world feels heavy.

Headlines will overwhelm. Injustices will sting. Crises, local, national, and global, will make your daily to-do list seem painfully trivial by comparison. You'll look at your calendar, full of meetings, projects, and business goals, and wonder: *Will any of this really matter in the grand scheme of things?*

It's human to feel that way, especially for leaders who care deeply.

But here's what I've learned: even small acts of purpose-driven work can be a form of healing, of progress, of hope. When you build a company that treats people with respect, delivers tangible value to clients, and creates space for others to thrive, you're contributing to the antidote. You're proving that business can, in fact, be a force for good.

You might not be solving every global problem. But you're doing something profoundly important: creating pockets of light, trust, and humanity that extend outward. The clients you serve carry those experiences into their own organizations. The employees you grow multiply that spirit within your company, bring it to new teams and new communities, and even into their homes.

Every time your business chooses transparent communication over silence, investing in people rather than cutting corners, long-term progress over short-term expediency, or simply kindness in the face of difficulty. You're making the world incrementally better. It may not make headlines, but it builds something much more enduring: faith in what's possible.

So, when the weight of the world makes your work feel small, pause and remember: your leadership is an act of hope. It may not fix everything, but it fixes something. It lights a path.

Keep going. Your example and the culture you're building matter more than you know.

With empathy and belief in your purpose,

ACTIVATE THE FLYWHEEL: THE LEADERSHIP SPECTRUM -- FROM ACKNOWLEDGEMENT TO ACTION

When the world feels heavy, it helps to focus on what you *can* control. Impact doesn't always come from grand gestures. It often begins with awareness, empathy, and small but meaningful acts. You have a range of agency when the outside world feels overwhelming or when global issues dwarf day-to-day work. The power of this idea lies in reframing helplessness into clarity: *there is always something you can do.*

1. Acknowledge (Lead with Humanity)

When the world feels unsteady, your first job is simply to recognize it. Don't rush to fix; start by connecting.

- Acknowledge the moment and how it affects your people and clients.
- Be visible. Be human. Say, *"This is hard,"* or *"We're all feeling this."*
- Allow space for empathy and understanding before moving forward.

2. Communicate (Provide Context and Clarity)

In uncertainty, silence amplifies fear. Communication: honest, transparent, two-way, is a powerful stabilizer.

- Share what you know, what you don't, and what you're doing to navigate forward.

- Reinforce purpose: why your work still matters and how you're contributing.
- Enlist feedback and perspective from your teams and from clients. Make it conversational.

3. Contribute (Align Action with Your Sphere of Influence)

Once you've grounded your team in clarity, move toward what's possible.

- Leverage your **core strengths:** *how can your people, products, or expertise help?*
- Act where you have influence. Support clients, community, or industry partners in ways that align with your purpose.
- This could mean sharing knowledge, offering time or talent, or providing financial resources when appropriate.

4. Amplify (Sustain and Spread Impact)

Keep the momentum alive by reflecting on and sharing what worked.

- Celebrate small wins and stories of impact.
- Reinforce the message that even small actions matter; collectively, those small actions create culture.
- Model consistency; hope is sustained through ongoing, visible effort.

FROM MY JOURNEY

Over the course of my career, there were countless moments when the outside world made work feel small. But none was more vivid or more defining than the early days of the 2020 Covid 19 pandemic.

We saw what was unfolding globally, but like many, we didn't think it would hit *us* quite so hard. Still, our leadership team came together to run "what-if" scenarios: contingency plans we hoped we'd never need. Looking back, I'm grateful we did, because the reality that followed was beyond anything we could have imagined.

At the core of our response was one simple but powerful strategy: **communication**. Open, transparent, frequent, and two-way. Things were changing daily, and since we were now 100% remote, we instituted weekly **Friday FaceTime meetings**: a space to connect, share updates, quell anxieties, and nurture the belonging we were all missing.

We built plans around caring for our people, our work, and our clients. Some of it was deeply human. We showed up for each other with patience, empathy, and grace. Some of it was operational—resetting expectations, defining new ways of working, and holding space for uncertainty.

And while the pandemic redefined what "normal" meant, we found meaning by doing what we did best: **listening, understanding, acting.** Since we were in the business of understanding consumers, we leveraged that expertise. We launched a nationwide, pro bono consumer survey to help our clients interpret how the world around their customers was changing and what they could do to support them.

It might have seemed small compared to the global scale of disruption, but in our sphere of influence, it mattered. It gave us purpose and a way to turn empathy into action. To be a force for good, even in chaos.

When the world feels big, and your work feels small, ask: *What's the next right thing within my control?* and take the actions needed to move it forward.

OPEN WHEN: YOU NEED TO INSPIRE HOPE

Dear Leader,

Business often measures leadership by hard outcomes: revenue, efficiency, shareholder value. Those matter, but there's another leadership skill that determines whether those results endure: hope.

Hope isn't the same as optimism.

Optimism assumes things will work out.

Hope is believing in a better future *and creating the pathways to get there.*

It's the spark that connects today's effort with tomorrow's impact. It's the belief that what we're doing now is building something that matters. Hope blends vision, agency, and determination -- the qualities that give people the courage to keep going, especially in uncertain times.

When you lead with hope, you give your team more than direction. You give them the energy to keep contributing, innovating, and believing that their work has purpose. Hope fuels resilience in adversity, commitment to long-term goals, and the will to keep creating value when others are ready to give up. In business terms, hope isn't fluff; it's *the foundation of sustainable impact.*

So how do you put hope into practice?

- **Articulate a compelling vision or a go-forward plan.** People need to know where they're headed and why it matters. Tie daily work to a bigger picture that extends beyond this quarter.
- **Be deliberate.** Balance today's realities with tomorrow's possibilities. Insert hope into both broad communications and one-to-one conversations.
- **Demonstrate belief and confidence.** Acknowledge challenges honestly, but pair truth with conviction in your team's ability to overcome them.
- **Create agency.** Invite people to co-create solutions. Hope grows stronger when people feel part of defining the path forward.

- **Be present and visible.** Your calm steadiness, especially during tough times, reminds people that progress is still possible.

Hope isn't blind positivity. It's honesty, paired with belief. It's reminding people that every small, purposeful action adds to something bigger, something enduring. When you cultivate hope, you create the conditions in which people see meaning in their work and clients feel confident in your partnership.

The magic of inspiring hope is that it doesn't just weather storms; it builds futures.

With you in tapping into the power of hope,

ACTIVATE THE FLYWHEEL: BUILDING YOUR CAPACITY TO INSPIRE HOPE

These practices strengthen your ability to inspire hope. They work best when you show up often: **visible, steady, and actively communicating.**

Practice	Why It Matters	Putting It in Play
End Every Update with a Nod Toward Tomorrow	Hope looks forward, so it grows when people can connect today's work to a meaningful future. It shifts focus from "what's happening" to "where we're headed."	Close meetings and updates with a forward-looking statement or question: "Here's how this moves us closer to our vision..." or "What's one thing we can do this week to move forward?

Practice	Why It Matters	Putting It in Play
Celebrate Small Wins	Progress fuels belief. Small, visible wins remind people that their efforts matter and that momentum is building.	Spot and recognize progress in real time: verbally, in messages, or in team huddles. Call out examples of perseverance or creativity that signal progress, not just completion. Visually map progress over time with milestone maps or progress trackers – share widely.
Ask Future-Oriented Questions	Hope lives in the ability to picture what's possible. Future-oriented questions unlock optimism and agency.	Pose questions like: What possibility excites you most about where we're headed? or If we got this right, what would it make possible for us, for our clients?
Balance Honesty and Belief	Hope is credible only when it's honest. Pair transparency about challenges with confidence in the team's ability to navigate them.	When delivering hard news, acknowledge the reality but also highlight progress, capability, and past wins. People can handle tough truths when they trust your belief in them.
Model Grounded Optimism	Your tone sets the emotional climate. Calm, grounded optimism fosters stability and motivation.	In your words and actions, demonstrate that challenges are part of the journey, not the end of it. Let steadiness and confidence project forward.

FROM MY JOURNEY

I've always believed that hope is the leadership X-factor. When it's done right, it's a true gift to those around you. But it requires finesse: a delicate balance of realism, honesty, compassion, and optimism. The goal isn't to offer blind reassurance or surface-level "rah-rah." It's to help people see the future clearly enough to move toward it, even when the present feels uncertain.

Two moments in my leadership journey made that truth real for me—both arriving during transitions, both requiring me to hold grief or complexity in one hand and possibility in the other. Both moments were times when I was stepping into a role once held by another, influential leader.

The first was when our founder, John, passed away. I remember waking up the day after his funeral with the heavy realization: *we are all hurting, yet we must go on.* As the newly appointed CEO, I knew the words I chose next mattered. We were raw. I was raw. Yet I knew I needed to address the entire organization with a message that acknowledged our loss honestly while helping people believe we could keep going.

I wrote and re-wrote that message, and I knew it would never be perfect. In it, I shared the simple belief that our greatest tribute to John would be to continue the work he started. I ended with something like, *"A year from now, a decade from now, we will look back with pride on how we came together to create this next chapter."* Looking back, that message became our shared bridge between loss and purpose.

Years later, when I stepped into the CEO role at Human8, I found myself leading through uncertainty once again. The organization was in transition. Multiple companies had been acquired, teams were at different stages of integration, and no one was operating at their peak. We were fragmented and tired. I had to acknowledge the current reality *and* paint a picture of what was possible, a path forward.

I introduced a simple mantra: **Stabilize. Harmonize. Optimize.** Those three words became more than a framework; they became a shared language of hope. They helped our people see beyond the complexity of the moment and gave us a roadmap to move forward one steady step at a time.

Both moments taught me an important lesson: hardship will always exist in business and in life. But hope is the bridge that helps people cross from what *is* to what *can be*. As leaders, our task isn't to make things easy. It's to make them possible.

OPEN WHEN: YOU'RE TEMPTED TO PRIORITIZE SHORT-TERM GAINS OVER LONG-TERM VALUE CREATION

Dear Leader,

Leading brings choices, and not all of them are clear-cut. Daily, the urgent competes with the important. And often, numbers, deadlines, or short-term targets whisper louder than your long-term vision. And the temptation to act will be real.

You'll be tempted to keep a high-performing employee who undermines your values because replacing them feels risky.

You'll be tempted to take on a client who isn't a fit because their logo would look great on your roster.

You'll be tempted to pause investments in people, innovation, or philanthropy when times get tough, telling yourself it's just for now.

But "just for now" decisions have a way of shaping "forever."

Sustainable businesses are built through a lens of long-term value creation: choices that may take longer to pay off but compound in trust, loyalty, and impact. Short-term gain can make a good quarter; long-term value builds a great company.

When you find yourself with this trade-off, pause and consider:

- *What will this decision mean for our business and culture six months from now?*
- *Does this decision reinforce or erode trust with our people and clients?*
- *Will this help us build momentum or debt we'll have to repay later? If it's debt, is it worth it?*
- *Is this decision aligned with where we're headed, or does it keep us stuck in today?*
- *If our financials looked different, would I make this same decision?*

Leading for the long-term takes focus, discipline, a little faith, and a lot of courage. It means saying no to work that doesn't align with your core. It means investing in people, innovation, and client relationships even when budgets are tight. It means holding firm when a decision is unpopular but right.

Remember: the health of your business isn't measured by this month's results alone but by how well you've positioned it to thrive five years from now.

Leadership is a long game. The decisions you make under pressure define not just your business but also your imprint as a leader.

So, when the temptation to grab the quick win hits, breathe. Sometimes it will be the right choice; sometimes it won't. Pause, revisit your long-term goals, your fundamentals, your people, and stay the course.

Your future self and the people and clients who believe in what you're building will thank you for it.

With conviction and clarity,

ACTIVATE THE FLYWHEEL: THE LONG-GAME LENS

Great leaders don't avoid trade-offs; they manage them with intention. Pausing to review decisions through a long-game lens ensures the decisions you are making now contribute to a healthy, sustainable organization in the long term.

When decisions feel urgent, pause and reflect through a longer lens:

- **Horizon Check – *What's the Time Frame?***
  Ask: *Am I solving for this quarter or laying groundwork for the future?* If it only benefits the now, explore whether it sacrifices tomorrow's strength.

- **Cultural Impact – *Who and What is Affected?***
  Consider how the decision affects the trust and engagement of employees and clients.
  Short-term wins that chip away at culture or other fundamental elements of what you are building rarely pay off in the long run.

- **Momentum – *Is this a Deposit or Withdrawal?***
  Determine whether the action creates sustainable energy (systems, innovation, loyalty)
  or future debt (burnout, rework, reputational repair).

- **Alignment Test – *Does It Honor Our Fundamentals?***
  Cross-check against your Purpose, Mission, Vision, Values, and Brand Promise.
  If it doesn't fit within them, it's probably not worth the trade.

- **Future-Self Reflection – *Will I Thank Myself Later?***
  Visualize your future self, looking back. *Are you proud or regretful?*
  Let that perspective guide your present-day courage.

FROM MY JOURNEY

Over the years, I've learned that **responding beats reacting every time**. Believe me, this was not always the case for me, but what feels urgent in the moment almost always benefits from a pause. I've also learned that every decision sets a **precedent**: a signal to your team about what matters and what to expect in the future.

I remember one instance when, after an especially demanding year, our leadership team wanted to reward employees with a fully paid week off over the holidays. On the surface, it was simple. But dig a layer deeper, and the decision had ripple effects. Closing the business for a week would cost us money. It could leave clients without support. *And, if we offered it once, would it be expected again?*

It still felt like the right thing to do – our people had carried us through a period of stress and strain. But before saying yes, we paused long enough to ask a few grounding questions:

- *What are the ramifications of this decision, positive and negative?*
- *What precedent does this set now and in the future?*
- *What expectations might it create for next year or the year after?*

That reflection didn't change our decision, but it changed our **approach.** We framed the paid time off intentionally, connected it to our values, and communicated it as a **special act of gratitude for extraordinary effort**, not a new, guaranteed benefit. That pause created clarity. The intention protected culture.

I share what may seem like a relatively small decision because it illustrates how quickly individual choices accumulate over time. What began as a one-time gesture eventually evolved into an annual, paid holiday shutdown, in addition to our existing time-off policies. It became a powerful satisfier for employees, a meaningful differentiator in our benefits, and a clear statement to both our people and our clients: we work hard, and we also believe in fully disconnecting, resetting, and renewing for the year ahead.

That experience taught me that, by leading with the long game in mind and pausing to reflect, we can move more deliberately. Short-term wins can feel gratifying, but they're not always rooted in long-term value. Every "yes" and every "no" becomes part of your cultural DNA. When leading, we're not just taking action today, we're seeding actions, expectations, norms, and possibilities that our teams will carry forward long after the moment has passed.

 OPEN WHEN: IT'S TIME TO GIVE BACK

Dear Leader,

There comes a moment—often after years of building, striving, and growing—when you finally look up from the grindstone and realize how far you've come. The business you once architected from sheer determination now stands on solid ground. You've built a team, a brand with a reputation, and a track record of success. And with that comes something else, a deep sense of gratitude.

At first, giving back may have taken the form of quick or reactive acts of generosity: sponsoring a local event, mentoring a peer or intern, or supporting a cause. But at some point, the impulse shifts from *giving when asked* to **giving with intention**. That's when you know it's time.

Giving back isn't about obligation; it's about coming full circle. It's about recognizing that success never happens in isolation. You've been molded and shaped by mentors who opened doors, clients who took chances on you, and employees who believed in your vision. Giving back is a way to say thank you and to pass that same opportunity forward.

There are many ways to give, and each one holds power:

- **Give your time.** Serve as a mentor, advisor, or voice of experience. Join industry or academic boards. Teach. Share what you've learned so others can rise faster and farther. Or volunteer in ways that align with community needs, company capabilities, or your employees' passions.
- **Give your talent.** Leverage your company's capabilities to advance your industry or community through pro bono projects, thought leadership, internships, or innovation partnerships that lift others.
- **Give your treasure.** Set aside profits to support causes that align with your values, your employees' passions, or your clients' communities. Even small, steady commitments make a lasting difference.

Over the years, I've learned that giving back connects to a higher calling to create positive impact in others' lives. Those "others" don't need to be within your company walls. In fact, broadening the reach often amplifies the influence, inviting your people to contribute in ways that extend beyond their daily roles.

When giving back lives as a shared priority, it helps everyone lift their gaze from the day-to-day to the bigger picture. It cultivates gratitude for what's been built together and widens perspective in a world that can easily pull focus inward. It's a reminder that we're not in it alone, and neither are others.

You've built something worth sharing. And when you share it, your wisdom, your resources, your capabilities, you turn company success into **collective progress**.

So, if you're feeling the pull to give back, listen to it. That's not a distraction from your purpose -- it's the next evolution of it.

With gratitude,

ACTIVATE THE FLYWHEEL: GIVING BACK WITH INTENTION

There's no single right way to give. These practices are meant to spark thought, not to prescribe. The most meaningful giving begins in the heart. Let your purpose lead the way, then build structure around it so generosity moves from impulse to intentionality and sustains impact over time. Big picture, you are moving from Heart → Strategy → Impact.

Align with Purpose

- Anchor your giving to what your business stands for.
- Ask: *How can our purpose show up in the way we give?*
- Focus on causes or initiatives that extend your mission, values, or community impact.

Engage Your People

- Invite employees to help identify where and how you give.
- Create opportunities for shared contribution: volunteering, matching gifts, pro bono work, mentorship.
- Involvement builds ownership and turns giving into part of your culture, not an obligation.

Leverage What You Do Best

- Look at your **time**, **talent**, and **treasure** through the lens of your unique capabilities.
- *What skills, tools, or expertise can make the biggest difference?*
- Purpose-aligned pro bono work often has stronger and longer-lasting effects than one-time donations.

Commit and Communicate

- Choose a rhythm that fits your business: quarterly focus areas, annual giving initiatives, or recurring partnerships.
- Share stories of impact internally and externally. Transparency keeps momentum and pride alive.

- Periodically ask: *Is our giving creating the impact we intended, both internally and externally? Are we investing where it truly matters to us?*
- Notice both tangible outcomes: hours volunteered, funds raised, people served, communities or causes improved, and intangible ones: employee pride, connection, and personal growth.
- Evaluate what's working, what isn't, and how your giving could evolve next.

FROM MY JOURNEY

For many years, our company gave back, but not in a particularly structured way. We supported university internship programs (those interns were often the spark of our future hires). We sponsored the occasional industry event or made donations when someone approached us. We gave, but it was largely *reactive*. Good-hearted, but not yet intentional.

Then one day, John, our founder, announced to the company that after conferring with the leadership team, we'd be contributing a percentage of profits to a local nonprofit. It was a proud moment. That single decision marked the beginning of a new mindset: that giving would be part of our organizational fabric, not an afterthought.

For a while, that local community organization became our anchor partner, receiving our time, talent, and treasure. But as our philanthropic spirit grew, so did our thinking. We began to ask: *What if our giving could reflect not only the purpose of our business but the passions of our people?*

So, we evolved. We introduced **bi-annual, all-company Give Back Days**, closing the business so every employee—remote team members included—could serve together in the community. We invested in travel and lodging so everyone could be part of it. Beyond those events, employees were encouraged to dedicate a set number of company-paid hours each year to volunteer with causes they personally cared about.

What came back to us were the stories—an abundance of them—of teams serving side by side. Repairing houses, cleaning up urban areas, planting trees, fostering animals, supporting shelters, mentoring kids, and partnering with organizations we might never have known on our own. Those stories were shared company-wide, sparking a collective pride and impact that extended far beyond the office walls.

What we realized: structured giving was an extension of our values, purpose, and culture. It reminded us that success brings privilege and with it, a responsibility to help others rise, too.

OPEN WHEN: YOU ACHIEVE SOMETHING WORTH CELEBRATING

Dear Leader,

You did it. You hit the goal, landed the client, completed the project, or launched the thing that once existed only as an idea. A milestone you worked toward has arrived, yet if you're like many leaders and me, your instinct is to move quickly on to the next thing.

Don't.

Pause.

Mark the moment.

Because celebration isn't fluff. It's energy and fuel.

Celebration serves as both acknowledgment and affirmation: of effort, of excellence, of shared success. It embeds memories that motivate future performance and deepens emotional connection to the work, the team, and the purpose behind it.

Celebration doesn't have to be grand to be meaningful. It can be as simple as:

- A sincere "you did it" spoken at the right time.
- A handwritten note recognizing specific effort.
- A team lunch or toast after a long push.
- A public recognition at an all-company meeting.
- A structured event that honors a major milestone achieved together.

What matters most isn't the form, it's the intention. When you take time to celebrate, you signal to your people that you see them and that their contributions matter.

Celebrations at the individual level, such as work anniversaries, promotions, or personal milestones, are just as important as team- or company-wide ones. Recognizing individuals strengthens belonging and pride; recognizing collective accomplishments connects progress and meaning to the grind. Together, they reinforce that every contribution moves the whole forward.

And the benefits multiply: recognition builds trust and confidence; trust fuels pride and belonging; pride and belonging generate the energy to take on the next opportunity, the next challenge.

Don't underestimate the power of marking success, big or small. The stories told in those moments: of perseverance, creativity, and collaboration, are the ones your culture stands on. They remind people not just *what* they accomplished, but who they became in the process.

So, before you charge ahead, take a breath. Gather your team. Reflect on what you've accomplished together and let yourself feel the joy, gratitude, and pride that come from shared achievement.

You've earned this. And so have they.

With appreciation and applause,

Why This Letter Lives in the Great Impact Section

Celebration is embedded here because it *amplifies impact*. When you pause to honor achievement, you transform outcomes into meaning. You create emotional resonance that strengthens connection, reinforces values, and sustains momentum across the Flywheel.

Impact doesn't just come from what you accomplish, it comes from the narratives created about how you *see*, *share*, and *celebrate* those accomplishments with others. Celebration offers an opportunity to "point to" progress connected to vision, values, purpose.

ACTIVATE THE FLYWHEEL: SCALING CELEBRATION WITH INTENTION

The table below is intended to inspire. The way that you acknowledge your people and celebrate is personal and needs to feel true to you as a leader and to your culture. No matter how you choose to celebrate, intentionality balances frequency with authenticity. The goal is to achieve both meaning and presence: ensuring people feel seen, valued as whole people, and connected to the greater impact their work creates.

Level	Purpose	Examples	Outcome
Individual	Recognize personal effort, growth, career milestones (work anniversaries, promotions, etc.), and life milestones (marriage, births, new pet, etc.)	• Handwritten notes of appreciation. • Shout-out in team meetings. • One-on-one acknowledgments after major contributions.	Build confidence, belonging, and emotional connection.

Level	Purpose	Examples	Outcome
Team/ Project	Reinforce collaboration, determination, and shared wins.	• Team lunches, informal bonding events. • Storytelling in all-company or broader group settings about how collaboration achieved goals.	Strengthens trust and reinforces culture through shared success.
Organization wide	Milestones that reinforce collective progress and purpose.	• All-company recognition events. • Milestone announcements tied to purpose and values. • Impact stories highlighting people and culture.	Fosters pride, purpose, and community around the company's broader goals and mission.

FROM MY JOURNEY

From the early days when there were only a handful of us crowded around shared desks to the years when the business had grown into a vibrant organization, celebration was always part of our DNA. It wasn't something we had to remember to do; it was simply how we operated.

Our day-to-day was often frenetic. Deadlines loomed. Clients needed answers yesterday. New work poured in. But no matter how busy things got, we made time to pause, even if it was just two minutes to say, *"Job well done."* Those small pauses mattered. They reminded us that people are whole people, not just workers crossing tasks off a list.

Celebration wasn't reserved for the big moments, though those were special too. Milestone anniversaries, reaching quarterly goals, and landing the next big client. The real heartbeat came from the everyday undercurrent: weekly client wins, new hires and promotions, positive client feedback, and small acts of collaboration or kindness that made tough days easier. Offering a few meaningful words of recognition in those moments became the red thread that wove progress and shared achievement through our culture.

For me, helping people know that I *saw* them and that they were important to the company and to me was at the core of leadership. Marking moments, big or small, was how we reinforced meaning, connection, and pride.

It didn't take long to realize that while big celebrations will always have their place, it's just as important to establish an *authentic cadence* of regular acknowledgment: a steady, human heartbeat that keeps people moving forward together.

OPEN WHEN: YOU NEED A STRATEGIC PLAN TO ALIGN YOUR VISION AND YOUR TEAM

Dear Leader,

You'll know when the moment arrives.

Sometimes it's when things are going well, momentum is strong, growth is accelerating, and you realize the organization needs more clarity, prioritization, and alignment to sustain it. Other times, it's when things feel uncertain. Maybe progress has stalled, the environment has shifted, or the path forward seems foggy. The vision is clear in your mind, but you can sense that not everyone sees it the same way or knows how to move toward it.

Either way, the signal is the same: **your vision needs some type of structure, a strategic plan to align your people and your future.**

The heart of strategic planning lies in creating the **structure and rhythm that connect vision, strategy, and execution**. The documentation and communication of the strategy may live in a polished deck, but that's just the window dressing. The strategy itself is how you translate where you are going into progress and ensure that your people, investments, and energy are moving in the same direction.

When I talk about strategic planning, here's what I mean:

- **Vision:** A vivid picture of where you want to be 7–10 years from now; a north star that brings coherence and purpose to decisions and inspires your people to move with purpose.
- **Strategy:** The roadmap of measurable goals and objectives that bridge aspiration and action. Strategy defines *how* you'll get there, what success looks like, and how you'll know if you're on track to succeed.
- **Execution:** The discipline of translating strategy into clear action plans, ownership, accountability, and timelines, embedding it into the company's quarterly and daily rhythm so progress becomes part of the culture.

When times are good, strategic planning prevents complacency by channeling momentum into meaningful direction. When times are hard, it is your stabilizer, helping you focus on what truly matters, prioritize resources, and make tough calls with more confidence.

In both cases, it creates **hope with structure**. Because strategy is, at its heart, an act of optimism: a belief that with clear goals, alignment, and consistent follow-through, the future you imagine is within reach.

So, when you sense it's time to get serious about strategic planning, whether you're chasing growth, optimizing your current state, or regaining footing, bring your leadership team together. Revisit your fundamentals. (Re)define your long-term vision. Translate it into measurable goals and a cadence that keeps the plan alive and accountable, not static.

When you do, you'll move from reacting to leading, from surviving quarter to quarter to intentionally writing the next chapter.

With strategic focus,

ACTIVATE THE FLYWHEEL: THE RHYTHM OF STRATEGIC CLARITY

Strategic planning is more than a plan on paper -- that's only the beginning. Success comes from internalizing an **organizational rhythm** of planning, measuring, adjusting, and communicating. When vision, goals, and progress are discussed regularly, strategy turns into a living, breathing part of the culture, not an annual exercise, but an everyday alignment mechanism.

This structure and cadence create the momentum that keeps vision alive, strategy in motion, and the organization accountable to execution. **Alongside this rhythm, it's critical to develop an organizational communication plan that reinforces alignment, clarity, and buy-in.**

Annually: Revisit Vision & Set Annual Goals

- Reaffirm your long-term **Vision** (7–10 years out).
- Define 3–5 measurable **Annual Goals** that move you closer to that vision.
- Communicate the "why" behind each goal so every team member understands their role in achieving it.

Quarterly: Align, Measure & Reset

- Set no more than 3-5 measurable **Quarterly Goals** that build toward annual outcomes.
  - » Assign a single, accountable owner to each goal to ensure clarity and follow-through.
- Review progress on the past quarter's metrics and lessons learned.
- Adjust course where needed to stay aligned with strategy.
- Re-energize the team with renewed focus, transparency, and a shared understanding of what matters now and next.

Monthly: Review & Refocus

- Track progress on key initiatives and milestones.
- Identify roadblocks early and resolve them quickly.
- Celebrate small wins to maintain momentum.
- Keep communication open and two-way. Progress reports aren't just numbers; they're opportunities for shared learning and continued alignment.

- Confirm top priorities for the week.
- Align team efforts on what matters most.
- Reinforce clarity through short standups or updates that keep everyone moving together.

FROM MY JOURNEY

If I had to narrow down the things I enjoyed most as a leader to my top five, strategic planning would make the list.

When we first began, our goals were mostly reactive, addressing what was right in front of us, fixing what needed improvement, and firefighting our way toward stability. But as we matured, those goals shifted. They became more proactive, less about responding to the present moment and more about writing our future. **The discipline of the process: setting goals, holding ourselves accountable, and communicating regularly with the organization, became its own source of strength.**

It was a discipline I learned, harnessed, and refined during my tenure at Gongos and later carried forward as a core discipline when I became Global CEO at Human8. I loved the discussions, the healthy debates, the clarity that would emerge from the process. Strategic planning wasn't just an exercise in setting goals; it was **an act of collective sense-making**.

So many times, I'd walk into one of our quarterly sessions feeling overwhelmed by everything that had transpired over the past quarter. Client demands, organizational shifts, unexpected curveballs. Yet by the end of each session, I'd feel reset. Calm. Clear. Re-anchored in our direction or confident in our re-direction.

For us, strategic planning was as much about **deciding what we wouldn't do** as what we would. Those conversations about "*no*" were often the most strategic of all. Prioritization became our protection. The guardrails against spreading ourselves too thin.

But it wasn't just about progress tracking. Our quarterly rhythm became a time to **reconnect as a leadership team**, to revisit our "why," and to take stock of how far we'd come. It was also a space for gratitude. A moment to pause, appreciate the wins, and recognize the people who made them possible.

Looking back, I realize strategic planning wasn't just a business process; it was a renewal practice. It gave us a shared language for direction and the discipline for achieving our goals; a rhythm that kept us moving forward together.

For additional guidance, see: *Establishing (or Re-Setting) Your Foundation, Open When: You're Defining Your Fundamentals.*

OPEN WHEN: YOU ARE READY TO SHAPE YOUR LEGACY – INTENTIONALLY

Dear Leader,

Legacy is often written little by little through daily decisions, conversations, and commitments that add up over time.

When you think about defining your legacy, it's tempting to picture something monumental: a breakthrough innovation, a widely recognized brand, a company name etched into the industry. But legacy isn't defined only by scale; it's defined by substance, by **significance**. It's about the **imprint** you have on the hearts and minds of the people, clients, and communities you serve, long after you've moved on.

Every leader leaves a legacy. The real question is how *intentional* you'll be about envisioning and defining yours.

At its core, your legacy lives in three dimensions:

- **The culture you build:** how people experience working with you, and what they adopt and carry forward.
- **The clients you serve:** how your work helps them grow, think differently, strengthen their business, or expand their possibilities.
- **The impact you extend:** how your business contributes beyond itself: to your industry, the community(ies) in which you operate, or a purpose larger than profit.

A **vivid vision of the future** is the foundation of legacy. It guides every choice you make. Without it, you risk leaving a legacy by accident; perhaps one defined by busyness instead of meaning.

In large organizations, legacy might take the form of a movement, a market shift, a philanthropic endowment, or a company culture that outlives its founder. In smaller organizations, it may be more intimate but no less powerful: leaders you've developed who are now influencing other companies, clients whose businesses are better because of how you served them, the ideas you've contributed that subtly (or significantly) advanced your field.

I encourage you not to leave legacy as a someday concept, but rather to consider it an *everyday* discipline. It's embedded in how you hire, how you handle mistakes, how you make decisions under pressure, and how you treat people when no one is watching.

So, pause and ask yourself:

- *What will endure because of the choices I'm making right now?*
- *How do I want people to describe the experience of working with—or for—this organization 5, 10, 20 years from now?*
- *What am I doing today that ensures this company (or team), and the people within it, will thrive beyond me?*

Legacy leaves both tangible and intangible value that continues, the culture that remains, the stories people tell. While it can't be forced, you can guide it by leading with clarity, consistency, and care.

Realize this: you are shaping your legacy every day. The question isn't *if* you'll leave one. It's *what kind?*

With conviction and purpose,

ACTIVATE THE FLYWHEEL: LEGACY IN MOTION

Your legacy is already taking shape through every decision, relationship, and story unfolding within your business today. *What do you want those narratives to say?* Use these prompts as a starting point. And remember, your legacy should reflect what matters most to you, your business, and your people.

People – The Culture You Build

The values, behaviors, and shared beliefs that influence how your people experience working with you and in your organization are a cornerstone of legacy. How you lead echoes in how others lead after you.

Practice Ideas:

- Codify your values and reinforce them through rituals and recognition.
- Invest in leadership development at every level, not just the top. Develop leaders who model the behaviors you want to encourage.
- Capture and share stories of values-in-action and celebrate behaviors that model them.
- Create moments that employees internalize to remember years later.

Guiding Questions: *What do I want people to say it felt like to work here? What lessons or habits do I want them to take into future roles? How am I preparing others to lead well beyond my tenure?*

Clients + Work – The Value You Create

Legacy also lives through the mark you make with the work itself, the thinking you advance, the problems you solve, and the relationships you cultivate.

Practice Ideas:

- Invest in long-term relationships built on trust and shared success.
- Deliver work that elevates and provokes deeper thinking or inspires change, not just meet requirements.
- Share knowledge generously through sharing perspective, thought leadership, and teaching.
- Create case studies, frameworks, or reusable IP that can outlive individuals.

Guiding Questions: *What do I want clients to say it felt like to work with us? What part of our brand promise do we want clients to associate with us years from now? How can our work help people grow beyond the engagement itself?*

Beyond the Walls – The Impact You Extend

With intention, legacy has an opportunity to expand beyond your walls into your industry, community, future generations of leaders, and the broader world around you.

Practice Ideas:

- Advance your field by publishing insights, defining standards, and pushing thinking.
- Commit intentionally to a give-back strategy: contribute time, talent, or money to causes that align with your values and purpose.
- Support emerging leaders; Mentor founders of other businesses.
- Serve on the boards of other companies, industry associations, or non-profits that align with your purpose and mission.

Guiding Questions: *Who will be better because we exist? What ripple effect do we want to create beyond revenue?*

FROM MY JOURNEY

If I'm honest, I didn't set out to *define* a legacy.In the early years, I was too busy building. Focused on people, clients, and making hard decisions that mattered in the moment. Legacy never crossed my mind, but if it had, I would've said it was something reserved for later, something you intentionally carve out when things finally slow down. But the truth is, legacy builds quietly while you're busy leading. You just don't see it right away.

For me, I started to feel it in unexpected ways—in the *returns*.

A note from a former employee thanking me for believing in them.

A client who left their company but called to bring us into their new one.

A leader who once worked alongside me, now leading others using the same language and lessons we shared.

Those moments reminded me that legacy isn't always something you leave behind; it can also be something you pass forward. It lives in the people who carry your words, your ways, your standards, and your hope into their next chapter.

The other side of legacy revealed itself in the *hand-off*.

Letting go of the company I helped build was both grounding and bittersweet. After selling, I admittedly hung out in a leadership role far longer than was necessary. But looking back now, I can see there's a quiet humility in realizing that it's not up to you anymore, it's up to them. That your work now depends on others, and that's exactly how it should be. Legacy, I've learned, isn't ownership; it's stewardship. It's having faith that the culture, values, and great work you've nurtured will continue to grow, evolve, and outlive you.

Looking back, I realize I was creating a legacy long before I ever named it. Through the people I developed, the behaviors I modeled, the principles I refused to compromise, and the trust I tried to build day by day. And even now, I'm still building, just in a different way. My lifelong passion for leadership, for learning, and for teaching what it means to lead with both head and heart continues. This book is part of that next layer, an attempt to share what I've learned so others can carry it further.

Legacy isn't as fancy as it sounds. Truly, it boils down to how far your influence travels, how others carry it forward, and the imprint you leave behind.

For additional guidance, see: *Establishing (or Re-Setting) Your Foundation, Open When: You're Defining Your Fundamentals.*

WHEN THINGS GET HARD

In this section, you will find letters to ***Open When*** you are facing moments that call for human resilience. These letters do not align with a specific Flywheel element but are here for you as you navigate what it means to be steady and lead through challenge and uncertainty.

Open When:

- You're Facing Loss or Crisis
- YOU are Burning Out
- Your People are Struggling
- You're Doubting Yourself
- You're Leading Through Uncertainty

BEFORE YOU BEGIN

Every leader will face moments that test their steadiness. When uncertainty, loss, or exhaustion make it difficult to move forward. These moments don't fit neatly inside the Flywheel or a strategy, but they certainly affect both. They can happen anytime to anyone.

This section is about those times.

When you must find your footing on shaky ground or while others are losing theirs.

When you need to lead with both strength and softness.

When the best thing you can offer isn't always a solution, but rather presence, transparency, and hope.

I was once told that the true test of a leader is their ability to lead through difficult times. The letters in this section are written for those difficult times.

Because these moments don't align cleanly with any single element of the Flywheel, I won't be guiding you to **Activate the Flywheel**. Instead, the invitation in this section is to **Lead the Moment:** to show up with steadiness and humanity. To show care for others, and for yourself, so that the Flywheel can endure even when forward motion may feel like it's paused.

Moments like these will never feel easy, but they can reveal your deepest leadership strengths. Fortunately, or unfortunately, how you show up in difficulty often is what people remember most about you.

OPEN WHEN: YOU'RE FACING LOSS OR CRISIS

Dear Leader,

There will come a day when something shakes your business. When a loss, setback, or crisis pulls the air from the room. It might be the departure of a key client or the loss of a long-time team member. It might be a financial shortfall, a restructuring, or something more personal. Whatever form it takes, it will test your steadiness, your voice, your heart, and quite possibly, your resolve.

In these moments, remember this: **how you respond and how you make people feel will be remembered far longer than the crisis itself.**

Loss and crisis can be analyzed through spreadsheets and strategy, but those alone won't heal them. These are *human experiences*, felt differently by every person involved. To lead through them requires empathy, transparency, and calm confidence. You are the one who helps others see the path forward when everything feels unsteady.

Begin by understanding who is affected and how this moment may land with them. Listen for their fears and speak to their questions directly—with both clarity and compassion. People don't expect perfection or every answer neatly tied up. But they *do* expect honesty and transparency.

When communicating:

- **Be transparent.** Share what you know and acknowledge what you don't. Silence breeds stories.
- **Show emotion but remain steady.** Vulnerability makes you human; calm confidence builds faith and trust. You can be both simultaneously.
- **Explain the why.** If it's a difficult decision like layoffs, restructuring, or changing direction, help people see the reasoning, even if they don't agree. Understanding is often the first step toward acceptance.

- **Provide direction.** Even a small sense of what comes next, what to expect tomorrow, restores hope and stability. Providing direction allows you to guide the narrative rather than let others fill in the gaps.

And please remember: **You are human, too**.

Even as you hold space for others, hold space for yourself. Crisis leadership is physically and emotionally draining. Take the pause. Seek counsel. Allow yourself to grieve, process, and recharge. Resilience doesn't mean being unshaken. **It's finding the strength to rise again**.

You won't handle everything perfectly, and that is okay. No one does. You'll learn, understand, and grow stronger from each experience. And if you lead with empathy, care, and courage, you'll give your people something even more powerful than answers. You'll offer trust.

And trust is what carries an organization through loss, crisis, **and** uncertainty and toward renewal.

You will come out of this stronger.

With belief in your resilience,

LEAD THE MOMENT: A SIMPLE CRISIS FRAMEWORK

When things get hard, use these four steps to lead with steadiness and compassion.

Step	Focus	Guiding Question	Example Actions
Recognize	Acknowledge what's happening with honesty and empathy.	Who is impacted, and how might this land emotionally and practically?	Name the situation clearly and objectively. Avoid minimizing or over-dramatizing. Express genuine care.
Respond	Communicate expediently. Do so calmly, transparently, and with heart.	What do people need to hear **and feel** from me right now?	Balance facts with compassion. Explain the "why." Outline immediate next steps.
Reassure	Provide stability and direction.	How can I help people feel safe enough to move forward?	Share near-term plans. Check in frequently. Solicit and answer questions. Reinforce shared strength.
Restore	Care for yourself so you can care for others.	What do I need to recover, process, and lead well tomorrow?	Debrief with trusted peers. Rest. Journal or reflect on lessons learned.

FROM MY JOURNEY

The hardest crisis communications I ever had to deliver were about letting people go, especially when it wasn't about performance, but about survival.

Several months into the Covid 19 pandemic, the financial reality hit hard. For the first time in nearly 30 years, we were facing downsizing. We pored over projections, ran cash flow models from every angle, and searched relentlessly for alternatives. No spreadsheet softened the truth: we would have to let valued teammates go.

I remember feeling deeply disappointed in myself. *Not on my watch*, I thought. We weren't the type of company that let people go when things got hard, yet here we were. These weren't just employees. They were colleagues and friends. The weight of that responsibility was crushing. Letting these people go wasn't just a financial decision; it was personal. These people were part of our "family." We were letting them go into a difficult job market. *Would they be okay?* It also felt like years and experiences of building the business together were walking out the door.

We spent days crafting how we would communicate with those leaving and those staying. We were committed to honesty, compassion, and dignity. Still, when the day came, delivering that message over video, looking into the eyes of people who trusted me, was excruciating. I had to find a way to provide both honesty and hope; to hold myself together, while acknowledging the pain and still helping everyone believe that a path forward existed. My voice shook. Tears were shared. Theirs and mine.

And yet, something remarkable happened afterward. Amid grief, there was grace. Most people leaving thanked us for transparency and for the experience gained with us. People who remained offered empathy back to us. They may not have liked the decision, but they understood it, and they trusted how it was handled.

Looking back, I don't remember the exact words I spoke that day. I remember the silence. The heaviness. And the compassion shown back to me. I also know that a quiet strength took root in me and others that day, to rebound even stronger than before.

That moment reinforced something I already knew, but this time it shouted in spades: steering through success is easy. Real leadership shows up when your heart is breaking, and you keep leading anyway with humanity, honesty, and hope. In a crisis, people might forget the details, but they will remember how you made them feel, and whether you helped them see a way forward that they could choose to believe in.

 OPEN WHEN: YOU ARE BURNING OUT

Dear Leader,

You probably didn't notice it at first.

The long days became longer. You couldn't quite stop putting more effort in. The fervor you once had for learning and bringing new ideas to life started to feel less possible, less energizing. The inbox expanded, the decisions became harder, and the joy you once felt in leading now feels distant.

You tell yourself it's just a busy season. But deep down, you know: *something's off.*

Burnout rarely arrives all at once. More often, it comes in disguised as dedication alongside the belief that if you don't hold it all together, things might crumble. It shows up when you start growing impatient, maybe even snippy, with people you care about. When your work-life balance tips beyond repair. When the things you once loved about your work start to feel like chores.

The good news? **You're not broken, you're human.** The same drive that built momentum can also deplete it. And the awareness that something doesn't feel quite right is not a weakness; it's a wake-up call.

Start by **pausing long enough to notice** what's happening. Burnout thrives in silence, speed, and a relentless head-down focus. Awareness and voicing your needs to someone you trust are the first steps back toward renewal.

Then, **reconnect with your purpose**. Remind yourself why you started this journey: what you set out to build, who you wanted to serve, and how your work contributes to something larger than yourself. Sometimes the goal hasn't changed, but the way you're approaching it needs to. Other times, the goal *has* changed, and it's time for honest reflection about your next step forward. Whatever the case, be real with yourself about what you need. A leader depleted is not good for anyone.

Finally, **design a more sustainable way forward.**

That might mean setting firmer boundaries, redistributing responsibilities, or empowering others more fully. It could mean reconnecting with peers or mentors who replenish your energy. Or simply allowing yourself to rest—not as a reward for productivity, but as a requirement for perspective.

Remember: your people take cues from you. If they see you operating at a relentless pace, they'll assume that's what success looks like. But when they see you prioritizing well-being, reflection, and renewal, you give them permission to do the same.

Leadership is about both endurance *and* sustainability. You can't pour from an empty cup.

Take a breath. Step back. Rest your mind. Refuel your spirit.

Because your people, and your purpose, need you at your best.

With understanding and encouragement,

LEAD THE MOMENT: SPOTTING YOUR OWN BURNOUT

Burnout is not a sign of weakness; it's a signal to pause and take care of yourself. Listen to it early to nurture strong and sustainable leadership.

Early Signs

Clues that you may be nearing burnout:

- You're noticeably short on patience.
- The work that used to energize you now drains you.
- You're always "on," but rarely present.

- Small wins feel invisible; small setbacks feel enormous.
- You can't remember the last time you felt mentally spacious or able to feel energized from learning and applying something new.

Micro-Resets

Small interventions that can create meaningful relief:

- **Pause before reacting.** Take a breath, literally. One deep breath can reset your nervous system.
- **Name it.** Saying *"I'm running on empty"* out loud invites support.
- **Step outside.** A short walk or change of scenery recalibrates perspective.
- **Reconnect.** Call a peer or mentor who can provide perspective or coach you on how to reset.
- **Protect the recharge.** Rest is not indulgence or earned by productivity; it's a necessity and required for leadership.

FROM MY JOURNEY

With *achievement*, *focus*, and *discipline* among my top five strengths (thank you, CliftonStrengths), I was terrible at spotting burnout in myself and even worse at treating it.

My stamina for working both *on* and *in* the business was that of an elite athlete. I often saw this as a strength, and in many ways it was. But it was also a liability to both my team and me.

For me, it meant I struggled to turn work "off." For my team, it meant I wasn't modeling healthy boundaries. Worse, I sometimes slipped into resentment, telling myself no one cared as much or worked as hard as I did. *Yikes*.

People often said to me, *"You make it look so easy."* And with grit and grace, I'd push forward, driven by purpose, determined to keep delivering for the business and everyone who counted on me. But it wasn't sustainable. I was setting an impossible standard. One that didn't serve anyone well.

Over time, I didn't become great at managing my own burnout, but I did learn a few counterbalances. One of the most effective: I began **prescheduling vacation time** at the start of every year, calendaring family trips and other small breaks months in advance. It gave me something to look forward to, and more importantly, created space I wouldn't allow myself to take in the moment.

I also **leaned heavily on peers and mentors**. People who'd been in my shoes, who understood the push-pull of leadership, and could help me regain perspective when I'd lost sight of my own limits. They challenged my assumptions about endurance and success, reminding me that sustainability isn't a sign of weakness but of wisdom. On their advice, I began building intentional renewal into my life: physical practices like running, yoga, and Pilates, and quieter forms of restoration such as journaling, long walks in nature, and time spent gardening and admiring hummingbirds. None of it changed my wiring overnight, but it helped replenish the energy I was so quick to spend.

It took time, and I never fully outgrew the tendency to push past my limits. But I did learn this: stamina isn't strength if it comes at the expense of self. The best leaders don't just endure; they take time to intentionally *restore*, for themselves and for the people who rely on them.

OPEN WHEN: YOUR PEOPLE ARE STRUGGLING

Dear Leader,

Even the healthiest teams will have moments when people struggle. Sometimes it's one individual quietly trying to hold things together. Sometimes it's a team showing signs of fatigue or disengagement. And sometimes, it's the whole organization navigating uncertainty, change, or loss.

Struggle is part of the human experience. But how you, as a leader, notice and respond to it can make all the difference.

The first step is to **stay attuned**. You can't support what you can't see or don't know. Build mechanisms to keep a pulse on your team's well-being, both formal and informal. Employee experience surveys provide useful signals, but the richest insights often come through *everyday connection*: regular check-ins, one-on-one conversations, curiosity-driven questions, and open forums that incite candor and safety. Coach your managers to spot early signs: shifts in tone, energy, attitude, or collaboration are often clues that something deeper is going on.

When you do notice a struggle, **listen first**. Resist the instinct to assume, fix, or prescribe. Create room for people to be honest about how they're doing without fear or consequence. If the challenge is personal, remind them you care about them holistically, not just as a worker. Often, what people need most isn't a solution; it's to feel *seen, heard, and understood.*

At the same time, great leadership balances empathy with accountability. Compassion doesn't mean lowering standards or ignoring what needs to get done. It means helping people find a sustainable path forward while feeling supported along the way. That balance is *compassionate accountability*—the courage to care deeply and keep moving.

When your people are struggling:

- **Listen with intention.** Don't rush to fill the silence or compare experiences. Let them tell you what they need.

- **Clarify their needs.** Ask, *Do you need someone to listen, OR Do you need someone to problem-solve with you?* Sometimes the answer is both.
- **Be transparent.** If you can't solve everything, say so. Clarity builds trust, even when the answers are hard or imperfect.
- **Offer flexibility.** Adjust priorities, timelines, or workload temporarily to create breathing space.
- **Point to the light.** If the challenge is temporary, help people regain perspective. They may not be able to see it yet.
- **Acknowledge effort.** Recognition, especially when energy is low, can rekindle resilience more than you think.

When people are struggling, presence and two-way communication are critical. You don't have to have all the answers, but you do have to show up with empathy, authenticity, and importantly, follow-through.

With care,

Camille

LEAD THE MOMENT: PRACTICING COMPASSIONATE ACCOUNTABILITY

Before you can support struggling employees, you have to be connected enough to notice. Regular check-ins, trust, and true human connection are the foundation. When people know they're seen and safe to speak honestly, leadership can balance both care and clarity without unintentionally softening expectations or eroding psychological safety.

Modeling the allyship between accountability and care shows people that you embody both, and your people learn that empathy can co-exist with excellence.

Step	Focus	Guiding Questions
Notice	Observe early signs, shifts, and signals.	What might this behavior be telling me?
Invite	Create space for honest conversation. Show that you value them as humans, not just what they produce.	How can I make it safe for them to open up?
Clarify	Understand needs, barriers, expectations, and be clear about what success looks like. What still must be achieved and why it matters.	What support or clarity will help them move forward? What expectations may need to be adjusted?
Align	Co-create realistic next steps and shared commitments.	What does progress look like for both of us? What support would help you achieve the desired outcome?
Support	Follow through on the support offered, check in regularly, recognize progress, and recalibrate when needed.	How will I stay present while showing care and upholding expectations? What is the cadence of follow-up?

FROM MY JOURNEY

Keeping a pulse on employees is one of the most important things a leader can do, and I say that from both sides of the desk. When people invest so much of themselves in their work, knowing someone notices and cares matters more than we often realize.

As a leader, I learned that regular check-ins: short conversations without a major agenda, can have an outsized impact. Even when I felt like I wasn't *doing* anything, simply listening helped people feel seen and valued. That steady presence often made all the difference.

And I know this firsthand because I once sat on the other side. Early in my career, I had a standing 9:00 a.m. Tuesday, touch base with John, our founder. On paper, it was an operational alignment meeting. In practice, it became something more. There were plenty of mornings I walked in exhausted, frustrated, or unsure of my progress. Yet nine times out of ten, I'd walk out feeling lighter, grounded, and reconnected.

What changed in that half hour? Usually, nothing dramatic. John didn't hand me solutions or take work off my plate. He listened. He asked thoughtful questions. He shared a perspective I couldn't yet see. Just voicing what was in my head, and feeling genuinely heard, was often enough to reset my outlook.

Those conversations were game changers for me. As my own leadership responsibilities grew, I made it a priority to offer that same kind of space to my team—not as a formality, but as a leadership rhythm. My goal was a ripple effect. A culture where leaders at every level checked in with genuine care, not just about the work, but about the *person behind it.* That steady rhythm became its own form of prevention, a proactive way to keep a pulse and spot signals before they became unmanageable.

Over time, I learned something simple but powerful: when my direct reports were okay, the organization had a much better chance of being okay. Sometimes the most impactful leadership comes from simply having a consistent presence that serves both accountability and compassion repeatedly.

OPEN WHEN: YOU'RE DOUBTING YOURSELF

Dear Leader,

There will be moments when you wonder if you're showing up in the right way for your team and for the seat you occupy in your company. You'll replay conversations in your mind, notice shifts in people's energy, or feel your own stamina slipping. And suddenly the doubts creep in: *Am I leading well enough? Am I the right leader for this moment? Is this role the right fit for me?*

Self-doubt doesn't disappear as you rise. If anything, leadership amplifies it. The stakes feel higher, the visibility is sharper, the potential for influence more profound. And because leaders often carry these fears quietly, they can feel heavier than they actually are.

But hear this clearly: **feeling unsure does not mean you're unfit to lead.** It means you're self-aware, reflective, and human.

When your confidence feels shaky, pause long enough to understand what's driving it. Sometimes the feeling is a signal that you are stretched thin or carrying undue pressure. Other times, it's simply the weight of caring deeply about your team and wanting to show up strong for them.

Keep these reminders close:

- **Manage your energy first.** How you feel is reflected in how you lead. If you're exhausted, burned out, or questioning yourself, your people will feel it. Press pause and take time to reflect. *Is what I'm experiencing a trend or a moment? What's really driving how I'm feeling right now?* Understanding the root cause matters. And then, take care of yourself - proactively and regularly. This is not an indulgence; it's leadership maintenance.
- **Demonstrate steadiness.** You don't have to feel fearless to lead with calm confidence. Showing up grounded, especially on hard days, strengthens trust and helps others lean in to follow your lead.
- **Model consistency.** People read your emotions more than you realize. Consistency builds trust; volatility erodes it. Teams can weather tough seasons if their leader is steady. Inconsistency: high one day, low the next, creates anxiety and hesitation.

- **Check your blind spots.** Seek perspective from trusted peers or mentors. The hardest behaviors to see are always our own, even for leaders.
- **Lead with authenticity.** Don't trade your style or shape-shift into the leader you think you *should* be. People trust what's real, vulnerable, and human more than polished performance.
- **Model balance.** If you never unplug, they won't either. Show your team what sustainable leadership looks like—not just what hard work looks like.

Self-doubt from time to time is normal, even healthy. What matters is having enough self-awareness to understand its source, learn from it, and keep leading through it. When you show up as your clear-minded and authentic self, you give your people the same permission to be human and still strive to be their best.

With you in the reflection,

LEAD THE MOMENT: LEADING THROUGH SELF-DOUBT

A simple leadership self-check for when you're questioning yourself:

1. Pause. Self-doubt feels urgent, yet still, take a moment to reflect.

- **Ask:** *What am I feeling now, and why? Was there a triggering moment or event?*
- **Look for:** Signs of fatigue, stress, overwhelm, and emotional carry-over from other areas of life.

2. Separate Fact from Story. Your mind can create narratives that aren't true.

- **Ask:** What objective evidence do I actually have? *What assumptions am I making?*
- **Look for:** exaggerations, misinterpretations, overgeneralizations, "I should" statements.

3. Check Alignment. Doubt often signals a values conflict rather than incompetence.

- **Ask:** *Is this a skills issue, a clarity issue, or a values issue?*
- **Look for:** unaligned values, unclear expectations, mismatched priorities

4. Seek Perspective: Self-doubt narrows your view; outside perspective can widen it.

- **Ask:** *Who can help me see this more clearly?*
- **Look for:** A trusted peer, mentor, advisor—someone who knows both your strengths and your blind spots. If you haven't already, consider investing in a mentor or coach; someone who can objectively listen, enable you to vent, and provide an outside perspective regularly.

5. Connect to What's True. Return to the strengths, skills, and experiences that brought you here.

- **Ask:** *What is true about my capabilities, impact, and track record?*
- **Look for:** past wins, moments of resilience, meaningful feedback.

6. Take One Grounded Step. Movement dissolves self-doubt faster than rumination.

- **Ask:** *What is the next best action I can take? What is one manageable step that would move things forward?*
- **Look for:** one clarifying conversation to ease uncertainty, one decision to unstick, and something you can delegate to reset your energy.

FROM MY JOURNEY

Self-doubt was never something I eliminated; it was something I learned to manage. Even at my most confident, it was there. Quieter on some days, much louder on others. With time and experience, I came to understand that not having everything figured out wasn't a disqualifier for leadership. It was simply part of the practice.

That understanding was put to the test when I stepped into the CEO role at Gongos.

When I transitioned from COO to CEO, replacing our founder, the shift happened overnight with no transition time. He was so much more than our CEO and founder. He was a revered leader, mentor, and friend to so many, both inside and outside our organization. Stepping into his shoes, I could practically feel the weight of expectations settle on my shoulders. Imposter syndrome wasn't subtle. It was screaming!

For a while, I measured myself against him, replaying decisions and interactions in my head, wondering whether I was leading "well enough" or whether people wished for him or someone else in the role instead of me. I wanted to honor him and his legacy, but without realizing it, I was also shrinking myself in the process.

The breakthrough came when I accepted a truth I already knew deep down: I was never going to be him, and I didn't need to be. He chose me as his successor for a reason. It was time to step forward, not as a replica, but as myself—with my own strengths, relationships, instincts, and way of leading.

I leaned on the people I trusted most, listening to their feedback and letting their confidence bolster mine. I invested in an outside mentor and surrounded myself with industry peers who helped me design a leadership approach that was both authentic to who I am and effective for the organization.

That experience taught me so many things. Among them, strong and authentic leadership emerges when you find and grow into your own shoes, even when uncertainty never fully disappears.

OPEN WHEN: YOU'RE LEADING THROUGH UNCERTAINTY

Dear Leader,

There will be (many) times when the path ahead feels foggy. When information is incomplete, signals are mixed, the context feels complex or ambiguous, and people are looking to you for clarity you don't yet have. These moments can test your confidence as much as any crisis or setback, and they can wear you down. Uncertainty is different than change; Change has direction, uncertainty does not. Leading when the future is unclear requires steadiness infused with the courage to act even with an incomplete picture.

Leadership is not about predicting the future; it is about preparing yourself and your people to move forward even when the path is uncertain.

Uncertainty is now a constant; markets shift, technology accelerates, assumptions change, and plans need rewriting. Many leaders wait for clarity before acting, hoping for reassurance, perfect data, or a sign that the turbulence will settle. But waiting for certainty is often the slowest and riskiest course of action.

Leading through uncertainty means trading the illusion of control for the discipline of courage: moving thoughtfully, humbly, and sometimes incrementally, instead of standing still. Indecision breeds stagnation. Some action, even imperfect, is better than none.

Here are a few principles to keep in mind when the fog rolls in:

- **Name what you know and what you don't.** Transparency is a stabilizing force in uncertain times. People can handle incomplete information, but silence fuels anxiety. Clarity builds trust, even when it is limited.
- **Focus on steadiness and direction, not prediction.** Even if you don't know exactly what's ahead, you can offer: *"Here's what matters right now." "Here's how we'll navigate through this." "Here's what won't be disrupted."*

- **Prepare people to adapt and flex their thinking.** Coach your team to explore "what if" scenarios, test assumptions, and pilot ideas. This builds the muscle to move within an environment that's not fully clear.
- **Take meaningful steps, not massive leaps.** When it's difficult to plan far in advance, break work into smaller cycles, set shorter time horizons, and check in often. Momentum beats paralysis because it enables learning. Progress, even imperfect progress, boosts confidence.
- **Model what you want others to feel.** People take emotional cues from your courage, your curiosity, and your calm confidence. Being grounded and present is more important than being fearless.

In addition to all of this, communicating meaningfully and frequently is essential. Your people need to hear your message repeatedly so they can gain courage and march forward aligned and with intent.

You are leading in a world where volatility and uncertainty have been normalized. Try not to let feeling unsettled break your spirit. It's normal to feel shaken, and, if anything, it is a good indicator that you're aware and attuned to the world around you and to humanity. Take courage and know that your presence and your willingness to lead by taking the next step forward are what your team needs most right now.

With you in the unknown,

LEAD THE MOMENT: NAVIGATING UNCERTAINTY

When the path isn't clear, create momentum by moving with intention. Remember: progress over perfection. These practices help you and your team act, learn, and adapt even in ambiguous conditions.

1. Reframe the Moment.

Uncertainty can feel like a limitation, but it can also open new possibilities. Shift your team's lens from *what is* to *what could be*.

Try a From/To Shift:

- FROM "wait for certainty" TO "learn our way forward."
- FROM "protect what we have" TO "explore what's possible."
- FROM "solve the whole problem" TO "identify the next smart step."

This reframing energizes creativity and begins to reduce fear.

2. Think in Scenarios, Not Predictions.

The goal in the face of uncertainty isn't to foresee the future. That's impossible. Instead, try building comfort operating within multiple futures.

Ask your team:

- *What if X happened tomorrow? How could we ready ourselves for it?*
- *What assumptions do we rely on that could break? What would we do?*
- *Where are we most exposed? Most resilient?*

Scenario thinking builds adaptability as a muscle and increases your ability to respond rather than react when surprises happen.

3. Reduce the Noise to Focus on What Matters.

When everything is important, nothing is important and in uncertain times, everything can feel urgent. It's not. Prioritize sharply.

Ask:

- *What is essential right now?*
- *What can we pause, stop, or say no to?*
- *Where will progress have the greatest impact?*

Prioritization is both a discipline and an act of protection—protecting your people and their energy.

4. Move in Small, Fast Cycles.

Big plans have more potential to collapse under uncertainty; small cycles thrive in it.

Try:

- 6–12-week execution windows.
- Frequent check-ins and micro-adjustments.
- Retrospectives to determine "keep, shift, stop."
- Celebrating small, quick wins that ignite momentum.

5. Communicate Early, Often, and With Intent.

People need you now. If you're quiet, silence creates more uncertainty, even fear. Your voice creates stability and direction.

Do:

- Share what you know (and don't know).
- Explain how decisions will be made.
- Repeat priorities often.
- Translate direction into meaningful next steps.
- Use language that builds both belief and ownership.

Communication is more than information sharing. If done purposefully, it's moving people.

5. Strengthen the Human Side of Leadership.

People watch your actions and behaviors more than your strategy. Model grounded curiosity and hope.

Practice:

- Naming the ambiguity without dramatizing it.
- Showing calm confidence.
- Inviting questions.
- Acknowledging emotion.
- Celebrating progress, not just outcomes.

Your steadiness becomes a stabilizing force.

FROM MY JOURNEY

One of the most important lessons I learned during my early tenure as CEO isn't something you wait out. It's something you prepare for. I had watched too many organizations grow larger and, unintentionally, slower: weighed down by bureaucracy, attached to predictability, and unable to respond quickly when the environment shifted. I never wanted us to lose our nimbleness. I believed strongly that we needed to be both disciplined *and* adaptable: structured enough to scale, yet flexible enough to navigate the unexpected.

To build that capability, our leadership team practiced moving through uncertainty before we were forced to. One of the most effective tools was a series of rapid-fire scenario sessions we held biannually. We posed specific "what if" questions: a major client loss, a major client gain, a sudden economic swing, a technology shift that could disrupt our proprietary software, etc., and brainstormed possible responses. We didn't pressure ourselves to get the answers "right." The value was in the thinking: stretching our imagination, breaking assumptions, and building confidence that we could handle whatever came our way. We tucked those plans away, and more than once, they became incredibly useful starting points when reality caught up to the scenarios we had envisioned.

During the Covid 19 pandemic, this preparation paid off. The world was shifting quickly, and the path ahead was too unpredictable for traditional annual planning. We moved to six-week strategy sprints instead. With our purpose in focus, we set priorities that mattered most at that time: staying close to clients and our people, and continually monitoring external signals that informed cultural shifts, service adjustments, marketing reframes, and business development needs. Those short cycles helped us stay aligned, responsive, adaptive, and connected at a time when everything else felt certain.

What these practices taught me is that navigating uncertainty requires the courage to move forward rather than defaulting to "wait and see." When teams stay curious, flexible, and grounded in short, steady steps, uncertainty feels less intimidating and more navigable together.

For additional guidance, see: *Beyond the Flywheel, Open When: You're Ready to Build Adaptability into Your Culture.*

BEYOND THE FLYWHEEL

In this section, you will find letters to ***Open When*** you're moving from managing performance to envisioning and creating the future. These letters are centered around future-focused leadership and the disciplines required to move beyond one cycle of business and do not align with one specific Flywheel element.

Open When:

- You're Ready to Build Adaptability into Your Culture
- Growth is Starting to Change Your Culture
- You Realize the Customer is No Longer at the Center
- Growth Requires More than What's Inside Your Walls
- It's Time to Reinvent
- It's Time to Sell (or Not)
- You're Navigating the Sale of Your Business
- You're Ready for Succession Planning

BEFORE YOU BEGIN

The work of leadership doesn't end when the Flywheel is turning smoothly. In fact, that's when a different kind of work begins. The kind that ensures momentum continues, evolves, and a healthy, sustainable business endures.

This section explores leadership moments that transcend the Flywheel. These moments are less about managing performance and more about architecting the future. They ask you to look ahead with clarity and courage, to anticipate change before it demands reaction, and to build mindsets and structures that outlast you.

Here, your role as a leader shifts. You are still responsible for execution, but also for orientation. Your eye must be on both the present and what's emerging next. The letters that follow focus on the disciplines that keep organizations relevant, resilient, and rooted in purpose over time: adaptability, cultural evolution, customer focus, reinvention, partnerships, succession, and continuity.

Because these moments are complex and deeply human, the letters in this section are intentionally longer. **Each is followed by "From My Journey," then a space for your own thoughtful consideration entitled "Your Turn."** The topics range from heavy to hopeful. All are designed to help you lead proactively so that your business doesn't just perform well today, but continues to evolve into a healthy, sustainable future.

OPEN WHEN: YOU'RE READY TO BUILD ADAPTABILITY INTO YOUR CULTURE

Dear Leader,

Just as adaptability is an invaluable trait in people, it's the defining capability of organizations that endure. In a world where markets shift overnight, technologies evolve daily, and client expectations change in real time, adaptability isn't just a behavioral trait; it's a strategy.

At its core, adaptability is the ability to swiftly adjust strategies and perspectives in the face of challenges—or opportunities—even the unexpected ones. To do this well, leaders and organizations alike must get comfortable with change *and* develop a growth mindset.

Creating a culture of adaptability means building the organizational muscle to flex without breaking. It takes both the ability to *lead* change and the capacity to *respond* to it. Each one is critical to long-term success. The goal is to create an organization that sees change not as a threat but as an opportunity to learn, grow, and gain an advantage.

When adaptability is part of your culture, your Flywheel spins stronger across every dimension:

- **Great People** stay curious and engaged because they're encouraged to learn, stretch, and experiment. They become nimble: able to flex into new roles and evolve their skills as the world changes.
- **Great Work** gets better because teams innovate and problem-solve in real time.
- **Great Clients** benefit from your continued relevance and foresight, often finding themselves ahead of change rather than reacting to it.
- **Great Impact** follows...because resilience creates sustainability.

So, how do you build adaptability as a core strength rather than an occasional reaction?

1. Embed it in a growth mindset.

A culture of adaptability begins with belief. The belief that individuals *and* the organization can learn and grow. Encourage curiosity. Reward learning and experimentation as much as outcomes. When leaders model asking, *What if?* rather than *What is?* they normalize evolution as part of the work.

2. Adopt an outside-in approach.

Adaptable organizations look beyond their own walls. Continuous scanning of markets, competitors, and client needs ensures relevance. These external inputs serve as the muse for evolution and innovation.

3. Prioritize progress over perfection.

In times of change, the ability to move quickly and learn as you go is more valuable than having all the answers. Create space for experimentation and iteration—pilot programs, scenario planning, and reflection points. Progress, not perfection, builds momentum. Celebrate small wins along the way.

4. Align systems and rewards.

Performance metrics, incentives, and recognition should reinforce flexibility, experimentation, collaboration, and initiative, not just efficiency or perfection. If you want people to adapt, make sure your structures don't punish them for trying.

5. Model steady flexibility at the top.

Your composure and willingness to pivot with purpose influence the culture far more than any plan or program. When leaders stay calm amid uncertainty and open to recalibration, adaptability takes hold as both modeled and expected.

Adaptability is a value creator because it safeguards what truly matters: relevance and resilience. It's what keeps your Flywheel turning through shifting client needs, emerging technologies, and evolving markets.

You don't need to predict the future; you just need to prepare your organization to respond well to it. Sometimes that means leading the change. Other times, it means having the agility to pivot. Either way, adaptability isn't a reaction; it's your competitive advantage.

With you in remaining relevant,

FROM MY JOURNEY

I've written and spoken often about managing and adapting to change because, truthfully, my career has been defined by it.

Sometimes I was *responding* to change—like deciding whether to leave a stable, well-known employer to become one of the founding members of a start-up, or stepping into the CEO and owner seat, literally overnight. Other times, I was creating it—like transforming our traditional marketing research agency into a customer-centric consultancy, expanding far beyond data collection to deliver deeper, more strategic value to clients or like rising to the challenge of the Human8 CEO role with the intent of creating harmony among ten disparate agencies.

My own experiences navigating these shifts became the foundation for how I later advised others through change management. But whether I was leading it or responding to it, one thing held true: adaptability was the constant.

Being adaptable meant staying curious, maintaining a voracious appetite not only for learning but for experimenting with new ideas. It meant being willing to fail when necessary and comfortable with pivots and course corrections when the situation required it. It meant embracing uncertainty as a teacher rather than a threat.

Even when I was the one driving the change, sleepless nights and self-doubt often came with the territory. But ultimately, building that adaptability muscle allowed both me and the teams and organizations I led to keep evolving, no matter what came our way.

YOUR TURN: BUILDING YOUR ADAPTABILITY MUSCLE

Ask Yourself:

Think of two defining moments in your leadership journey: one where you *initiated* change, and one where you *had to respond* to it.

- *What helped you adapt in each moment?*

- *What did those experiences reveal about your resilience, your flexibility, and the way you move through uncertainty?*
- *How might those lessons strengthen your organization's ability to adapt in the future?*

Thinking About Your Organization:

- *Where do you notice rigidity showing up in your organization today? What beliefs, habits, or structures might need to evolve?*
- *What external signals (market shifts, client behaviors, emerging technologies) are telling you it's time to adapt?*
- *When was the last time you chose progress over perfection? How did that decision open new possibilities?*
- *How well does your current culture reward curiosity, experimentation, and learning? Where might fear of getting it wrong be holding people back?*
- *What's one small adaptive move you could make in the next 30 days that would strengthen your organization's resilience?*

OPEN WHEN: GROWTH IS STARTING TO CHANGE YOUR CULTURE

Dear Leader,

Every organization has a culture: a collective set of beliefs and behaviors that define how it feels to work there and to do business with you. It's the lived experience of your purpose, your values, and your brand promise.

As your organization grows and the world around you shifts, your culture will shift too. That's normal. It's natural. In fact, it's healthy. But it can also feel unsettling, especially for those who've been part of the story from the early days.

Long-tenured employees may find themselves reminiscing about the *good old days*, noticing that what once felt small and familiar now feels larger, more complex, maybe even a little less personal. It's easy to romanticize what was. But evolution is part of endurance. A thriving culture doesn't stay fixed, and it certainly doesn't let complacency settle in. A thriving culture stretches, adapts, and matures as the business does.

The key is knowing what makes your organization *uniquely you* and being intentional about nurturing those qualities as you grow. This is where **your Fundamentals** come back into play. They're your cultural compass, helping you hold onto what's essential while creating space for new people, new ideas, and new ways of working to shape what's next.

And here's an important distinction:

Protecting your culture can sometimes sound defensive, as if you're guarding it from change.

Nurturing your culture is different. It reflects a growth mindset and the willingness to preserve your core identity while allowing it to evolve with new people, new partnerships, leadership transitions, and opportunities.

Guideposts for Nurturing Your Culture

- **Revisit Your Fundamentals**
  Go back to your purpose, vision, mission, values, and brand promise. *Are they still clear? Still true? Still guiding how you operate day to day?*
- **Identify the Beliefs and Behaviors That Enable You to Thrive**
  What behaviors, beliefs, and rituals have always made your culture strong, both internally and externally? What must be intentionally modeled and celebrated to keep your ethos alive?
- **Spot the Habits That Hold You Back**
  Which behaviors or unspoken norms might now be limiting growth? Where do new employees feel stuck or bump into rigid processes that no longer serve the organization?
- **Surface What's Crept In**
  Over time, every culture accumulates a few unintended behaviors or "shadow values." Don't ignore them, name them. Ask whether they serve who you are today and who you want to grow into.
- **Stay Curious, Not Defensive**
  Culture is shared, not held by one person or a small group. When something feels different, get curious. Growth doesn't have to mean losing who you are if you are intentional about understanding what makes your culture **your** culture and translating it to stay relevant *and* authentic.

So, when you feel the pull between nostalgia and progress, remember: the goal isn't to protect the past, it's to nurture what's timeless within it, and let that guide how you grow forward. It's a tricky balance, but I know you can do it.

With heart and humility,

FROM MY JOURNEY

I believe it was Peter Drucker who said, *"Culture eats strategy for breakfast."* And he was right. If you're struggling with culture, you'll struggle to execute strategy, no matter how thoughtful your plan.

I've long believed culture is a competitive advantage when it's healthy and aligned. But I've also seen firsthand how it can morph into a constraint when it's not evolving at the same pace as the business.

During periods of high growth, we often found ourselves unable to train or promote fast enough to keep up with demand for senior talent. We'd bring in what looked like a great hire: strong experience, aligned values, but once they joined, they'd encounter what we jokingly (and somewhat proudly) called *"the Gongos way."*

Our culture, which had served us beautifully for years, became unintentionally rigid. We didn't leave enough space for new ideas or outside experience to influence how we worked. What we saw as consistency and excellence, others experienced as inflexibility. And for senior-level hires eager to contribute, it was discouraging to feel like their perspectives weren't fully welcomed or valued.

Eventually, we were able to name this pattern and recognize it not as a flaw but as a natural outcome of growth. What had made us great at one stage was now holding us back from the next.

Among many efforts to understand and evolve culture, we introduced growth-versus-fixed-mindset training not as a cure-all, but to provide people with a shared language and perspective. It helped us reconnect to our *why* while making space for new *hows*. The goal wasn't to protect our culture from change, but to nurture what mattered most through change.

The key to intentional cultural shifts is helping people **see the benefit of new behaviors** so that their beliefs can evolve with them. Like many meaningful changes, this requires a shift in mindset and time. **But when people understand *why* a shift matters, not just *what* needs to change, they can embrace growth as part of the organization's story rather than a threat to it.**

YOUR TURN: NURTURING CULTURE AS YOU GROW

As your organization grows, culture naturally evolves—whether you intend it to or not. Being prepared begins by being tuned in. Use the questions below to pause, notice what's shifting, and choose what to nurture forward.

- **What about your culture is core, and what is contextual?**
  What beliefs, behaviors, or rituals are essential to who you are? What ones served you well early on, but may no longer fit the scale or complexity of today?
- **Where do you see signs of cultural tension?**
  What do long-tenured employees miss or feel protective of? Are these non-negotiables, or can they be softened?
  Where do newer team members experience friction or unspoken rules?
- **What behaviors are actually being rewarded?**
  Beyond stated values, what actions lead to recognition, influence, and advancement? Do these behaviors reflect the culture you want going forward?
- **What must evolve for your culture to support growth?**
  What mindsets or ways of working may need to shift? What is one behavior you can model, or one conversation you can begin, to help that evolution take hold? What can you do to prepare people to evolve with the organization?

For additional guidance, see: *Establishing (or Re-Setting) Your Foundation, Open When: You're Defining Your Fundamentals*

OPEN WHEN: YOU REALIZE THE CUSTOMER IS NO LONGER THE CENTER

Dear Leader,

When most businesses begin, they focus on a customer need. That clarity fuels the launch, sharpens decisions, and keeps early teams aligned. In the beginning, the customer is unmistakably the "North Star" of the business, central to decision-making.

But as growth takes hold, something subtle often shifts.

Conversations begin to center more on internal priorities: profitability, productivity, efficiency, offerings, and market share. These are important questions, necessary ones. Yet when they dominate, they can begin to overshadow the very reason your business exists: to serve your customers.

Many organizations say they are customer-centric. Far fewer practice the discipline of keeping the customer at the center as business complexity increases. Customer focus doesn't maintain itself. It requires vigilant listening and constant recalibration, especially as success, scale, and structure create distance between decision-makers and the people they serve.

Growth can be noisy. And without an intentional focal point, that noise can drown out the customer's voice.

Here's a simple way to test your North Star: **pay attention to where your time, energy, and conversations are going.**

Are discussions primarily about maximizing financials, improving efficiency, and pushing products or offerings? Or do they also include questions like:

- *Are we still deeply aligned with what our customers truly value?*
- *Are we structured to deliver the experience they need, not just the one that's easiest or most efficient for us?*
- *Are we listening closely to what the market needs, not just what we already sell?*

When the customer remains the central focus, everything else aligns: strategy, operations, innovation, and financial health. But when the customer fades into the background, decisions optimize internally while relevance erodes externally.

Keeping the customer as your North Star doesn't mean ignoring financial performance. It means remembering that profit follows value, not the other way around. When you consistently create meaningful value for customers: when you help them succeed, solve what matters most to them, and evolve alongside them, your business grows more resilient.

When the noise of growth starts to drown out your customer's voice, pause. Reorient. And ask yourself whose needs are truly guiding your decisions.

The surest way to create lasting value is to never lose sight of the people you exist to serve.

With you in keeping true north,

FROM MY JOURNEY

During my tenure as CEO at both Gongos and Human8, I had several wake-up moments when I realized our leadership conversations had drifted way too far from the customer. We all knew we were here because of our deep commitment to serving our clients. Yet, paradoxically, we were spending very little time with them as our focal point. Something was off.

It wasn't intentional. The customer still mattered deeply. But operational priorities, internal complexities—the real work of running a growing and transforming organization—had somehow snuck in to take precedence. At times, we would go weeks without explicitly inserting the customers' voice into the room. And occasionally, I wasn't sure we had the *right* people in the room to represent that voice, rather than relying on secondhand interpretations. I distinctly remember asking myself one day: *When was the last time I actually interacted with a customer?*

That realization stopped me.

I knew it wasn't enough to say we were customer-centric—honestly, *who would claim otherwise?* To truly practice customer centricity, we needed to create intentional space for it. That meant reshaping our agendas—collectively and personally.

Yes, we regularly reviewed the pipeline and revenue. But we went a layer deeper by introducing two additional practices. First, each leadership team member was accountable for bringing one story from a client or market interaction to our weekly huddles. Second, we began inviting frontline team members into leadership meetings so we could hear customer stories directly. Successes and friction points alike. Moments where we were delivering extraordinary value, and moments where we were falling short.

I also knew that if I expected the organization to "walk the talk," I needed to do the same. I set a personal quota: every month, I committed to interacting with a set number of customers through virtual conversations or on-site visits in their own environments. That time was dedicated to immersing, listening, and understanding what was changing in their world, and to sharing perspectives back when it was useful. That proximity grounded me. It became a guardrail against assumptions about what our customers truly wanted and needed.

Quarterly, our client leaders were also responsible for bringing the voice of the customer into our strategic planning: what they were hearing, what was shifting, and the patterns or early signals emerging across accounts. Combined with my own conversations and our regular client pulse surveys, this input often surfaced insights about where we needed to adapt our offering, improve the client experience, or even rethink elements of our longer-term strategy and innovation pipeline.

Looking back, those moments of drift were disappointing yet also important reminders. In a growing organization, customer focus doesn't sustain itself; it competes with countless other priorities. Customer focus must be revisited, reintroduced, and sometimes reimagined over and over again. And if the customer is truly to remain your North Star, it isn't a responsibility that can be fully delegated. It must be claimed as a leadership priority because when you pause and ask *why your organization exists at all*, the answer begins and ends with the customer.

YOUR TURN: RE-CENTERING ON THE CUSTOMER

As your organization grows, don't let your customer focus get weighed down by competing priorities. Use the prompts below to pause, recalibrate, and reclaim your North Star.

- ***Where does the customer show up in your leadership conversations today?***
  When was the last time the customer's voice meaningfully influenced a decision—not just metrics, but your strategy, practices, capabilities, or experience? Who is (and isn't) in the room when customer-related decisions are made? Are these people close to the customer's voice or once removed?

- ***What currently competes for/takes priority over the customer, and why?***
  What internal priorities or conversations most often crowd out customer focus? Are those priorities serving the customer?

- ***How close are you, personally, to your customers right now?***
  When was the last time you listened directly, without an agenda, to what customers are experiencing? What assumptions might you be making that getting closer could correct?

- ***Are you listening and acting?***
  Where are you strong at gathering customer insight, but slower to respond? Where might you be acting quickly without first truly understanding customer needs?

- ***Does the way you're organized reflect the client as your North Star?***
  As organizations scale, structure can prioritize efficiency over the customer experience. Revisit whether your teams' workflow and decision paths are designed to serve client needs first, or whether the client has shifted to secondary to internal needs and priorities.

- ***If the customer were sitting at your decision-making table, what would change?***
  What decisions, meetings, measures, or behaviors would look different? How would the conversation or resulting actions change? What is one intentional shift you could make to ensure the customer remains central as you grow?

OPEN WHEN: GROWTH REQUIRES MORE THAN WHAT'S INSIDE YOUR WALLS

Dear Leader,

Whether from the moment you open your doors or years later when your Flywheel is spinning or any point in between, there will come a time when you realize there's wisdom in looking outward to amplify your ability to create value for clients.

In our fast-changing world, very few businesses grow on their own. Clients expect speed, personalization, and seamless solutions that often require a combination of strengths no single organization can deliver. The most adaptive leaders recognize this, and instead of trying to be *everything to everyone*, they focus on being *exceptional at what they do best* and partnering purposefully for the rest.

A strategic partnership is a purposeful alliance between organizations that combine their unique strengths to create new value that neither could achieve alone. Think of strategic partnerships as ecosystem building, and when done right, they offer the potential to extend your leadership capacity, accelerate innovation, and open new pathways to create value for your clients **and** for your people.

Start With Why Together?

Every strong partnership begins not *with what's in it for us?* but with *what problem can we solve better, together?* The best collaborations are rooted in an outside-in orientation, with the primary focus on creating new value for clients. This mindset provides the clearest pathway for mutual growth.

Ask yourself:

- *What customer need or opportunity are we jointly addressing that we couldn't fulfill on our own?*
- *How will this partnership make life easier, better, or more inspiring for our shared audiences?*
- *Does the collaboration feel additive?*

Look for these Five Fits:

- **Market Disruption**
  Seek partnerships that create surprise and delight, not incremental improvement. When two brands combine their strengths to solve a long-standing pain point in a fresh way, customers take notice.
- **Synergy That Expands Reach**
  The best partnerships multiply exposure to like-minded audiences. When aligned, each brand lends the other a halo effect, resulting in a more fluid, cohesive journey for customers.
- **Credibility and Capability Exchange**
  For startups, a partnership can fast-track legitimacy and scale. For established players, it can inject innovation and agility. Ideally, each partner elevates the other.
- **Values Alignment**
  Shared ethics, integrity, and customer-first philosophies are non-negotiable. The partnership will only go as far as the trust and mutual respect that underpin it.
- **Clarity of Roles and Strengths**
  Define who does what early and revisit it often. Partnerships fail when overlap breeds confusion. They thrive when each party leans into their core competency and respects the other's expertise.

Measure What Matters Most

- Beyond metrics like revenue or reach, the real measure of a successful partnership is **the creation of unforeseen value for the customer.**
- *Did your collaboration unlock something neither could have achieved alone?*
- *Did it strengthen your people, your offerings, your brand, your customer portfolio?*

Strategic partnerships, at their best, ***expand what's possible****—for your business and the ecosystem around it.*

With optimism and openness,

FROM MY JOURNEY

From the moment we opened our doors, we realized that going it alone would make for a longer, slower road to getting our Flywheel spinning at the speed we needed for sustainable growth. In the early days, our challenge was diversifying our client base. If you've read some of my earlier reflections in the Great Clients section, you'll remember that we were 100% embedded in the automotive sector for our first few years—a risky proposition, to say the least.

Our first real strategic partnership came when we joined forces with an outside consultant who specialized in a methodology that required marketing research expertise. He had ample experience with the other elements of the offering, but not the consumer research side, and we were the missing piece. In terms of capabilities, together, we fit like two puzzle pieces. Our strategic partnership created a win-win: his client base introduced us to industries we hadn't yet touched, giving us credibility and access that would have been difficult to achieve on our own, and our expertise filled a gap in his offering, enabling him to show up with a one-stop solution for his clients.

That early experience planted a seed. As our business grew and became more complex, we developed a discipline we called **value chain analysis**: a regular review of our capabilities and core competencies that helped us decide whether to *build, buy, or partner.* Over time, this framework became a simple but powerful decision lens for our growth strategy:

- **Build:** Leveraging our own people, resources, and innovation to create new capabilities or offerings from within.

- **Buy:** Acquiring an existing capability, technology, or company to accelerate growth or fill a critical gap more quickly than building internally.
- **Partner:** Forming a purposeful alliance with another organization to combine complementary strengths and co-create new value, avoiding redundancy.

These conversations became a consistent and essential part of our strategic planning rhythm. What we learned was that the "right" answer, whether to build, buy, or partner, can evolve as markets shift, technologies advance, and customer expectations rise. What once made sense to build internally might later call for creating an ecosystem externally.

The key is to stay open and fluid, with a process that forces you to regularly look up and out. Strategic partnerships thrive in companies that don't cling to ownership for ownership's sake but instead commit to collective value creation.

And perhaps the greatest gift of these partnerships? **The two-way learning that happens when both organizations fully collaborate to rise together.**

YOUR TURN: SEEING BEYOND YOUR WALLS

Take a moment to look across your business: your people, capabilities, and ambitions for growth. Often, healthy organizations flex between building, buying, and partnering; adapting their growth path to change.

Consider where internal strength ends and external opportunity may begin.

Ask yourself:

- *Where do we have capability or capacity gaps that slow us down or limit what's possible?*
- *Which parts of how we create value are becoming harder to differentiate, or are becoming more commoditized?*
- *What capabilities could we buy to close a critical gap faster, better, or more efficiently than building internally?*

- *If we stopped developing X, what would that free up – for our people, our focus, and our pocketbook?*
- *How often do we pause to re-evaluate these choices as markets, technologies, and customer needs evolve?*
- *How often do we/should we pause to re-evaluate these decisions in the context of evolving markets, technologies, and customer needs?*

OPEN WHEN: IT'S TIME TO REINVENT

Dear Leader,

If you're leading an enduring organization, there will come a time when you ask yourself: *Will what we've always done sustain us into the future?*

You may already feel that what once worked isn't working as well. Growth slows. Momentum feels harder to sustain. The context around you begins to shift, prompting you to question the very foundation of your model.

The reasons vary, but the signal is the same: **it's time to evolve to stay relevant.**

Reinvention begins by recognizing those early signs of obsolescence. They might show up as client needs shifting, competitors innovating faster, talent leaving for "fresher" opportunities, or internal processes that once felt efficient now feel outdated. Keeping a constant pulse on the external world: market trends, cultural shifts, and technology, ensures you're not caught flat-footed when reinvention calls.

When assessing the need for reinvention, look broadly:

- **Market and industry:** *Where is our industry heading? Are new entrants rewriting the rules?*
- **Technology:** *What tools, platforms, or data sources are changing expectations?*
- **Society and culture:** *How are people's values, priorities, and behaviors evolving, and how might that reframe demand?*
- **Your clients:** *What new needs are going unaddressed? Do your current capabilities help clients stay ahead?*
- **Your organization:** *Are you leading in relevance and differentiation or simply iterating on the past?*

Reinvention is about pivoting with purpose, not panic. **It's having the courage to disrupt yourself before the world does it for you.** Think of it as stepping into the calm eye of the storm rather than being swept up in its chaos.

Vision fuels reinvention, but buy-in sustains it. Involve key stakeholders early: employees, clients, partners, board members, investors. Invite them to help imagine the next chapter. Your reinvention may create a context in which not everyone chooses to continue the journey with your organization, and that's okay. Clarity about where you're headed and what it will take to get there creates alignment for those who remain and peace for those who move on.

When leading reinvention, remember three essentials:

- **Anchor the "why."** People need to understand not just what's changing, but *why*. Paint a vivid picture of the risk of standing still and *not* evolving, reinforced by client needs and market realities.
- **Define the "how."** Translate your vision into tangible steps, milestones, and behaviors that show progress and build belief. Talking about change without equipping people to act on it breeds frustration.
- **Clarify "what's in it for me."** Resistance is human. Help employees, clients, and partners see how the reinvention benefits them. Momentum builds when people feel personally connected to the outcome.

Reinvention is one of the hardest and most courageous acts of leadership because it means letting go of something that's still working, just not well enough for the future. But it's also one of the most rewarding, because it renews energy, relevance, and purpose.

When you sense that quiet tug, that it's time to evolve, don't wait for the market to decide for you. Step boldly into the eye of the storm.

With courage and clarity,

FROM MY JOURNEY

There are moments when success itself becomes the risk. When what brought you here may not be enough to carry you forward. We found ourselves at such a moment as early signals suggested our industry and our clients were on the cusp of rapid change. We began to ask ourselves: *What will the future demand of us? Will what made us successful today still be enough tomorrow? How do we remain relevant for a healthy, sustainable future?*

The forces reshaping our industry were already visible. Access to consumer data was proliferating, automation was accelerating, and client expectations were evolving at unprecedented speed. The traditional marketing research model that had served us so well was becoming increasingly commoditized.

For us, restless dissatisfaction had always been part of our DNA. We'd never been content to rest on what was working. We were wired to ask, *What's next?* That mindset pushed us to anticipate change and act with intention, rather than react to it. But instead of making reinvention all about us, we took an **outside-in** approach: evolving in concert with the changing needs of our clients, their customers, and the broader marketplace.

Unlike many in our industry, who pursued growth through mergers and acquisitions, we chose to grow organically. It was a more demanding path. Slower, riskier, but deeply authentic. We transformed from a traditional research agency focused on primary data collection into a customer-centric consultancy. Instead of simply delivering insights, we helped clients integrate multiple sources of data, translate understanding into action, and embed that understanding into how their organizations operated. That meant supporting insight integration, commercialization of opportunities, change management, and the design and implementation of both consumer and employee experience programs. It required adding new skill sets to those that already existed, new structures, and an entirely new way of thinking about value creation—moving from informing decisions to helping drive them. Over time, this shift allowed us to partner more deeply with senior leadership teams and contribute to initiatives that shaped strategy, culture, and growth, not just marketing decisions.

Reinvention, we discovered, isn't a single initiative or a program; *it's a mindset*. It reminded us that an enduring organization comes from movement, not maintenance. And it taught us that when reinvention is guided by purpose, vision, and an outside-in perspective, it is one of the most powerful expressions of continuity there is.

YOUR TURN: LEADING REINVENTION FROM THE OUTSIDE IN

The best reinventions rarely start from the boardroom; they start with the world around you.

Take time to look outward before you look inward:

- *What shifts in your customers' or clients' needs, behaviors, or expectations could redefine what "value" means in your business?*
- *Which societal, cultural, or technological forces are quietly reshaping your market or your people?*
- *How often do you intentionally invite external voices (clients, partners, industry peers, board members, investors) to challenge your assumptions?*
- *If you viewed your organization entirely through your clients' eyes, what would you change first?*

Reinvention both protects and expands relevance. The outside world is always signaling what's next. **The question is: *are you listening closely enough to hear it?***

Conceptualizing your reinvention is the first step. Here are a few additional reflections to aid your journey:

- **Internal Readiness:** *What fears, attachments, or beliefs make reinvention difficult? What support will you need to deliberately pave the pathway to change?*

- **Alignment and Stakeholders:** *Whose buy-in will be required for reinvention? How can you engage them early to co-create the next chapter with you?*
- **Authenticity of Path:** *What would it take to ensure your evolution feels true to your values, not just the market's demands?*

For additional guidance, see: *Great People, Open When: You're Navigating Change* and *Beyond the Flywheel, Open When: You're Ready to Build Adaptability into Your Culture.*

OPEN WHEN: IT'S TIME TO SELL (OR NOT)

Dear Leader,

Few decisions are as complex or as personal as deciding whether to sell the business you've built. If you've poured years of your life, energy, and identity into it, your company isn't just a financial asset. It's a living part of you—the people, the stories, the risks you took, and the impact you made along the way.

When you begin to wonder whether it's time to sell, remember: this isn't just a transaction. **It's a transition**. And like every transition, it deserves clarity and intention beyond the numbers.

As Bo Burlingham writes in *Finish Big*, the best exits are the ones planned long before they're executed. Whether that moment is on the near horizon or years away, taking time now to define what "a good exit" means to you is one of the greatest gifts you can give yourself **and** your organization.

When you begin contemplating transition readiness, **market timing and personal alignment** are both significant factors. You'll know it's time not only when the business is valuable to others, but when you can envision your next chapter with purpose and peace.

Guideposts to Consider:

- **Check your why.**
  Are you selling out of fatigue, opportunity, legacy planning, or the pull toward something new? Naming the *why* clarifies whether selling is truly the right path or whether reinvention **or** renewal might meet the same need.
- **Consider all stakeholders.**
  Selling affects more than you. It touches employees, clients, partners, and even your family. The right buyer should feel like a continuation of your values and new opportunities for your team.
- **Balance the tangible and intangible.**
  Numbers matter, but so do purpose, impact, brand equity, and peace of mind. Spreadsheets can tell you what your business is worth, but only you know what it's worth to you.

- **Imagine life after.**
  Picture your next chapter without this business. **Does it fill you with excitement or uncertainty?** If the vision energizes you, selling may be right for you. If it feels like loss without renewal, perhaps your work here isn't finished yet.

Whatever you decide, know this: selling is part of your story, but it doesn't define it. What you built through Great People, Great Work, Great Clients, and Great Impact continues to live on through you, your next adventure, and the reverberating effects of your leadership.

And choosing *not* to sell can be just as powerful. It's a reaffirmation of belief—a conscious decision to keep building something meaningful.

Whichever path you choose, may you do it with clarity, intention, and peace.

With respect and understanding,

FROM MY JOURNEY

This is the first time I've put pen to paper about my decision to sell. Saying it was difficult is an understatement.

The decision came two years after the Covid-19 pandemic began—a period that tested every ounce of endurance I had. Leading through those years meant managing constant uncertainty, caring deeply for our people and clients, navigating the first reduction in force in nearly 30 years, and trying to preserve our sense of belonging while many resisted returning to the office. We invested enormous energy in redefining new ways of working, both for ourselves and alongside our clients.

We rebounded. In fact, 2021 became a record year for us. But despite the success, I knew something inside me had shifted. It wasn't just fatigue; I'd been tired before. This was something deeper. A tug that said, *You've built this chapter... but maybe it's time for a new one.*

Nearing my mid-50's, I felt that pull more clearly. I began to sense there was "something else out there." Another way for me to make an impact beyond Gongos. That realization came with both peace and grief. After over 30 years of building, leading, and stewarding the business, I knew the time was approaching to begin rounding out this chapter.

I quietly set a three-year horizon for myself. The only person I shared it with was my husband, who agreed that it might be time for us to move forward into our next chapter. And as soon as I made that decision, the universe seemed to affirm it. Within months, three different and appealing companies reached out about potential acquisitions.

I'd been approached before and usually entertained those conversations out of curiosity. But this time was different. I now had clarity about why I might sell, and that shifted everything. Over the course of a year, I went back and forth, weighing the pride of what we'd built against the possibilities of what could be next. The company was strong, the culture vibrant. We still had so much potential. Yet I also knew that joining a larger global organization might allow us to amplify our purpose; to bring our mission to more clients, more markets, more people.

That conviction ultimately guided my decision to sell. **For me, the decision carried two intentions: expanding what we had created to a broader stage and making space for the beginning of my next chapter.**

YOUR TURN: DEFINING YOUR WHY BEFORE YOU SELL

Plenty of very useful frameworks exist to help you think through exit-readiness from the financial, operational, and legal perspectives. I highly recommend using them for their intended purpose.

These reflection prompts are meant **to help you think through your inner landscape:** identity, purpose, personal readiness, and emotional clarity. Before considering a sale, pause to explore your why beyond the numbers.

- ***What's really driving the thought of selling?*** *Is it exhaustion, curiosity, opportunity, or a desire for reinvention?*

- ***How aligned is your decision with your values and vision?*** *Does selling advance the legacy you've built or risk diluting it? Consider the implications of each.*

- ***When you imagine life after the sale, what do you see?*** *Do you feel excitement for what's next, or a sense of loss?*

- ***If you chose not to sell right now, what would you need to rekindle energy and clarity?*** *What support or renewal might shift your perspective? What would make staying feel purposeful?*

- ***How ready are you to step out of the identity you've held as a leader of this business?*** *Where is that identity anchoring you, and where might it be holding you back?*

- ***What future impact will be possible because of this decision for you? For your company?*** *How might selling advance your purpose, people or your own personal contribution in ways staying might not?*

- ***If nothing changes in the business over the next 12 months, would you still want to sell?*** *What does your answer reveal about urgency, readiness, and your deeper motivations?*

For additional guidance, see: *Beyond the Flywheel, Open When: You're Navigating the Sale of Your Business.*

OPEN WHEN: YOU'RE NAVIGATING THE SALE OF YOUR BUSINESS

Dear Leader,

No matter how well-prepared you think you are, navigating the sale of your business will test your patience and resolve. It's an emotional roller coaster, a strategic challenge, and a deeply human process all at once. The spreadsheets, negotiations, and legal reviews are just the surface. Underneath are the intangibles: the relationships, the history, the trust, and the hopes you've poured into what you've built.

Expect sleepless nights as part of the process. You will find yourself moving between excitement and grief, confidence and doubt—sometimes in the same hour. That's normal, and it reflects how much you care.

Guideposts are numerous, and here are several to help point you in the right direction:

- **Know your value.** Before negotiations begin, understand both your financial worth and your emotional worth. Work with professionals to determine valuation, but also reflect on the intangible assets: your reputation, client trust, and culture, which make your company unique. Consider things like: *Is my business model scalable? Do we have valuable intellectual property? Do we have a well-known brand?*
- **Choose your partner, not just your price.** Selling is not only about numbers. It's about fit. Evaluate potential buyers for alignment with your purpose, values, and people. The right partner has the potential to amplify your mission if that's important to you.
- **Be clear on what's expected of you after the sale.** Many deals come with transition requirements: staying on to integrate teams, reassure clients, or sustain performance metrics. Clarify scope and timing early so expectations are manageable. Know what you are willing, and not willing, to commit to.

- **Enlist outside advisors.** Surround yourself with trusted financial, legal, and accounting advisors, or even a broker, so the details are well-managed, and your energy can stay focused on the bigger picture. A broker can also open doors to buyers you may not have considered.
- **Communicate strategically.** Be thoughtful about who to involve and when. Over-disclosing too soon can spark anxiety; waiting too long can breed mistrust. Beyond outside advisors, identify a small internal circle you trust as thought partners and sounding boards.
- **Keep your head and your heart in balance.** Expect moments of defensiveness, nostalgia, even grief. Balance logic and intuition. Revisit your *why* regularly—it will steady you when emotions spike, or negotiations shift.
- **Prepare for emotional whiplash.** The sale rarely unfolds in a straight line or on the original timeline. Offers shift. Terms evolve. Confidence wavers. Allow yourself to feel it all, but don't let temporary emotions drive permanent decisions.

Once the sale goes through, a different type of work begins. Determining when and how to communicate both internally and externally requires a thoughtful approach. Transition periods are delicate because you are bridging the gap between "what was" and "what's next." You may be called on to lead through integration, reassure clients, or help set new rhythms for the team.

There's a balance to strike between staying to guide and leaving to grow your next chapter. It's unrealistic to think that your culture and values won't change. They will. The question becomes: *How much influence can you (and should you) have over stewarding the next phase of the company's story?*

The sale of your business does not mean the end of your leadership; it simply rescopes its reach. The lessons, relationships, and impact you've created will carry forward in ways you may never fully see.

Move through this process with confidence and care. You've built something worth buying—and more importantly, something worth continuing, just in a new form.

With respect and so much empathy,

FROM MY JOURNEY

From the first exploratory conversations to signing the final paperwork, the sale of our company took about sixteen months, but it felt much longer. The process was intense, all-consuming, and at times surreal. What no one prepares you for is this: you must keep running the business as usual while managing the constant distraction of something that easily is a full-time job in itself.

For most of that journey, only two people inside the organization knew: my CFO and one other trusted leader, someone I had long observed making objective, company-first decisions. Keeping the circle small was intentional. I knew how much anxiety early disclosure could create, and until I had not only an offer but due diligence that I felt confident in, I didn't want to burden the team with uncertainty that might never materialize.

Because several companies approached us, I chose not to hire a broker. Instead, I built my own deal team, people who knew me and the business intimately: my CFO, my attorney, our accounting firm, and my strategic-planning mentor. All three had experience with M&A and, more importantly, with us. They were trusted voices at the negotiating table and helped me stay grounded in what mattered most for both the business and me, personally.

There were many moments we almost walked away... right up to the final day. I reminded myself often that the acquiring company would be doing its due diligence on us, and that we had every right to do the same. Selling your company is not about proving your worth; it's about confirming mutual fit. The deal must feel like a win-win.

When deciding among three interested companies, I created my own set of non-negotiables.

- **Fit with culture and mission.** I wanted our purpose to endure beyond the sale.
- **People first.** No redundancies, and new growth opportunities for our team.
- **Autonomy and flexibility.** The ability for me to stay, or leave, on my own terms.

- **Value and fairness.** I knew my minimum based on professional valuation, but I also had *my number*—one that factored in intangibles like brand equity, client trust, and 30 years of sweat equity.

In the end, I didn't accept the highest financial offer. I chose the partner I believed would best carry our vision forward and would not create redundancies in staff: a global company without a U.S. footprint. We would be their North American presence and a chance to amplify our mission on a bigger stage.

Did I make the right choice? I'm honestly not sure. No matter how much diligence you do, no partnership unfolds exactly as imagined. Cultures merge differently in practice than on paper. You have to make peace with that. What matters most is knowing your non-negotiables, asking hard questions, and walking away from the deal if alignment falters.

Looking back, I learned that selling a business marks a continuation of leadership just expressed in a different form. Entering the process with open eyes, clear priorities, and conviction in what truly matters provides the steadiness needed to navigate the uncertainty that follows.

YOUR TURN: DEFINING YOUR NON-NEGOTIABLES (BEFORE YOU SELL)

Use this exercise to clarify what must be true for you to feel at peace with a sale. Capture honest answers first, then translate them into *Must-Haves, Nice-to-Haves*, and *Deal-Breakers*. Think of your non-negotiables as elements that will protect what matters most to you so that moving through the sale with confidence, integrity, and peace is possible.

Values and Legacy

- *What parts of our culture/way of working make us unique?*
- *What legacy do I want protected (for people, clients, brand, industry)?*
- *Where am I willing to flex—and where am I not?*

People Outcomes

- *What outcomes do I require for my team (e.g., roles retained, no forced redundancies, growth paths)?*
- *Who are my critical keepers? What commitments do I need from them?*

Brand Promise

- *What must remain true about how we serve clients (quality, access to our team, pricing philosophy, responsiveness)?*
- *Are there any key accounts needing special protection or transition plans?*

Financial Thresholds

- *What is my floor (minimum valuation) and why?*
- *Beyond price: what structure terms matter (cash vs. earnout, escrow, working capital, timing)?*

Post-Sale Role & Timeline

- *How long am I willing to stay? In what capacity?*
- *What autonomy, decision rights, and exit flexibility do I need?*

Strategic & Cultural Fit

- *How closely must the buyer's mission and operating style align with ours?*
- *What are my "yellow flags" (signals we're not aligned) vs. "red flags" (stop the deal)?*

Brand, Autonomy & Integration

- *What guardrails do I need around our brand, product or capabilities, and pricing autonomy?*
- *What level of integration (light, phased, full) is acceptable—and at what pace?*

Diligence I Require from Them

- *What internal docs/metrics do I need (org design, culture, references from other companies acquired, employee retention history, client concentration, business development statistics, integration track record, financials, ethics)?*
- *Who do I need to meet (leadership team, operators, HR lead, integration lead, board, outside investors)?*
- *Are there other companies that have been acquired? Can I meet the owners of those companies to understand their acquisition journey?*

For additional guidance, see: *When Things Get Hard, Open When: You're Leading Through Uncertainty* and *Beyond the Flywheel, Open When: It's Time to Sell (or Not).*

OPEN WHEN: YOU'RE READY FOR SUCCESSION PLANNING

Dear Leader,

If you've read the *Great People* section on developing successors, you already know that succession planning starts long before an exit is on the horizon. But when you're preparing for your own transition, it requires deeper reflection and intention.

The question isn't *if* you'll transition; of course, you will. But, **how well you'll prepare your organization and its people for what comes next.**

Too often, succession planning lives in the background. You tell yourself there's time. You assume people will know what to do. Good intentions can't substitute for real preparation.

Succession often fails due to years of quiet delay. Use these guideposts to begin preparing for your own transition.

1. Start Early and Stay Honest

The best time to begin your succession planning is before you think you need to. A thoughtful, multi-year plan gives you space to develop and test your future leaders rather than rush to replace them under pressure. Start by asking yourself: *If I weren't here tomorrow, who would step in? What non-negotiables in terms of skills, experiences, behavioral qualities, and mindset are important for this position? Who shows real potential, not just competence?*

2. Cultivate Readiness

One of my greatest learnings came when I stepped into the CEO role earlier than expected. John and I had discussed transition, but there wasn't enough time to fully prepare for the ownership side of leadership. The learning curve was steep, not because of will or commitment, but because some lessons simply require lived experience. Give your future leaders that experience now. Invite them to board meetings, strategic discussions, and difficult decisions.

Cultivating readiness is as important as naming a successor.

3. Anchor the Transition in People and Culture

Every company's evolution depends on its people. As you transition, ensure your leadership handoff protects what's most sacred: your values, your purpose, your culture. Your successors may lead differently (and they should). Still, the organization's heartbeat must remain aligned with its core promise to employees and clients alike.

4. Balance Urgency and Deliberation

Succession planning rarely feels urgent until it's too late. The process requires balancing decisiveness with patience. Waiting for a perfect moment is unrealistic. Start small: document your key responsibilities, relationships, and decision spaces. Build clarity around ownership, governance, and communication. Then, revisit and refine. Make it a living document that evolves with your role and the organization.

5. Don't Do This Alone

Your transition isn't just yours. It's part of the organization's journey and story. Invite others into the process early. Transparency builds trust and helps your team see change as continuity rather than loss. Done well, succession strengthens confidence and energizes the next generation of leaders to carry the work forward in their own way.

You may not be able to predict every circumstance, but you can intentionally help people prepare to thrive beyond your tenure. This turns leadership into legacy.

With the long game in mind,

FROM MY JOURNEY

Succession planning is something I often thought about, in principle. I believed in its importance. I documented what I thought would be required and intentionally developed people in many areas of my role. But I'll admit, I struggled when it came to designating *the person* who would eventually succeed me.

I could see a group of people who, together, possessed the right combination of skills, experience, and leadership potential, but no single individual had the *whole shebang*. In hindsight, I see that as a real misstep on my part. I'm not sure if it was hesitation, optimism, or fear that kept me from making that call. Maybe it was all three.

Part of it, I think, was deeply emotional. The business was my baby. I had helped nurture it from its earliest days, shaping not just the strategy but the soul of the organization. I had a comprehensive handle on the business—both executional and visionary—and that blend of EQ and IQ made it hard for me to imagine anyone stepping in with the same care and context.

Looking back, I wish I had been more deliberate and more objective. I wish I had recognized sooner that the goal wasn't to find a replica of me. It was to prepare the organization for what it needed *next*.

That, I believe, is the hardest truth for many founders and long-tenured leaders: **succession planning requires enough emotional distance to see the business clearly.** Only then will you see what it needs. Cloning your leadership style is impossible, but creating the conditions for new leadership to thrive is absolutely possible.

If I could do it again, I would spend more time openly exploring both internal and external possibilities, naming the gaps I saw, and giving the organization permission to evolve beyond me.

YOUR TURN: INTENTIONAL TRANSITIONING

Succession planning requires identifying what the organization needs in its next leader and preparing it to be ready.

Use the prompts below to reflect honestly on what your organization will need next, and what you may need to let go of to support it. **Enlist a partner, either inside or outside the organization, to help you remain objective.**

- ***If you weren't here tomorrow, what would break? What would hold?***
  What decisions, responsibilities, relationships (both internal and external) are overly dependent on you? Where have you already built strength and continuity beyond yourself?

- ***What leadership capabilities does the organization need next? Where do you need to protect against "more of the same?"***
  How might the future demand different skills, experiences, and styles than those that served you well? What gaps would a successor need to fill?

- ***Where might emotion be clouding objectivity?***
  What fears, attachments, or assumptions make it difficult to name or prepare a successor? What would change if you viewed this decision from an outside perspective? What would change if you viewed the organization's long-term needs instead of your own identity?

- ***How can you create readiness without control?***
  What exposure to responsibility or experiences could you begin sharing now? Where could you step back to allow others to step forward?

WHAT YOU CARRY FORWARD

This book was never meant to be consumed in sequence or completed. It was meant to be opened and returned to again and again. Like the letters that inspired it, it was written for moments you may encounter as you lead and grow your purpose-driven endeavor, and as you continue to deepen your leadership practice.

As you've read through one or many of the letters, my hope for you is that you see this clearly: **just as growing a business unfolds across seasons and cycles, so does growing as a leader.** Leadership is humbling in that way. Like any meaningful craft, it is a practice. There is always a new experience, a new lesson, a new lens through which to see your work and yourself.

And it is deeply rewarding, especially when you allow leadership to be about something larger than you.

A key tenet to remember moving forward: readiness **is not the strongest prerequisite for leadership. Willingness is.**

Willingness to step forward when the path isn't fully clear. Willingness to take initiative when others hesitate. Willingness to engage even when you don't feel completely prepared.

THE LEADER YOU ARE GROWING INTO

I wrote this book from a place of deep passion for leadership development, yours and my own, and with real empathy for how difficult leadership is today. While the Flywheel provides structure for the book, it grew out of lived experience: one moment leading to another, patterns revealing themselves through reflection and practice.

What emerged from those experiences, and I hope, through your time with these pages, is the possibility of meaningful shifts in how you see yourself and your role as a leader. If you've been reflecting as you read, you may already notice subtle changes.

You may be less focused on having the right answers and more committed to *listening and asking better questions.*

You may be more comfortable *with the humility of naming uncertainty* rather than masking it with confidence.

You may feel a deeper responsibility not just for outcomes, but *also for the people creating them.*

None of this is accidental. At its best, leadership deepens our capacity to understand and to serve.

You don't lead from a title. You can lead from any seat. And it's never too early to begin by showing up, taking initiative, and holding the success of the team and organization ahead of your own.

In a world defined by complexity, where change is constant, clarity is fleeting, and discomfort is shared by leaders and teams alike, I know you see that a special kind of leadership is needed. One grounded not in force, but in humanity and presence. Not in certainty, but in courage. Not in perfection, but in progress. One that holds high expectations while honoring the people who carry them forward.

You've seen how **Great People, Great Work, Great Clients, and Great Impact** are not steps to complete, but a rhythm to create. **A way of orienting yourself when the noise gets loud and the path forward feels unclear.**

In times of uncertainty, we can't control everything, but we *can* control what we come back to.

- We can invest in our people and ensure their voices are heard, even when results feel fragile.
- We can focus on meaningful work that elevates both our clients and our brand.
- We can serve clients as partners, listening deeply rather than treating relationships as transactions.
- We can define impact not just by scale, but by significance.

This rhythm doesn't remove uncertainty, but it gives you something steady to hold onto as you move through it.

Always calibrating between one foot grounded in the here and now. One foot intentionally stepping into the future.

Now, You Are the Author

This is where the voice of this book shifts.

Because from here on out, **you** are the one writing the letters.

I invite you to imagine the *Open When* letters you'll create:

- For yourself now, when leadership feels uncertain or heavy
- For your future self, who has left behind a meaningful impact
- For a future team member, navigating their first big stretch
- For a fellow leader, standing at the edge of a difficult decision

What would you want them to remember?
What perspective would you offer?
What truth would you pass along that is earned through your own experience?

Writing those letters, literally or metaphorically, is an act of reciprocity. It's how leadership multiplies. It's how wisdom moves forward, person to person; it's your legacy in motion.

And it's how you stay accountable, not just to results, **but to who you want to be along the way.**

FROM MY JOURNEY: WHEN WALKING AWAY WAS THE RIGHT WAY FORWARD

One of the hardest leadership decisions I've ever made was stepping down from the CEO role at Human8 less than a year after accepting it.

When I sold Gongos, I invested in Human8 and became a managing partner during a period of rapid acquisition. As the integration progressed, it became increasingly clear that the leadership needed for the next season of the business would be different. The leadership that had served us well during the acquisition was not what the organization needed as it moved into full integration. Now we needed to bring cohesion, harmony, unified goals, shared meaning, and metrics of success across ten companies under one brand umbrella.

As a significant shareholder and a tenured CEO who had transformed her own business through organic growth, the integration of new capabilities, and long-term, values-led decision-making, I was asked to consider stepping into the Global CEO role. I was intrigued by the challenge and inspired by the vision of creating a cohesive, global consultancy, and I accepted.

What I underestimated was how fundamentally different the operating environment would be.

I had grown Gongos organically. My leadership team and I made decisions through a long-term lens, grounded in purpose, values, people, and clients—trusting that financial results would follow. Human8, however, was majority owned by private equity. While the Board and I believed we were aligned on vision, mission, values, and strategy, it quickly became clear that we were operating from different paradigms.

My belief was simple: focus on the Flywheel and financial results will follow. The reality was equally clear: financial results had to come first.

This wasn't about private equity being right or wrong. It was about fit. At this stage of my career, I knew my strengths as a leader: purpose-driven, values-based, people- and client-centered, long-term strategy-focused. And I knew, just as clearly, that those strengths were not what the business needed in that moment or under that level of financial pressure.

So, I made a decision that was both deeply difficult and deeply clarifying.

I was honest with the Board about the misalignment between what the role required and how I led. I stepped aside so that we could find the right leader for that season. I helped identify the next CEO and stayed to ensure a thoughtful, responsible transition.

This was hard in every way: emotionally, professionally, and personally. I questioned myself. I wondered what story would be told. I asked myself whether I should just stay and endure. In many respects, staying would have been easier than being honest.

But none of that outweighed what I knew to be true: staying would have required me to compromise how I lead and who I am.

Stepping away wasn't quitting. It was choosing alignment. It was creating space for the right leader for that season of the business and honoring the leader I know myself to be.

If this story offers you anything, I hope it offers permission.

Permission to listen and trust yourself when something feels misaligned.

Permission to honor your strengths instead of forcing them into the wrong context.

Permission to step away with integrity, knowing that leadership is not defined by the role you hold, but by the values you refuse to compromise.

A FINAL TRUTH TO TRUST

If there's one myth worth letting go of as you move forward, it's this: that good leaders have it figured out. They don't.

What they *do* choose is practice: reflecting, adjusting, listening, continuously learning, and trying again. They choose progress over perfection, especially when the stakes are high and the path forward feels messy or blurred.

You will get things wrong. You will misread situations. You will second-guess yourself. You will wish you'd handled some conversations differently.

These things are all important leadership moments that strengthen your practice.

What matters most is not avoiding missteps, but responding to them with humility, accountability, and care. While polished "wins" may feel good, you will be remembered for the way you repair after mistakes, the way you learn and adapt, the way you keep yourself and your people moving forward even in the face of adversity.

Leadership will always be hard.

The context will keep changing.

Certainty will remain elusive.

The way you show up will matter more than you know. Often in ways you will never fully see, but trust, others will fully feel.

When the moment comes, and I promise it will, when you wonder if what you're doing is enough, please remember: You don't have to lead perfectly. You don't have to have it all figured out. You just have to choose to lead with purpose, intention, and care.

The next step is yours.

VOICES THAT WALKED WITH ME

None of us becomes a leader alone. Along the way, I leaned on the wisdom of countless others: authors, thinkers, mentors, and practitioners whose ideas inspired, grounded, challenged, and motivated me to act and to change.

I relied heavily on my monthly *Harvard Business Review subscription.* More than once, it felt as though they were reading my mind, the cover topic landing squarely on something we were navigating in real time, or an aspiration I was quietly holding.

I also read constantly. My reading list included contemporary books, but I also returned to the same titles again and again, engaging with their ideas, testing them, and applying what I learned to the company and the people I was leading. I could offer a long list of titles that I held in my hands over the years, but instead, I've chosen to share the ten books and authors I leaned into the hardest. These are the ones that hold significance for how I think about leadership and the core elements of the Flywheel: people, work, clients, and impact.

While many of these books were written years ago, their insights have proven enduring, and returning to them over time only deepened their relevance for me.

When You're Defining What Kind of Leader (and Company) You Want to Be

These are the works that helped me form context and influenced how to define success, growth, and purpose.

- ***Small Giants* by Bo Burlingham:** A powerful reminder that success doesn't have to mean bigger at all costs. This book helped me see that choosing *who you want to be* as a company and *how you define growth* are two of the most important leadership decisions you'll make.
- ***The Art of Possibility* by Rosamund Stone Zander and Benjamin Zander:** Expanded how I think about leadership, mindset, and what is possible when you reframe how you see the world. An empowering philosophy I frequently leaned on came from this book: *Leading from Any Chair.*

When You're Learning How to Lead People More Effectively

These helped me better understand people, me included. I like to think they helped me lead with much greater awareness and intention.

- ***Strengths Based Leadership* by Tom Rath and Barry Conchie:** Grounded my belief that great leadership starts by understanding and amplifying strengths, not fixing people. It also helped me understand the most important leadership qualities that solidify a reason to follow.
- ***Emotional Intelligence 2.0* by Dr. Travis Bradberry and Dr. Jean Greaves:** A practical guide that strengthened my self-awareness, empathy, and emotional discipline in real leadership moments (and my personal life, too)

When You're Building Great Work (and the Conditions for It)

These influenced how I think about creativity, teams, and the environments where people do their best work.

- ***Creativity, Inc.* by Ed Catmull:** A behind-the-scenes look at building a culture where creativity, candor, and trust coexist and where leaders actively remove fear.
- ***Scaling Up Excellence* by Robert I. Sutton and Huggy Rao:** Helped me think more clearly about what *should* scale, what shouldn't, and why excellence requires discipline, not just ambition.

When You're Trying to Turn Belief into Action

These voices helped me translate purpose, clarity, and intent into action.

- **Simon Sinek:** *Start with Why*, *Leaders Eat Last*, and *The Infinite Game* helped me articulate purpose and adopt a longer-term view of leadership and competition while also prioritizing people's ability to thrive through empathy and accountability.

- **Patrick Lencioni:** While I have read almost all of Lencioni's books, the two that I leveraged most: T*he Advantage and The Five Dysfunctions of a Team*, reinforced my belief that organizational health, trust, cohesion, communication, and clarity are the foundation of enduring performance.

- **Chip Heath & Dan Heath:** *Switch and The Power of Moments,* provided a frame for how I think about leading change and designing moments, for both my team and our clients, that create lasting impact.

- **Tom Peters:** *In Search of Excellence and In Pursuit of WOW* reinforced the importance of bias for action, exceptional client experiences, embracing continuous change and evolution, and the energy required to make excellence real, not theoretical.

ACKNOWLEDGMENTS

A plaque sat on the shelf of my office throughout my years as owner and CEO of Gongos and later Human8. It read: *"We are all faced with a series of great opportunities brilliantly disguised as impossible situations."*

This book exists because of my lived experience with moments just like that. What initially felt impossible only became an opportunity because of the people who trusted me—enough to believe in a vision, enough to follow, and generous enough to give pieces of themselves along the way. In doing so, they helped mold me as a person and as a leader. I am deeply grateful for the leaders, colleagues, mentors, clients, family members, and friends who walked that road with me.

Through seasons of uncertainty and transition, many stood beside me with the steady belief that we were building something special together. Others listened patiently every time I said, *"I have a crazy idea..."* The kindness, generosity of spirit, and camaraderie I experienced were more than one should be afforded in a lifetime. If you were part of that journey and are reading this book, I hope you see and feel a part of yourself woven throughout these pages.

At the center of it all is my husband, **Erik Higley**, my partner in every sense of the word. From the beginning, we chose a path that didn't always follow traditional roles; instead, we built a partnership grounded in trust and a willingness to leverage each other's strengths without ego. Together, we've built a vibrant family life, raising three children to adulthood while both remaining deeply engaged in work that matters. Erik's support has continued throughout the writing of this book through his patience, serving as a sounding board, and giving me the space to write and to step into a meaningful next chapter.

Certain ideas have also inspired this work. *A Roadmap for Seamless Transitions in Leadership* by **Bill Hermann** and **Gordon Krater** influenced my thinking at an important moment in my leadership journey. Their *Wheel of Progress*, a framework for sustaining culture and continuity during leadership transitions, stayed with me and helped spark what became the Flywheel you encounter in this book. While their work centers on transitions, I adapted and expanded the underlying idea to the broader, day-to-day work of building healthy, sustainable businesses where people, work, clients, and impact continuously reinforce one another. I'm grateful for their contribution to the leadership conversation and for the role their thinking played in shaping my own.

My daughter, **Claire Higley**, strengthened and supported my vision for the book's iconography: a hand-drawn, human feel, something you might sketch together in a one-on-one mentoring session. Her creativity (and patience) brought that spirit to life on the page.

My sincere thanks to my book coach, **Linda Griffin**, for her guidance as I navigated the unknown path of writing my first book. Her support made the endgame feel possible.

Early concept evaluators provided honest feedback and encouragement to move forward: **Lori**, **Sam**, **Bobby**, and **Drew**. And beta readers: **Brooke**, **Kevin**, **Robyn**, and **Tim** gave their time and thoughtful perspective. The book is stronger because of you!

Modern tools supported the writing of this book. **I used them responsibly—without outsourcing my conscience, my experience, or my voice.** The ideas, perspectives, and stories shared here are my own, shaped by lived experience and careful reflection. Any tools I used served only to help clarify, refine, and strengthen the expression of those ideas.

Finally, to the readers holding this book: thank you for taking a chance on this *Open When* concept. It's different, I know. But my hope is that its content and format empower you to pause, reflect, and lead with intention. If these letters meet you in moments that matter with even a bit more confidence and hope, then this work accomplished what I hoped it would.

ABOUT THE AUTHOR

Camille Nicita Higley is a leadership advisor, former CEO, and a voice in human-centered, purpose-driven leadership. Over the course of a 30-year career, she has built and led organizations and advised many others, grounded in the belief that performance and humanity are not competing priorities but reinforcing ones.

Camille began her career as one of the founding members of Gongos, later becoming partner, COO, and then CEO and owner. Under her leadership, the firm experienced consistent growth, exceptional client and employee retention, and a reputation for innovation in helping Fortune 500 companies make more human-centered decisions. She led the company through its successful sale to Human8, marking the culmination of a three-decade journey building a values-driven, high-performing organization.

Following the acquisition, she served as Managing Partner, CEO, and Board Director of the combined global organization, where she expanded her perspective on leadership at scale and within a complex, globally integrated environment.

Her work centers on helping organizations align people, work, and clients in ways that create value for all stakeholders: employees, customers, and shareholders alike. She has served on both corporate and nonprofit boards and is recognized for building high-performing cultures that adapt and thrive over time.

Today, Camille is a mentor to founders and executives of small to mid-sized firms, bringing practical wisdom and lived experience to the moments that define leadership. A lifelong student of leadership, she remains committed to the belief that business, at its best, is a force for good – an idea that inspired her authorship of *Open When*.

She lives in Southeast Michigan with her husband and their West Highland Terrier and is the proud mother of three adult children.

www.ingramcontent.com/pod-product-compliance
Lightning Source LLC
LaVergne TN
LVHW090549110826
845146LV00001B/71

* 9 7 9 8 9 9 5 4 4 7 8 0 1 *